THE STATE OF FOOD AND AGRICULTURE 1995

MRT-PER

THE STATE
OF FOOD
AND
AGRICULTURE
1995

FOOD AND AGRICULTURE ORGANIZATION OF THE UNITED NATIONS
Rome, 1995

The statistical material in this publication has been prepared from the information available to FAO up to June 1995.

The designations employed and the presentation do not imply the expression of any opinion whatsoever on the part of the Food and Agriculture Organization of the United Nations concerning the legal status of any country, territory, city or area, or of its authorities, or concerning the delimitation of its frontiers or boundaries. In some tables, the designations "developed" and "developing" economies are intended for statistical convenience and do not necessarily express a judgement about the stage reached by a particular country or area in the development process.

David Lubin Memorial Library
Cataloguing in Publication Data

FAO, Rome (Italy)
The state of food and agriculture 1995.
(FAO Agriculture Series, no. 28)
ISBN 92-5-103700-0

1. Agriculture.   2. Food production.
3. Trade.

I. Title   II. Series

FAO code: 70   AGRIS: E16 E70 K01

Printed in Italy

Foreword

As we get closer to a new millennium, I believe the time has come for a global mobilization to address the biggest problems of today's world: hunger and food insecurity. It is in this spirit that I took the initiative of convening a World Food Summit for November 1996, which will gather in Rome heads of state and government from all regions in the world.

Our expectations of this meeting are, first, to attract the world's attention to the fact that, in spite of major increases in global food production, hunger and malnutrition are still massively present in our contemporary world. The day-to-day human suffering and devastation caused by this scourge are far greater in scale than those caused by any war, epidemic or natural disaster, yet too few people have any precise perception of the nature and magnitude of the problem. Although ours is an "information age", food insecurity tends to attract media coverage only when exceptional events bring to light some of its most dramatic manifestations.

Second, the Summit will convey the fundamental message that the deaths and suffering associated with food insecurity are as unnecessary as they are intolerable. The end of hunger and malnutrition, far from being a utopian or poet's dream, is within the reach of our modern society's technology, resources and understanding of the underlying problems. Recent history offers outstanding examples to show that even massive and extreme food insecurity problems can be overcome.

Finally, understanding and awareness of this global problem must translate into broad support of and commitment to effective policy action. The Summit will provide an occasion for country representatives at the highest political level to examine the various dimensions of world food security and adopt a number of basic principles and commitments, as well as a plan of action. I am confident that the Summit will meet the hopes and expectations of millions of people and provide the impulse and inspiration for a major mobilization towards food security for all.

FAO is making a special effort to provide the Summit with adequate information and analytical support on the multiple conceptual, technical and policy dimensions of the food problem. As a further contribution to the debate, food security will be the theme of a comprehensive review in the 1996 issue of *The State of Food and Agriculture*.

The theme of food security is also prominent throughout this year's edition of *The State of Food and Agriculture*. Within widely differing situations and developments, the general picture emerging from this report is one of encouraging progress in many areas that directly or indirectly benefit food and agriculture. Indeed, the year 1994-95 has seen a strengthening of world economic recovery after the slowdown of 1990 to 1993; further progress in economic liberalization and reform in many countries; a recovery in international commodity prices that has provided many agricultural exporting economies with the foreign exchange earnings that will, it is hoped, enable them to consolidate the basis for sustained growth. These welcome developments in the global environment, together with a number of important achievements in individual regions and countries, configure what will probably be remembered as a period of opportunity and hope for many countries in the developing world.

Yet, least of all can we afford complacency. Along with the new opportunities, old problems and new risks emerge. The turbulence in financial markets of late 1994 was a reminder of the way market perceptions and economic situations can change in the face of persisting economic imbalances. There is a global economic recovery under way – but millions of people, mainly in African countries that are less well integrated into the world economy, are yet to see its benefits. While we must welcome important advances in macroeconomic and sector policy reform, the poor are particularly vulnerable in the short and medium term even to changes that are expected to benefit them in the long term. The windfall gains from stronger commodity prices represent financial relief and a developmental opportunity for agricultural exporters, but this period cannot be expected to last for long and the windfalls must be seen in the context of the previous protracted decline in real commodity prices and the deep structural imbalances in agricultural markets. Agriculture has benefited from the improved economic environment in many countries, yet production performances have remained inadequate in much of the developing world and some countries, no less than 15 of which are in Africa, are currently facing severe food shortages. Furthermore, the recent tightening in cereal markets and the prospect of declining government stocks in the major exporting countries, raise again the issue of the adequacy of such stocks in a global food security context. These developments coincide perversely, and disquietingly, with a trend towards reduced flows of food aid and external assistance to agriculture.

The problems in agricultural markets are the central theme of this year's special chapter, Agricultural trade: towards a new era?, an issue that also has major direct and indirect food security implications. This report points out that agricultural trade has expanded considerably in the past decades giving consumers access to more, better and cheaper food, while also being an important source of employment and foreign exchange. However, the gains from agricultural trade have been extremely uneven and markets remain plagued by distortive intervention and protection.

These issues are discussed against the background of the major changes in the economic, institutional and market environment for agricultural trade in the recent past. It is suggested that a "new era" may be emerging with the deregulation of the world economy, the increasing presence of the developing countries in world markets, the major transformations in the former centrally planned economies, the movement towards regional trade arrangements and changes in the world trade markets and rules following the conclusion of the Uruguay Round. Furthermore, this report addresses the complex and controversial issue of how trade interacts with environmental protection and the sustainability of production.

The trading order that will emerge from such an increasingly complex interplay of factors and influences is difficult to foresee. We may expect that a more liberal and integrated environment will boost trade, encourage efforts towards competitiveness and generate welfare overall. However, the impact of the Uruguay Round might turn out to be small in the short term and is likely to have uneven effects across countries and specific markets. Current expectations are for little change in the international prices of tropical products and somewhat higher prices for temperate products, indicating an asymmetric distribution of opportunities, risks and losses in the various situations. Furthermore, in spite of the general move towards more open and disciplined trading regimes, protectionism in traditional and new forms is likely to continue plaguing agricultural markets. Thus, food-deficit countries are likely to face higher import costs and the poorest of them possibly greater food insecurity, at least initially, while market access and competitiveness will remain difficult problems for many developing countries, even those that are better endowed for agricultural production and exports.

It is my hope that this report will contribute to greater awareness of not only the new opportunities, but also the old and new problems and uncertainties that will have to be faced by the international community in the "new era" that is unfolding.

Jacques Diouf
DIRECTOR-GENERAL

Contents

PART II
REGIONAL REVIEW

PART III
AGRICULTURAL TRADE: ENTERING A NEW ERA?

EXHIBITS

BOXES

TABLES

FIGURES

Acknowledgements

The State of Food and Agriculture 1995 was prepared by a team from the Agriculture and Economic Development Analysis Division led by F.L. Zegarra and comprising P.L. Iacoacci, G.E. Rossmiller, J. Skoet, K. Stamoulis, R. Stringer and S. Teodosijevic. Secretarial support was provided by S. Di Lorenzo and P. Di Santo. Computer and statistical support was provided by G. Arena, T. Sadek and Z. Pinna.

Contributions and background papers for the World review were prepared by G. Everett, M. Palmieri, F. Sandiford, M. Spinedi, P. Wardle and G. Zanias.

Contributions and background papers for the Regional review were prepared by M. Ahmad, G.S. Bhalla, A.Z. Ghezawi, K. Gray, U. Grothe, S. Hafeez, M. Harley, A.S. Jabarin, F. Kuba, D. Van Atta and J. Weeks.

The special chapter, Agricultural trade: entering a new era?, was prepared on the basis of contributions from D. Hathaway, T. Josling and P. Konandreas. Helpful comments and suggestions were provided by J. Greenfield.

The State of Food and Agriculture 1995 was edited by J. Shaw. The graphics were prepared by M. Cappucci and the layout by M. Criscuolo with C. Ciarlantini. The cover and illustrations were produced by Studio Page.

Glossary

ACM
Arab Common Market
ACP
African, Caribbean and Pacific States
ACS
Association of Caribbean States
AfDB
African Development Bank
AIACE
Almaty International Agricultural
Commodities Exchange
AMPCO
Agricultural Marketing and Processing
Company
AP
Andean Pact
APEC
Asian Pacific Economic Cooperation
Council
AsDB
Asian Development Bank
ASEAN
Association of Southeast Asian Nations

CACE
Central African Customs and Economic
Union
CACM
Central America Common Market
CAP
Common Agricultural Policy
CARICOM
Caribbean Community and Common Market
CARs
Central Asian republics
CBI
Caribbean Basin Initiative
CCECs
Central and Eastern European countries
CCET
Centre for Cooperation with Economies in
Transition

CER
Closer economic relations
CGIAR
Consultative Group on International
Agricultural Research
c.i.f.
Cost, insurance and freight
CIS
Commonwealth of Independent States
CMEA
Council for Mutual Economic Assistance
CNP
National Production Council
CUSTA
Canada-US Free Trade Agreement

DES
Dietary energy supplies

EACM
East African Common Market
EC
European Community
ECCAS
Economic Community of Central African
States
ECLAC
Economic Commission for Latin America
and the Caribbean
ECO
Economic Cooperation Organization
ECOWAS
Economic Community of West African States
EEA
European Economic Area
EEP
Export Enhancement Program
EFTA
European Free Trade Association
EHDAEs
Economies highly dependent on agricultural
exports

EU
European Union

FDC
Food-deficit country
FTA
Free trade agreement

GATT
General Agreement on Tariffs and Trade
GDP
Gross domestic product
GNP
Gross national product

HYV
High-yielding varieties

IBRD
International Bank for Reconstruction and Development
ICREA
International commodity-related environmental agreement
IDA
International Development Association
IEA
International environmental agreement
IEFR
International Emergency Food Reserve
IMF
International Monetary Fund
IRRI
International Rice Research Institute
ISO
International Sugar Organization
ITO
International Trade Organization
ITTO
International Tropical Timber Organization

LAFTA
Latin American Free Trade Area
LAPC
Land and Agricultural Policy Centre

LDC
Least-developed country
LIFDC
Low-income food-deficit country

MERCOSUR
Southern Common Market
MFN
Most favoured nation
MOS
Ministry of Supply
MTNs
Multilateral trade negotiations

NAFTA
North American Free Trade Agreement
NBK
National Bank of Kazakhstan
NGO
Non-governmental organization
NIS
New Independent State
NPC
Nominal protection coefficient
NTB
Non-tariff barrier

OAU
Organization of African Unity
OECD
Organisation for Economic Co-operation and Development
OPEC
Organization of the Petroleum Exporting Countries

PDS
Public distribution system
PECC
Pacific Economic Cooperation Conference
PHARE
Action Plan for Coordinated Aid to Poland and Hungary
PLO
Palestine Liberation Organization

PROs
Protracted refugee operations
PTA
Preferential Trade Area for Eastern and
Southern African States

RTA
Regional trade arrangement

SAARC
South Asian Association for Regional
Cooperation
SACU
Southern Africa Customs Union
SADC
Southern African Development Community
SAFTA
South Asian Free Trade Agreement
SAP
Structural adjustment programme
SPC
State Property Committee
SPS
Sanitary and phytosanitary
SSC
State Statistical Committee

TBTs
Technical barriers to trade
TBVC states
Transkei, Bophuthatswana, Venda and the
Ciskei
TFP
Total factor productivity

UNCED
United Nations Conference on Environment
and Development
UNCTAD
United Nations Conference on Trade and
Development
UNDP
United Nations Development Programme
UNEP
United Nations Environment Programme

UNOSOM
United Nations Operation in Somalia
USDA
United States Department of Agriculture

VAT
Value added tax

WAEC
West African Economic Community
WFM
World food model
WFP
World Food Programme
WHO
World Health Organization
WTO
World Trade Organization

Explanatory note

The following symbols are used in the tables:

-	=	none or negligible
...	=	not available
1993/94	=	a crop, marketing or fiscal year running from one calendar year to the next
1992-94	=	average for three calendar years

Figures in statistical tables may not add up because of rounding. Annual changes and rates of change have been calculated from unrounded figures. Unless otherwise indicated, the metric system is used.

The dollar sign ($) refers to US dollars. "Billion" is equal to 1 000 million.

Production index numbers

FAO index numbers have *1979-81* as the base period. The production data refer to primary commodities (e.g. sugar cane and sugar beet instead of sugar) and national average producer prices are used as weights. The indices for food products exclude tobacco, coffee, tea, inedible oilseeds, animal and vegetable fibres and rubber. They are based on production data presented on a calendar-year basis.[1]

Trade index numbers

The indices of trade in agricultural products also are based on *1979-81*. They include all the commodities and countries shown in the *FAO Trade Yearbook*. Indices of total food products include those edible products generally classified as "food".

All indices represent changes in current values of exports (f.o.b.) and imports (c.i.f.), all expressed in US dollars. When countries report imports valued at f.o.b. (free on board), these are adjusted to approximate c.i.f. (cost, insurance, freight) values. This method of estimation shows a discrepancy whenever the trend of insurance and freight diverges from that of the commodity unit values.

Volumes and unit value indices represent the changes in the price-weighted sum of quantities and of the quantity-weighted unit values of products traded between countries. The weights are, respectively, the price and quantity averages of *1979-81*, which is the base reference period used for all the index number series currently computed by FAO. The Laspeyres formula is

---

[1] For full details, see *FAO Production Yearbook 1993*.

used in the construction of the index numbers.[2]

Regional coverage

Developing countries include sub-Saharan Africa, Latin America and the Caribbean, the Near East and North Africa[3] and Asia and the Pacific.[4]

Developed countries include: the industrial countries and economies in transition.[5]

Country and city designations used in this publication are those current during the period in which the data were prepared.

---

[2] For full details, see *FAO Trade Yearbook 1993*.

[3] The Near East and North Africa includes: Afghanistan, Algeria, Bahrain, Cyprus, Egypt, Islamic Republic of Iran, Iraq, Jordan, Kuwait, Lebanon, Libyan Arab Jamahiriya, Morocco, Oman, Qatar, Kingdom of Saudi Arabia, the Sudan, Syrian Arab Republic, Tunisia, Turkey, United Arab Emirates and Yemen.

[4] Asia and the Pacific also includes the former Asian centrally planned economies: Cambodia, China, Democratic People's Republic of Korea, Mongolia and Viet Nam.

[5] The "industrial countries" include: Australia, Austria, Belgium, Canada, Denmark, Finland, France, Germany, Greece, Iceland, Ireland, Italy, Japan, Luxembourg, the Netherlands, New Zealand, Norway, Portugal, Spain, Sweden, Switzerland, United Kingdom and United States. The "economies in transition" include: Albania, Bosnia and Herzegovina, Bulgaria, Croatia, Czech Republic, the former Yugoslav Republic of Macedonia, Hungary, Poland, Romania, Slovakia, Slovenia, Yugoslavia, SFR and the former Soviet republics.

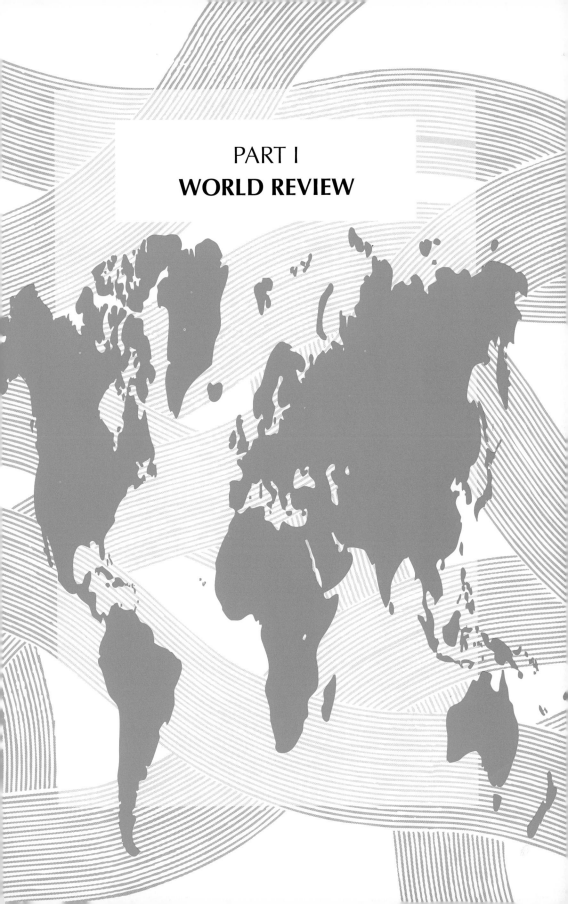

PART I
WORLD REVIEW

WORLD REVIEW
I. Current agricultural situation – facts and figures

1. CROP AND LIVESTOCK PRODUCTION IN 1994

- Globally, 1994 was yet another lacklustre year for food and agricultural production, as world crop and livestock output increased by only 1.8 percent having stagnated the previous year.

- Crop and livestock production in the developed countries expanded marginally by an estimated 0.3 percent, following a 3.8 percent contraction in 1993. In the developing countries as a group, production is estimated to have increased by 2.8 percent, slightly above the expansion rate of the preceding year.

- The single most important factor contributing to the global increase in agricultural production in 1994 was the spectacular recovery in production in the United States, following the sharply reduced 1993 harvests. Close to ideal growing conditions led to unusually high yields for major crops. This, together with the highest ever livestock production, led to an expansion in agricultural production of no less than 16 percent.

- In Central and Eastern Europe and the former USSR, agricultural production contracted by as much as 16 percent in 1994 following several years of decline. Most of the contraction occurred in the area of the former USSR. In Central and Eastern Europe, agricultural production declined by an estimated 7 percent, mainly as a result of drought-reduced crops in Poland which more than offset expansions in other major producers such as Hungary and Romania.

- Among the other developed country regions, production declined substantially in Australia and more moderately in the EC.

- The 2.8 percent increase in developing country crop and livestock production implied a 0.9 percent increase in per caput terms. This is a meagre gain compared with average annual production increases of 3.3 percent during the 1980s and of 3.2 percent from 1990 to 1993. Furthermore, performances varied significantly among the developing country regions with only Latin America and the Caribbean and the Far East recording increases above the rate of population growth.

- The strong production growth achieved by Latin America and the Caribbean represented a recovery from the severe setback of 1993, which itself followed several years of mediocre performance. The expansion in 1994 is largely accounted for by significant increases in Argentina and Brazil, while only a modest increase is estimated for Mexico and a contraction for Colombia.

- In the Far East, production growth decelerated in 1994 although it remained well above the rate of population growth. The People's Republic of China maintained robust agricultural growth, but unfavourable weather held back agricultural output and the rate of expansion fell below the average of the preceding five years. India experienced a relatively favourable agricultural year with production growth accelerating after a somewhat sluggish 1993.

- At 1.9 percent, the increase in crop and livestock production in the Near East and North Africa is an improvement over the performance of 1993, but still implies a further decline in per caput production. The growth in production in the region is largely attributable to an estimated 35 percent increase in Morocco, where production recovered after two years of sharply drought-reduced levels. In Egypt, production in 1994 is estimated to have declined by 2-3 percent, following five years of sustained increases in per caput production. The 1 percent decline estimated for Turkey marks the fourth consecutive year of declining per caput production.

- Sub-Saharan Africa experienced yet another poor agricultural year, as crop and livestock production increased by only an estimated 2 percent. Thus, after a temporary halt in 1993, the region returned to the path of declining per caput agricultural production which commenced in the early 1970s. Among the larger producing countries, relatively positive performances were recorded by Nigeria, which has seen continuous gains in per caput production levels since 1988, and Kenya, although its 7.5 percent increase represented only a partial recovery from the devastations caused by drought in both 1992 and 1993. A decline in production is estimated for Zaire and only a marginal increase is expected in the United Republic of Tanzania.

Exhibit 1

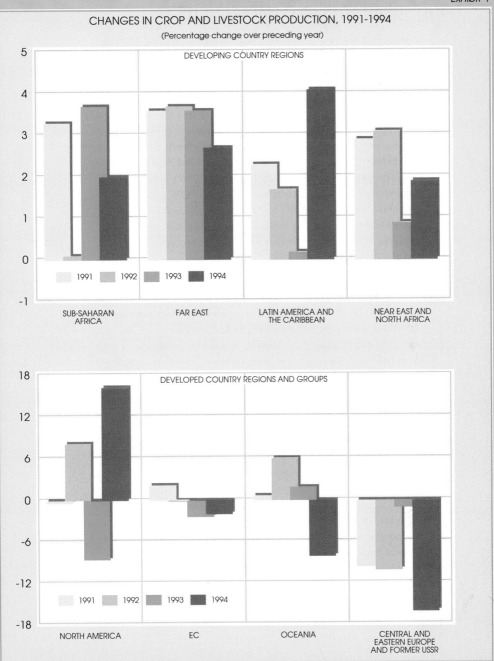

CHANGES IN CROP AND LIVESTOCK PRODUCTION, 1991-1994
(Percentage change over preceding year)

DEVELOPING COUNTRY REGIONS

1991   1992   1993   1994

SUB-SAHARAN AFRICA   FAR EAST   LATIN AMERICA AND THE CARIBBEAN   NEAR EAST AND NORTH AFRICA

DEVELOPED COUNTRY REGIONS AND GROUPS

1991   1992   1993   1994

NORTH AMERICA   EC   OCEANIA   CENTRAL AND EASTERN EUROPE AND FORMER USSR

Source: FAO

2. FOOD SHORTAGES AND EMERGENCIES

• Africa, where 15 countries currently require exceptional and/or emergency food assistance, remains the continent most seriously affected by food shortages.

• A massive cereal deficit for 1995/96 is forecast for southern Africa reflecting drought-reduced harvests in many countries. Rains in *Botswana, Lesotho, Namibia, South Africa,* parts of *Swaziland, Zambia* and *Zimbabwe* have been poor and national crops will be well below average. Southern parts of *Malawi* and *Mozambique* have also been affected by drought. The subregion's import requirements are set to rise dramatically in 1995/96 and local emergency interventions will be necessary for drought victims. *Angola* will remain heavily dependent on relief assistance in 1995/96, in spite of some improvements in the security conditions and a marginal increase in 1995 production.

• In spite of some good harvests, large-scale emergency assistance will be needed in eastern Africa throughout 1995. Food production in *Burundi* and *Rwanda* has failed to recover fully, although there have been some good rains for the 1995 first season crops and increased distribution of farm inputs. In Rwanda, following favourable weather conditions and timely provisions of agricultural inputs, the 1995 second season harvest increased substantially from the previous year, but remained well below average as a result of reduced plantings. In Burundi, the harvest outcome is likely to be compromised by renewed outbreaks of hostilities and a tense security situation in many areas. Large numbers of internally displaced and vulnerable persons in both countries continue to require emergency food assistance. Civil strife in the southern *Sudan* continues to hamper relief activities, while the departure of the United Nations Operation in Somalia (UNOSOM) from *Somalia* raises the likelihood of renewed food problems being caused by a deteriorated security situation. Localized droughts in *Ethiopia* and *Uganda* have necessitated emergency food interventions. Food distribution will still be required in 1995 to cover the needs of the most vulnerable people in *Eritrea.*

• Overall the food supply situation is satisfactory in western and central Africa, reflecting above-average to record harvests in most countries. However, food production and distribution in *Liberia* and *Sierra Leone* continue to be hampered by civil strife. Desert locusts may also develop in northwestern Africa from infestations at present in *Mauritania*. In central Africa, the food supply position remains tight in the urban areas of *Zaire* as a result of economic instability, high inflation and a tense political situation.

• Elsewhere the continuing factional fighting in *Afghanistan* has caused further displacement of people who, together with destitutes and returnees, will continue to be in need of international food aid in the months ahead. In *Iraq,* the food and nutritional situation remains grave, mainly as a result of the difficulties encountered by the government in financing imports. A recent UN Consolidated Interagency Humanitarian Programme for 1995-96 stresses that the country's needs are enormous and cannot be met solely through humanitarian assistance programmes.

• In *Cambodia,* large numbers of vulnerable people are at risk of starvation in the areas worst affected by drought and floods in 1994. In *Mongolia,* after a poor 1994 harvest, the already tight food supply situation is expected to aggravate further until the next harvest in September. In *Nepal,* serious food supply difficulties are reported from the areas hit by drought in 1994.

• In *Haiti,* the food supply situation is improving, but economic assistance is needed for the supply of coarse grain, bean seeds and other farm inputs for the planting of the second season crop.

• In *Bosnia and Herzegovina,* in the embattled area of Bihac the entire population is severely affected by shortages of food and relief assistance is critically needed. In Sarajevo deliveries of food aid are extremely difficult and food market prices are too high for a large part of the population.

• In *Armenia,* the food supply situation and living conditions of the urban population have eased somewhat during the past year but remain difficult. In *Azerbaijan* and *Georgia,* foreign exchange constraints and disruption to trade as a result of the conflict in Chechenya have limited food imports.

• In *Moldova,* the tight grain supply situation caused by last year's poor harvest has eased, but vulnerable groups are still in need of food assistance.

- In *Tajikistan,* the grain supply situation is extremely tight; domestic grain production is small and lack of foreign exchange or barterable goods severely constrains imports. In *Kyrgyzstan,* budgetary constraints will necessitate substantial quantities of food aid.

Exhibit 2

FOOD SUPPLY SHORTFALLS* REQUIRING EXCEPTIONAL ASSISTANCE

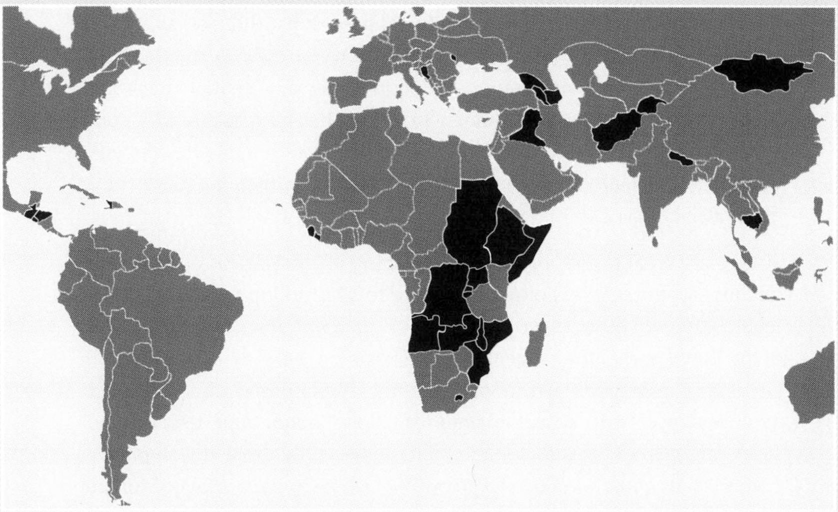

Source: FAO, Global Information and Early Warning System, April 1995

* In current marketing year

3. CURRENT CEREAL SUPPLY, UTILIZATION AND STOCKS

• World cereal production in 1994 is estimated to be over 1 953 million tonnes, 3 percent higher than the reduced harvest of 1993 and above the average of the last five years. Most of this increase, however, reflects a strong recovery in coarse grain production, especially in the United States. Rice output also rebounded strongly in 1994 whereas wheat production fell significantly, mainly as a result of reduced production in the developed countries, especially Australia and the Commonwealth of Independent States (CIS).

• Global cereal stocks for crop years ending in 1995 are forecast to decline, for the second consecutive year, to 311 million tonnes. At this level, total cereal stocks would be only 17 percent of trend utilization; i.e. at the lower end of the range the FAO Secretariat considers the minimum necessary to safeguard world food security. The largest decline is expected for wheat, especially wheat inventories held by major exporters. Rice stocks are also forecast to contract, although mainly in the developing countries, as global production growth fails to keep pace with consumption requirements. By contrast, coarse grain carryovers are anticipated to recover from their low opening levels, as a result of higher production in the United States.

• Early production prospects for 1995 point to some recovery in wheat, but to a reduction in coarse grain production. Wheat output is currently forecast to increase by around 4 percent to 550 million tonnes, with most of the increase coming from the developed countries, especially Australia and the EC. Total wheat output is also forecast to rise in the developing countries, with most of the increase expected to come from Asia. In Africa, on the other hand, wheat production is forecast to be smaller this year, mainly because of the drought in Morocco. Early prospects for world coarse grain production in 1995 point to a 5 percent fall to around 840 million tonnes. Most of the decline is expected in the developed countries (especially the United States, the CIS and South Africa), while in the developing countries total coarse grain production is forecast to increase, slightly exceeding last year's above-average crop.

• The 1995/96 supply and demand situation, even if there is another good paddy crop, implies that world cereal supplies will tighten further, so that the stock to utilization ratio could fall even lower than the minimum safety range. Both wheat and coarse grain stocks are forecast to be drawn down further, even though world utilization is expected to remain below trend and largely unchanged from 1994/95. The situation might prove even more delicate as wheat carryovers are projected to fall to around 106 million tonnes, the lowest volume since the beginning of the 1980s.

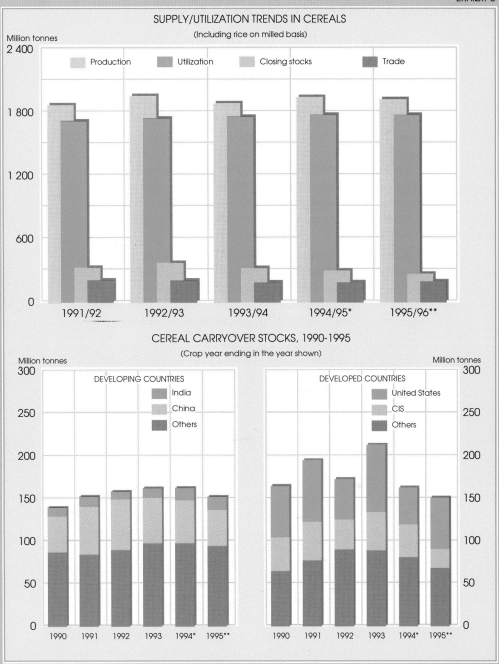

Exhibit 3

SUPPLY/UTILIZATION TRENDS IN CEREALS
(Including rice on milled basis)

Million tonnes

Legend: Production · Utilization · Closing stocks · Trade

1991/92   1992/93   1993/94   1994/95*   1995/96**

CEREAL CARRYOVER STOCKS, 1990-1995
(Crop year ending in the year shown)

Million tonnes

DEVELOPING COUNTRIES
- India
- China
- Others

1990 1991 1992 1993 1994* 1995**

Million tonnes

DEVELOPED COUNTRIES
- United States
- CIS
- Others

1990 1991 1992 1993 1994* 1995**

Source: FAO

*Estimate   **Forecast

4. EXTERNAL ASSISTANCE TO AGRICULTURE

• Over recent years, external assistance to agriculture has tended to decline both as a share of total official development assistance and in absolute terms. Measured in constant 1990 prices, commitments to agriculture declined from US$12 700 million in 1990 to $9 882 million in 1993 (excluding commitments from the United States for 1993; these commitments had been $506 million in 1992). The decline was far more pronounced for multilateral than for bilateral assistance. Indeed, multilateral assistance dropped in constant prices from $8 071 million in 1990 to an estimated $5 716 million in 1993, mainly as the result of close to a halving of commitments from the International Development Association (IDA), the soft-lending branch of the World Bank, and a reduction by almost two-thirds in commitments from the regional development banks.

• Preliminary data for 1994 point to a further decline in multilateral commitments, to $5 716 million in 1990 prices, mainly accounted for by lower commitments from the regional development banks. World Bank commitments are expected to increase slightly, thanks to a partial recovery in IDA commitments from the sharp reduction of the previous year.

• The declining trend in external assistance to agriculture is a major source of concern, occurring at a time when many low-income agriculture-dependent countries are facing increasing difficulties in exploiting the potential of their agriculture as a support of overall development, poverty reduction and food security.

Exhibit 4

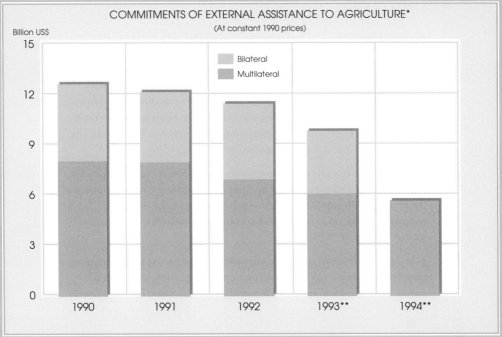

COMMITMENTS OF EXTERNAL ASSISTANCE TO AGRICULTURE*
(At constant 1990 prices)

Billion US$

Bilateral
Multilateral

1990   1991   1992   1993**   1994**

Source: FAO and OECD   *Note:* The 1993 bilateral figure excludes the United States.   * Broad definition   ** Preliminary

5. FOOD AID FLOWS IN 1994/95

• Shipments of food aid in cereals during 1994/95 (July/June) are estimated to be 9.8 million tonnes. This is 20 percent below the previous year's level of 12.6 million tonnes and 35 percent below the 1992/93 level of 15.1 million tonnes, mainly because of the reduced level of donor budgetary allocations. One early indication that this trend may continue is that, under the new Food Aid Convention that was expected to come into effect on 30 June 1995, the total minimum cereal aid commitment has been drastically reduced from 7.5 to 5.4 million tonnes.

• Although the composition of low-income food-deficit countries (LIFDCs) has changed to include 12 new countries of Central and Eastern Europe and the former USSR, sub-Saharan Africa still continues to be the major recipient of food aid in cereals and accounts for more than 40 percent of total shipments to LIFDCs.

• In addition to cereal commodities, donors are providing ever-increasing quantities of non-cereal commodities, comprising mainly vegetable oil, pulses, dairy products, meat and fish and other high-value commodities. In 1993, 1.9 million tonnes of these commodities were shipped and, in 1994, 1.6 million tonnes.

• As of March 1995 pledges to the 1995 International Emergency Food Reserve (IEFR) amounted to 280 288 tonnes of food commodities. For 1994, IEFR pledges amounted to 1 185 733 tonnes of food commodities, of which 927 639 tonnes were cereals and 258 094 tonnes other foodstuffs.

• In addition to IEFR contributions, by the first quarter of 1995 a total of 260 196 tonnes of cereal and non-cereal commodities had been pledged under the subset of World Food Programme (WFP) regular resources to meet the requirements of protracted refugee operations (PROs). The level of pledges to PROs in 1994 amounted to 691 976 tonnes of cereals and 89 142 tonnes of other commodities.

• As of March 1995 total pledges by 30 donors to WFP's regular resources for the biennium 1995-96 stood at US$288.8 million, representing 19 percent of the pledging target of $1.5 billion. Of the total amount pledged, $181.7 million was in the form of commodities and $107.1 million in the form of cash. In the previous biennium, 1993-94, pledges by 61 donors reached $988 million, representing nearly 66 percent of the pledging target of $1.5 billion. Of the total amount pledged $641.4 million were in the form of commodities and $346.6 million in the form of cash.

Exhibit 5

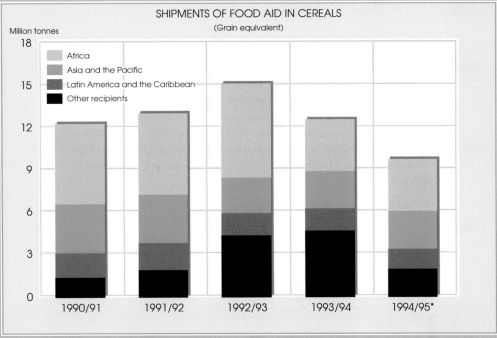

SHIPMENTS OF FOOD AID IN CEREALS
(Grain equivalent)

Million tonnes

- Africa
- Asia and the Pacific
- Latin America and the Caribbean
- Other recipients

1990/91   1991/92   1992/93   1993/94   1994/95*

Source: FAO   *Note:* Years refer to the 12-month period July/June   * Estimate

6. INTERNATIONAL AGRICULTURAL PRICES

• Confirming the tightening wheat market situation, *wheat* export prices have risen considerably in 1994-95. *Maize* export prices also strengthened during the first months of 1995, mainly reflecting adverse weather conditions for planting in North America. International *rice* prices were relatively weak in the second half of 1994 but recovered in early 1995 because of the large increase in import demand from Bangladesh, China and Indonesia. Among the different types of rice, the prices of lower qualities rose the most, boosted in part by the absence of China, which is normally a regular supplier of such rice, in the international market and by reduced supplies from Pakistan and Viet Nam.

• Prices of *oils* and *fats* had risen to record levels by the end of 1994 as a result of tightness of supplies. They remained high through March 1995 but, under the influence of abundant crop supplies and a substantial replenishment of world stocks, a downward movement started in April 1995 and could continue until the end of the season. The supply of *oilcakes* and *oilmeals* far exceeded demand and their prices decreased sharply after October 1994. The FAO index of international market prices for these products during the October 1994 to May 1995 period was 7 percent below the 1990-94 five-year average.

• Tighter world *sugar* supplies in 1994, which were at their lowest level in six years, caused sugar prices (International Sugar Organization [ISO] daily price) to rise sharply during the year. The price reached its five-year high during the first quarter of 1995. Prices subsequently weakened as a result of improved production in a number of key countries and forecasts of substantially larger crops in 1995/96.

• In 1994 prices in the world *coffee* market were volatile as a result of tight supplies, frost damage in Brazil and speculation activity. Prices rose sharply in September 1994, reaching more than three times the average level of 1993, and then fell to about US$3 000 per tonne by the end of the year. Prices remained around $3 200 to $3 500 per tonne during the first four months of 1995 reflecting stable market conditions.

• After significant increases in 1994, in the first four months of 1995 *cocoa* prices remained at their highest level for five years. The high prices reflected a tight market situation resulting from world consumption exceeding production over the 1992/93 to 1994/95 period. However, following indications late in the season that the 1994/95 supply deficit was less than anticipated as a result of higher production from the Côte d'Ivoire and Ghana, prices declined in May 1995.

Exhibit 6

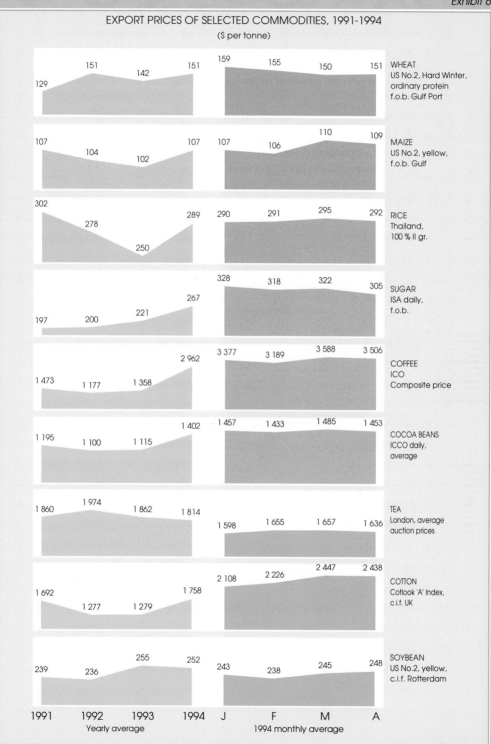

EXPORT PRICES OF SELECTED COMMODITIES, 1991-1994
($ per tonne)

	WHEAT US No.2, Hard Winter, ordinary protein f.o.b. Gulf Port
	MAIZE US No.2, yellow, f.o.b. Gulf
	RICE Thailand, 100 % II gr.
	SUGAR ISA daily, f.o.b.
	COFFEE ICO Composite price
	COCOA BEANS ICCO daily, average
	TEA London, average auction prices
	COTTON Cotlook 'A' Index, c.i.f. UK
	SOYBEAN US No.2, yellow, c.i.f. Rotterdam

WHEAT: 129, 151, 142, 151 | 159, 155, 150, 151
MAIZE: 107, 104, 102, 107 | 107, 106, 110, 109
RICE: 302, 278, 250, 289 | 290, 291, 295, 292
SUGAR: 197, 200, 221, 267 | 328, 318, 322, 305
COFFEE: 1 473, 1 177, 1 358, 2 962 | 3 377, 3 189, 3 588, 3 506
COCOA BEANS: 1 195, 1 100, 1 115, 1 402 | 1 457, 1 433, 1 485, 1 453
TEA: 1 860, 1 974, 1 862, 1 814 | 1 598, 1 655, 1 657, 1 636
COTTON: 1 692, 1 277, 1 279, 1 758 | 2 108, 2 226, 2 447, 2 438
SOYBEAN: 239, 236, 255, 252 | 243, 238, 245, 248

1991 1992 1993 1994   J F M A
Yearly average   1994 monthly average

Source: FAO

- World *tea* prices declined further in 1994 from the depressed level of 1993, and this trend continued for the first four months of 1995. The prolonged situation of depressed prices reflected an imbalance of the world tea market with the growth of export supplies surpassing that of import demand.

- World *cotton* prices reached record high levels in early 1995. In the face of strengthened demand, coupled with production shortfalls in many countries, stocks were drawn down markedly in 1994 and into 1995. As a consequence, prices in April 1995 were pushed to around 20 percent above those prevailing at the beginning of the year and 35 percent above those of April 1994.

7. FISHERIES: CATCH DISPOSITION AND TRADE

- In 1993 the *world catch* and *culture* of fish and shellfish reached about 101.4 million tonnes, from 98.8 million tonnes in 1992. In recent years both marine and freshwater capture fisheries have slightly declined, while aquaculture production has increased, reaching 15.9 million tonnes (excluding plants) in 1993.

- Among major producers China and Peru expanded production significantly in 1993, while decreases were recorded for Chile and the Russian Federation.

- The increases in *marine catches* have come, since 1983, primarily from four shoaling pelagic species and Alaska pollack. Catches of cods, hakes and haddocks have been in steady decline, with the exception of increased haddock catches in the northeast Atlantic after 1991.

- Many heavily fished stocks require urgent rehabilitation and action towards this end will involve reductions in fishing effort. A number of states have already addressed the problem of overcapacity in fishing fleets by initiating the scrapping or decommissioning programmes. To rebuild stocks effectively and to increase yields in the longer term reductions in fishing effort will mean reductions in world landings in the short to medium term.

- The steady increase in *inland fisheries* appeared to peak in 1990 at approximately 6.5 million tonnes and subsequently stabilized at a slightly lower level. In 1992 Asia produced 54 percent of the world inland catch and Africa contributed 25 percent. Nearly all inland resources show symptoms of excessive exploitation.

- *Aquaculture production* from inland waters (9 million tonnes in 1992) is higher than aquaculture production in marine waters (4.9 million tonnes in 1992) but rapid increases (recently of about 2 million tonnes annually) are recorded for both. The bulk of production is from developing states – Asia is by far the main contributor with 84 percent of world aquaculture production in 1992.

- Estimates of the disposition of world catch in 1993 indicate an increase of 1.7 percent in fish used for human consumption to 72.4 million tonnes.

- International *trade in fishery products* increased by 1.8 percent between 1993 and 1992, with the total value of exports exceeding US$41 billion. The share of developing countries in world exports of fishery products increased by 8.4 percent to $21 billion.

- Developing country exports in 1993 represented 32.6 percent of their total catch as compared with 55.6 percent for developed countries. In spite of this, developing countries as a group recorded an increasingly positive trade balance in fishery products, which reached $13.4 billion in 1993.

• Thailand became the main fish exporter in the world, overtaking the United States. Total Thai exports were $3.4 billion in 1993, an 11 percent increase over 1992. Japan maintained its position as top importer; in 1993 it imported some $14.2 billion, which accounted for 32 percent of world fish imports in value terms.

Exhibit 7

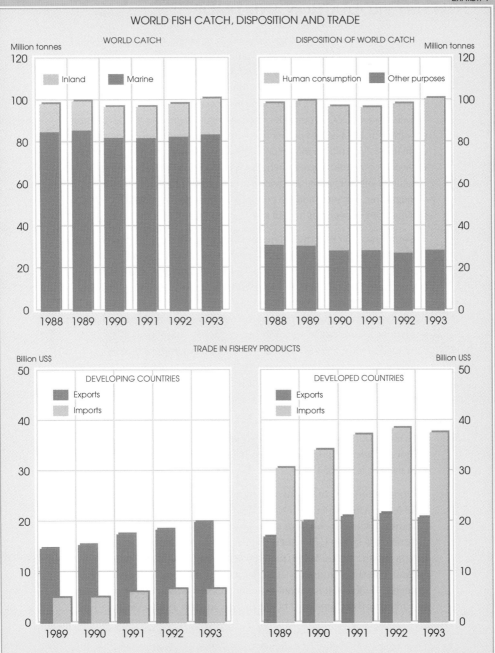

WORLD FISH CATCH, DISPOSITION AND TRADE

Source: FAO

8. FORESTRY PRODUCTION AND TRADE

• World *roundwood* production expanded considerably in 1994 to reach 3 460 million m³. However, this was still below the peak level of 1990 because of continued depressed production in the countries of Central and Eastern Europe and the former USSR. Output of industrial roundwood recovered notably in the Organisation for Economic Co-operation and Developement (OECD) countries and continued to grow in the developing countries. In 1994, world production of industrial roundwood was an estimated 1 555 million m³ – 6 percent below 1990 levels. Production of *fuelwood* continued to grow in the developing countries, where it constitutes 80 percent of roundwood production, reflecting increased demographic pressures and the continuing dependence of rural communities on wood as a main source of energy.

• North American roundwood markets had witnessed a price explosion in 1993 which was caused particularly by logging restrictions in the Pacific Northwest of the United States. Prices returned to more normal levels as a United States federal court, in mid-1994, temporarily lifted the logging ban in the protected federal public forests of the Pacific Northwest. Tropical log supply was affected by several environmental and sustainable management restrictions introduced by major Asian producers. These measures continued to have an upward effect on prices of all tropical timber products. Several consuming countries have started to substitute temperate timber for tropical timber, thus favouring exports from temperate countries, such as Chile and New Zealand, over exports from the large Asian market.

• Production of *wood pulp* in 1994 recovered strongly as the demand of the paper industry was stimulated by booming markets in the EC and North America. Trade and prices of pulpwood and wood chips increased markedly from the low levels of 1993.

• World production of *sawnwood* recovered slightly in 1994 from the low 1993 levels with increases in North America, the EC and Scandinavian countries. Prices of coniferous sawnwood, although levelling off from the peak reached in 1993, remained high. Countries in Central and Eastern Europe and the former USSR, with the exception of the Baltic states, continued to suffer from dramatic output drops. The Russian Federation recorded a further fall in output of coniferous sawnwood that was estimated at 9 million m³ or 35 percent below the already low 1993 level.

• Production of tropical sawnwood in 1994 continued its slow growth, with a higher share being utilized domestically within producing countries, thus reflecting the trend towards increasing internal manufacture of further processed products.

Exhibit 8A

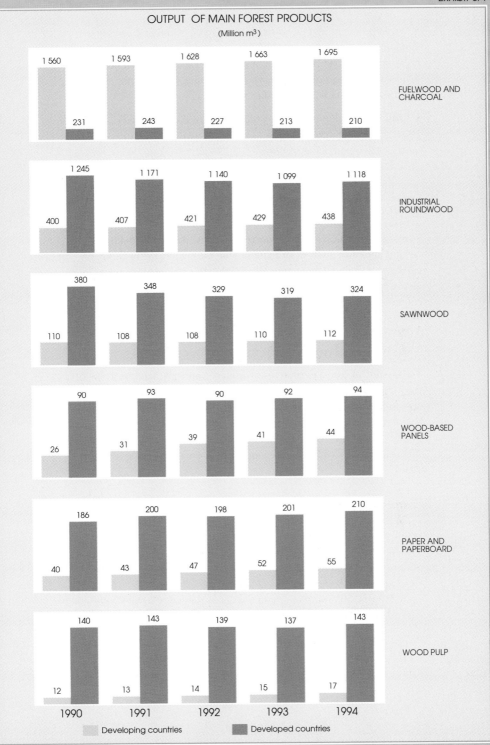

OUTPUT OF MAIN FOREST PRODUCTS
(Million m³)

FUELWOOD AND CHARCOAL

| 1 560 | 1 593 | 1 628 | 1 663 | 1 695 |
| 231 | 243 | 227 | 213 | 210 |

INDUSTRIAL ROUNDWOOD

| 1 245 | 1 171 | 1 140 | 1 099 | 1 118 |
| 400 | 407 | 421 | 429 | 438 |

SAWNWOOD

| 380 | 348 | 329 | 319 | 324 |
| 110 | 108 | 108 | 110 | 112 |

WOOD-BASED PANELS

| 90 | 93 | 90 | 92 | 94 |
| 26 | 31 | 39 | 41 | 44 |

PAPER AND PAPERBOARD

| 186 | 200 | 198 | 201 | 210 |
| 40 | 43 | 47 | 52 | 55 |

WOOD PULP

| 140 | 143 | 139 | 137 | 143 |
| 12 | 13 | 14 | 15 | 17 |

1990　1991　1992　1993　1994

Developing countries　　Developed countries

Source: FAO

• World production of *wood-based panels* grew a further 4 percent in 1994. Growth was more sustained in tropical developing countries where plywood production has enjoyed a very fast growth in the last decade thanks to the export-driven expansion of dynamic industries in Southeast Asian countries such as Indonesia and Malaysia.

• World production of *paper and paperboard* grew by a further 5 percent in 1994, continuing a decade-long ascending trend of the industry. Significant increases in output were recorded for the EC (8.5 percent), North America (4.5 percent) and the countries of Southeast Asia, while production continued to drop in the former USSR countries and in some Eastern European countries. The demand for certain paper grades was so tight that prices, after the severe declines of 1993, reached unprecedented levels.

• World production of *wood pulp* recovered markedly in 1994 by 5 percent, after five years of stagnation. This was mainly the result of the tightness of waste paper supplies which led the price of waste paper to increase fivefold in 1994. Environmental constraints in the developed countries severely limited the expansion of the present wood pulp capacity. As a result prices of wood pulp started to move up very sharply in the last part of 1994, returning to the former record levels of 1990, while international stocks of wood pulp diminished sharply.

• The value of world *trade* in forest products, after the decline of 1993, expanded in 1994 by an estimated 5 percent, reflecting the strong recovery of pulp and paper export prices and a generalized increase in export volumes. In addition, international export prices for logs, sawnwood and wood-based panels remained high. The volume of world trade expanded for all forest products with the exception of the log and tropical sawnwood trades.

Exhibit 8B

EXPORT VALUE OF MAIN FOREST PRODUCTS
(Billion US$)

INDUSTRIAL ROUNDWOOD

SAWNWOOD AND WOOD-BASED PANELS

Developing countries   Developed countries

Source: FAO

WORLD REVIEW
II. Overall economic environment and agriculture

WORLD ECONOMIC ENVIRONMENT
The year 1994 and the first half of 1995 have seen a gradual acceleration of world economic activity, with an increasing number of countries improving their economic performance. According to IMF, the growth in global output in 1994, at 3.7 percent, was the highest so far for the decade and current forecasts point to a slight acceleration of world economic growth to about 3.8 percent in 1995. The growth in the volume of world trade is also estimated to have accelerated, from about 4 percent in 1993 to 9.4 percent in 1994, and is forecast to expand by a further 8 percent in 1995.[1]

In the *industrialized economies,* the revival in growth took place in the context of low, although in some countries rising, inflation and generally prudent fiscal and monetary policies. Fiscal consolidation has remained high on these countries' policy agendas and interest rates have tended to rise as concerns shifted from economic recession to a possible resurgence of inflation. The recovery now under way has resulted in some reduction in unemployment rates, but these remain very high in some countries.

The *transition economies* in Central and Eastern Europe and the former USSR showed contrasting performances. Poland, Hungary, the Czech Republic and Slovakia – where the institutional and structural reforms are already well advanced – all showed positive growth rates in 1994 and, except for Hungary, are expected to accelerate the rate of economic expansion further in 1995. The economic recession also appears to have bottomed out in the Baltic states. On the other hand, the Russian Federation and most states in the former USSR faced further sizeable declines in economic activity during 1994 and 1995 (see Regional review of Central and Eastern Europe, p. 165).

Economic activity has remained dynamic overall in the *developing countries,* with GDP growth exceeding 6 percent in 1994 and forecast to continue expanding at a slightly lower rate in 1995. The favourable economic outlook reflected a combination of

---

[1] IMF. 1995. *World Economic Outlook,* May 1995. Washington, DC.

Figure 1

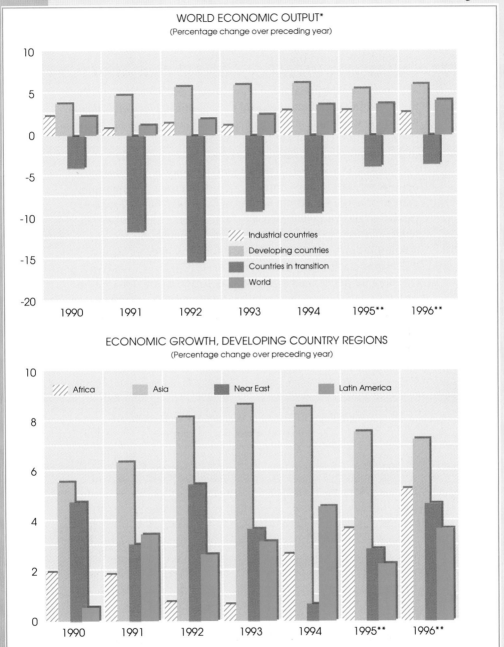

WORLD ECONOMIC OUTPUT*
(Percentage change over preceding year)

Industrial countries
Developing countries
Countries in transition
World

ECONOMIC GROWTH, DEVELOPING COUNTRY REGIONS
(Percentage change over preceding year)

Africa   Asia   Near East   Latin America

Source: IMF   * Real GDP or real NMP   ** Projections

external and domestic developments. External factors included the strengthening and spread of the recovery in the developed economies boosting trade and investment flows; the gains, albeit slow and uneven, in trade liberalization, along with the acceleration of regional integration (discussed in Part III, p. 199); the strengthening of international market prices of several major traded commodities; and large capital inflows which, although slowing in the wake of the Mexican crisis, appear to have resumed as the confidence of financial markets is being restored.

Domestic factors that contributed to the improved economic outlook for developing countries included further progress in market-oriented economic reform; successful stabilization in many countries, shown by widespread – and in some cases dramatic – reductions in inflation rates; and greater political and social stability in some countries and areas formerly affected by civil strife and armed confrontation.

Economic performances varied widely across the different countries and regions, however, as did the relative importance of the various domestic and external factors underlying them (see Regional review, developing country regions, p. 75).

As regards the *economic outlook,* Project LINK projections for 1996-98 point to annual growth rates of about 2.6 percent in the

Figure 2

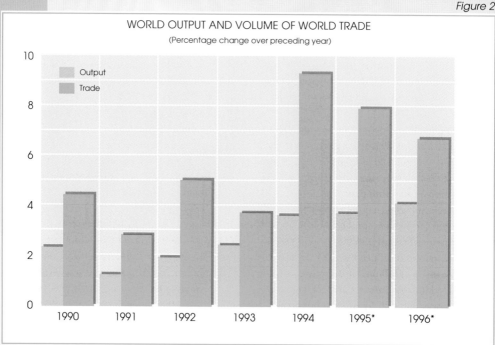

WORLD OUTPUT AND VOLUME OF WORLD TRADE
(Percentage change over preceding year)

Output
Trade

1990   1991   1992   1993   1994   1995*   1996*

Source: IMF

* Projections

BOX 1
EXTERNAL DEBT SITUATION OF DEVELOPING COUNTRIES

External indebtedness continued to be a major problem for many developing countries in spite of improvements in some crucial indicators of debt servicing and net transfers, and progress in debt restructuring and reduction.

The total developing country *external debt stock,* which at the end of 1993 reached US$1 812 billion, was estimated to be $1 945 billion at the end of 1994, up by 7 percent in nominal terms. The share of developing country long-term debt held by official creditors – bilateral lenders and multilateral institutions – continued to rise and was expected to account for 51 percent of total developing country long-term debt by the end of 1994, compared with a share in 1982 of only 35 percent.

The *increase in debt stock* is explained by: *i)* substantially higher total net flows on debt, estimated at US$108 billion in 1994, mainly in countries that have not rescheduled their debts and in some Latin American countries that have overcome their commercial debt problems; *ii)* the cross-currency valuation effect calculated on long-term debt and IMF credit increased the debt stock by a projected $25 billion; *iii)* rescheduled interest will add another $20 billion. On the other hand, officially supported debt and debt service reduction operations, market buy-backs and debt-equity swaps, as well as debt forgiveness (especially in support of the devaluation of the CFA franc) were expected to reduce the debt stock by almost $12 billion. Furthermore, accumulated interest arrears were expected to fall by over $8 billion as a result of the conclusion of restructuring arrangements.

External long-term *debt to agriculture* (broadly defined), of which 91 percent is owed to official bilateral and multilateral creditors, reached almost US$75 billion in 1993.

The estimated total *debt service payments* on all debts in 1994, at US$199 billion, represented an increase of 4 percent in nominal terms over 1993. The *total debt service to export ratio,* which in 1993 rose to 18 percent, reversing the downward trend of the previous few years, was expected to improve in 1994 by declining to 17 percent. The *debt to GNP ratio,* which has increased steadily during the 1990s, was estimated to reach almost 41 percent in 1994, the highest level since 1987.

Net transfers on total debt (i.e. disbursements minus total debt service payments), which had been negative since 1983, implying an outflow of resources from developing countries, turned positive in 1992. This reversal consolidated more recently as transfers to developing countries of almost US$29 billion and $25 billion were estimated in 1993 and 1994 respectively. The situation differed in the two more indebted regions, however. For Latin America and the Caribbean, after a positive net transfer on debt of almost $5 billion in 1993, a negative transfer of $10 billion was estimated for 1994. By contrast, in 1994 sub-Saharan Africa was estimated to have a positive net transfer, amounting to $2 billion, for the first time since 1980.

Aggregate net resource flows (which include other forms of external financing besides debt-related flows) to all developing countries, after declining for several years up to 1987, have increased every year since, both in real and nominal terms, reaching US$213 billion in 1993 and an estimated $227 billion in 1994. A striking feature is the surge in *private flows,* which in the 1990s have become the most important component of aggregate net long-term resource flows to developing countries. These increased from $159 billion in 1993 to an estimated $193 billion in 1994. In 1993 private flows, mainly portfolio equity investment, foreign direct investment and debt-creating flows, accounted for 75 percent of the total net aggregate long-term resource flows against 44 percent in 1990. However, it is a small group of countries, mainly middle-income East Asian and Latin American, that have expanded their access to private capital flows. In absolute terms the People's Republic of China and Mexico have been the largest beneficiaries. Although almost 30 percent of net long-term private flows are debt-creating they are not due to commercial banks as they were in the 1970s, but are in the form of bonds issued by a limited number of countries that have gained the necessary creditworthiness.

Source: World Bank. *World Debt Tables 1994-95*. Washington, DC.

Figure 3

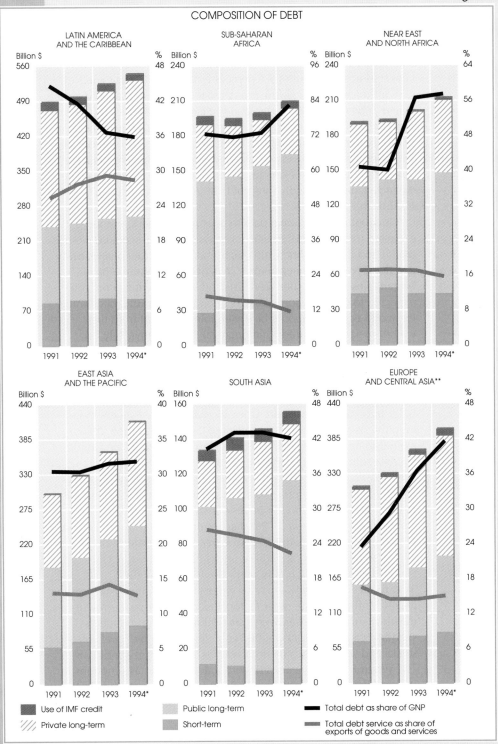

COMPOSITION OF DEBT

LATIN AMERICA
AND THE CARIBBEAN

SUB-SAHARAN
AFRICA

NEAR EAST
AND NORTH AFRICA

EAST ASIA
AND THE PACIFIC

SOUTH ASIA

EUROPE
AND CENTRAL ASIA**

Use of IMF credit   Public long-term   Total debt as share of GNP

Private long-term   Short-term   Total debt service as share of exports of goods and services

Source: World Bank, *World Debt Tables, 1993-94*

* Projections   **Including former USSR

developed countries (accelerating in Japan and Europe and slowing in the United States); 4.5 percent in the transition economies of Europe; 3 percent in the CIS, where a return to positive growth is expected from 1996; and 5.6 percent in the developing countries.

World economic growth is expected to be driven to a large extent by dynamic trade. World merchandise exports are forecast to expand by about 10 percent per year (7.5 percent at constant prices) with the developing countries, including those of South and East Asia, showing the fastest growth in both exports and imports. Some improvement is expected in the developing countries' trade balances, more markedly those of Latin America and the Caribbean.

A less polarized regional pattern of economic performance is expected to emerge in 1996-98, with the fastest growing economies (South and East Asia and China) moderating their rate of expansion and the low-growth ones (mainly in Africa) accelerating theirs. Nevertheless, the gap between fast- and slow-growing economies is expected to remain wide. Those economies better integrated into the world economy should be better able to benefit from the overall expansion of trade and financial flows. Conversely the poorest countries, which also tend to be those less integrated and less exposed to external competition, would benefit less from the improved environment. Another factor influencing performance differential across regions is likely to be the direction of their trade links. In particular, Asia and Africa would benefit relatively more from the rising economic dynamism of Japan and Europe, their main trading counterparts, while the slower growth in the United States would negatively affect Latin America and the Caribbean.

A factor of considerable importance for the economic prospects of the developing countries will be the future course of commodity prices. The strengthening in prices of many agricultural commodities in 1994 and 1995 has resulted in large windfall gains to many developing countries. However, the longer-term outlook is for a gradual weakening of these prices. Their surge was caused by various factors of which only one – the recovery in the industrialized countries – may be expected to continue exerting a positive influence. The other factors that played a greater role in the price surge, however, were transient in nature: production shortfalls caused by bad weather coinciding with low levels of stocks and supply adjustments to earlier poor market conditions. The World Bank projections (incorporated as basic assumptions in Project LINK forecasts) point to a 2.5 percent yearly decline in the prices of agricultural commodities and a 5-6 percent yearly decline in those of beverages between 1996 and 2004. Only timber is expected to appreciate, by about 2 percent a year.

Agricultural outlook

Figure 4 summarizes Project LINK forecasts for overall and agricultural output, exports and imports. Noteworthy features include:

- Prospects for overall economic and agricultural growth appear significantly brighter than were forecast last year. This is true for the developing countries as a whole and, to varying degrees, all individual regions.
- The expected growth in agricultural output is forecast to be significantly higher than the average of the 1980s. For the developing countries as a whole, the average yearly growth in agricultural GDP in 1994-98 is forecast at 5.7 percent, compared with 3.7 percent during the 1980s. The comparable figures for the two periods are 2.2 and 1.2 percent for sub-Saharan Africa; and 3.8 and 2.3 percent for Latin America and the Caribbean. In Asia and the Pacific agricultural GDP should expand at approximately the same pace as it did in the previous decade, while in the Near East and North Africa region some slowdown is expected.
- In general, agriculture is forecast to expand at a slower pace than other sectors – this is as expected given the generally low responsiveness of agricultural demand to changes in income.[2] The contribution of agriculture to overall growth is expected to vary, generally reflecting the relative importance of agriculture in the different regions' economies.[3] Nevertheless, it is in Asia and the Pacific, the region with the highest agricultural share of output, that the greatest gap is expected between GDP and agricultural GDP growth rates. Such expectations are in line with past trends characterized by a rapid process of industrialization in the region.
- In spite of its significantly lower dynamism compared with other sectors, agricultural GDP growth in Asia and the Pacific is still forecast to be the highest among the developing country regions. Again, this would be a continuation of past trends as

---

[2] The income elasticity of demand for agricultural products in the developing countries is typically of the order of 0.1 to 0.4, compared with 0.7 to 3.4 for manufactured goods.

[3] The share of agriculture in GDP is estimated at 18 percent in sub-Saharan Africa; 24 percent in Asia and the Pacific (35 percent in China); 17 percent in the Near East and North Africa; and 9.6 percent in Latin America and the Caribbean.

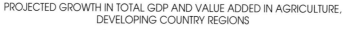

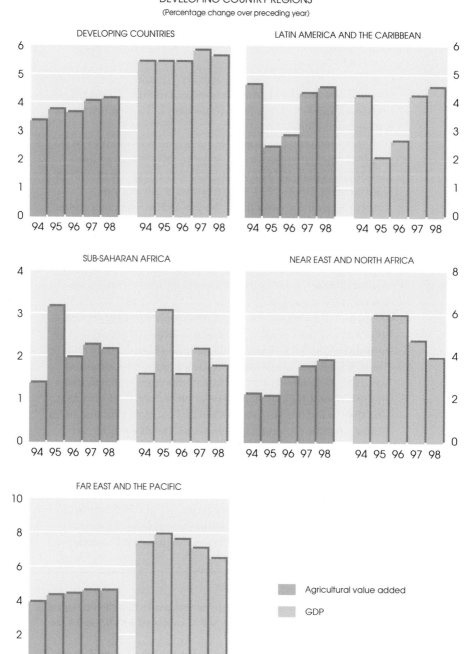

Figure 4

PROJECTED GROWTH IN TOTAL GDP AND VALUE ADDED IN AGRICULTURE,
DEVELOPING COUNTRY REGIONS
(Percentage change over preceding year)

Source: Project LINK and FAO

Note: all figures are projections

would be, on the opposite side, the lowest regional growth rates forecast for sub-Saharan Africa. For Latin America and the Caribbean the projected levels of agricultural GDP growth in 1995-98 would represent a vast improvement over the mediocre performances of the 1980s and 1990s.

Forecasts for total and agricultural trade in the developing country regions are summarized in Figure 5. The general picture is one of a strong increase in total exports in 1994 and 1995, spearheaded by booming agricultural exports; a sharp deceleration in the growth of agricultural exports in the following years, but still with a strong expansion of total exports; and a much lower expansion of total and agricultural imports, enabling sizeable improvements in trade balances. These general expectations are examined in the following section focusing on those countries for which agricultural trade matters most.

Outlook for developing country economies highly dependent on agricultural trade

This section examines the economic and agricultural prospects of two groups of countries regularly monitored in *The State of Food and Agriculture*: economies that are highly dependent on agricultural exports (EHDAEs); and low-income food-deficit countries (LIFDCs) that face particular problems in financing their food imports (FDCs). The country composition of these groups is shown in Tables 1A and 1B. The following section presents a special analysis of the problems and issues facing FDCs.

Given its pronounced agricultural export orientation, the EHDAE group is forecast to benefit greatly from the recent increase in commodity prices. Its agricultural export growth is expected to accelerate from 4 percent in 1993 to 10 percent in 1994 and then settle at around 6 percent per year for 1995-98. EHDAEs in Africa are forecast to enjoy a more dramatic but short-lived commodity price bonanza than those in Latin America and the Caribbean. Agricultural export growth in the African countries in this group is expected to bounce to over 20 percent in 1994 but then to slow down to only 3-4 percent in 1995-96. This may be explained by the more narrow agricultural export base of African countries and by the strong weight of single commodities such as cocoa, for which market prospects do not appear encouraging in the long term.

The strengthening of commodity prices should contribute to a significant improvement in the terms of trade, purchasing power of agricultural exports and trade balances of these countries.

Again, however, such improvements are forecast to be dramatic

Figure 5

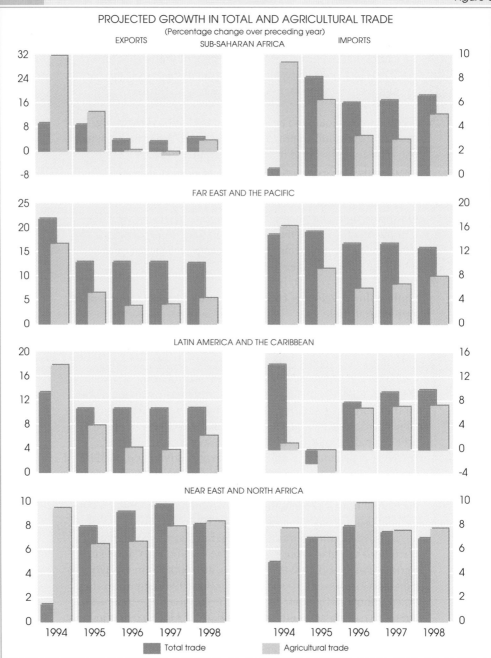

PROJECTED GROWTH IN TOTAL AND AGRICULTURAL TRADE
(Percentage change over preceding year)

EXPORTS   IMPORTS

SUB-SAHARAN AFRICA

FAR EAST AND THE PACIFIC

LATIN AMERICA AND THE CARIBBEAN

NEAR EAST AND NORTH AFRICA

1994 1995 1996 1997 1998   1994 1995 1996 1997 1998

■ Total trade   ▨ Agricultural trade

Source: Project LINK and FAO   *Note:* all figures are projections

TABLE 1A

Economies highly dependent on agricultural exports[1]

Sub-Saharan Africa	Latin America and the Caribbean	Asia and the Pacific
Côte d'Ivoire	Argentina	Sri Lanka
Malawi	Paraguay	Thailand
Zimbabwe	Honduras	Afghanistan
Mali	Cuba	Viet Nam
Sudan	Uruguay	Malaysia
Madagascar	Brazil	
Burundi	Guatemala	
Cameroon	Costa Rica	
Ghana	Colombia	
Liberia	Saint Vincent and	
Uganda	the Grenadines	
Kenya	Ecuador	
Ethiopia	Guyana	
Rwanda	Belize	
Swaziland	Dominica	
Mauritius	Nicaragua	
Central African Republic	El Salvador	
Tanzania,	Dominican Republic	
United Republic	Sao Tome and Principe	
Chad		
Burkina Faso		
Somalia		
Benin		
Guinea-Bissau		
Gambia		

[1] Countries for which agricultural, fishery and forestry exports were equivalent to 20 percent or more of their total export earnings, or 20 percent or more of their total imports, in 1988-90.

but also short-lived. In African EHDAEs, after a long period of almost uninterrupted deterioration, the barter terms of trade of agricultural exports improved by an estimated 25 percent in 1994 and an improvement of a further 7 percent is forecast for 1995. This would enable the purchasing capacity of agricultural exports to increase by about 24 percent in 1994 and 3.3 percent in 1995. However, these gains are forecast to be largely eroded in the following years, as the deteriorating trend of agricultural terms of trade is expected to resume in 1996. The forecast trends are similar, though less pronounced, for EHDAEs in Latin America and the

TABLE 1B

LIFDCs with the lowest capacity to finance food imports (FDCs)[2]

Sub-Saharan Africa	Latin America and the Caribbean	Asia and the Pacific	Near East and North Africa
Cape Verde	Haiti	Samoa	Egypt
Gambia	Nicaragua	Bangladesh	Yemen
Lesotho	Dominican	Cambodia	Sudan
Djibouti	Republic	Afghanistan	
Mozambique		Nepal	
Guinea-Bissau		Laos	
Somalia		Sri Lanka	
Comoros		Maldives	
Sierra Leone			
Ethiopia			
Burkina Faso			
Togo			
Senegal			
Benin			
Rwanda			
Mali			
Mauritania			

[2] LIFDCs for which food imports accounted for 25 percent or more of their total export earnings in 1988-90.

Caribbean. In particular, gains in purchasing capacity of agricultural exports are forecast to be relatively small in 1994-95 but the successive deterioration is also expected to be more gradual and moderate.

FDCs present the somewhat paradoxical feature of being both food-import dependent and agricultural export-based economies. Indeed, several countries belong to both the FDC and EHDAE categories. The increase in commodity exports can be expected, therefore, to have mixed effects for this group. On the one hand, their rising food import costs are likely to become more of a financial burden (even though the cereal price increases following the GATT Uruguay Round and agricultural reform in major exporting countries may be smaller than were suggested by early estimates – see Part III, p. 199). On the other hand, these countries will also benefit from the increase in prices of several of their main export products. The net result of these opposing influences is expected to be positive in the short term, as food import costs in FDCs are forecast to rise at a slower pace than export earnings from agriculture (approximately 7 percent and 18 percent per year, respectively, in 1994-95). In the longer term (1996-2000), however, the growth in food import costs is expected to rise to over 8 percent per year, while that in agricultural export earnings is forecast to decelerate sharply to less than 2 percent in 1996-97 and to increase only moderately thereafter. The agricultural trade deficit is forecast to narrow initially (from $US2.5 billion in 1993 to $2 billion in 1994 and $1.8 billion in 1995), but widen again to $3-3.5 billion in the following years. The overall trade deficit, estimated at about $17 billion in 1994 (about the same as in 1993), is forecast to increase slightly in 1995 and more markedly in the following years.

A number of observations can be drawn from the above review. Two general influences will largely determine the economic and agricultural outlook of the developing countries; the first of these is the expected continuing improvement in the global economic environment, which the developing countries will both contribute to and benefit from. The second influence is the strengthening of international prices of several important export commodities. The two influences are interrelated, to the extent that, on the one hand, better economic conditions can be expected to sustain the demand for and prices of agricultural commodities, while, on the other hand, the windfall gains from improved commodity markets not only provide a welcome boost to many stressed economies, but also generate opportunities for consolidating stabilization and reform, thus enabling countries to take better advantage of the improved economic environment. The latter effect is, however, conditional on a number of factors. There is a well-documented tendency for long-strained governments and individuals to consume, rather than capitalize on, sudden and large windfalls. The risk of this happening is all the more pronounced if complacent perceptions emerge on the nature and sustainability of such windfalls.

In the worst of scenarios, the windfall gains would contribute little to enhancing growth and welfare in the long term. In the short term they would create immediate financial management difficulties and "Dutch disease" effects leading to excessive currency appreciation and competitive losses. In other words, the windfalls may create as many problems as they solve and may mean, for the countries concerned, an eventual return to the *status quo ante*.

However, sound and timely policy action can avert this negative turn of events. Such action involves: first, a full awareness of the narrow base and transient nature of the commodity price bonanza; second, that governments view the bonanza as a developmental, rather than a short-term political opportunity; and third, that the right choices are made among a wide range of policy options. For instance, windfall gains can be used to invest in the most productive sectors or to encourage a broad-based participation of less favoured segments of the society. Governments may place priority on reducing macroeconomic imbalances and debt or decide that productive investment comes first. Financial resources may be used on domestic assets, programmes or projects, or invested in a diversified international portfolio as a means of reducing risks. The relative merit of the various options will depend on country-specific needs and circumstances. It is important, in any case, that due priority be given to the agricultural sector, bearing in mind its food security and economic role in the countries concerned and the disastrous sequels of past policies that neglected or overtaxed the sector.

WORLD REVIEW
III. Selected issues

FOOD IMPORTS AND EXPORT PERFORMANCE IN LOW-INCOME FOOD-DEFICIT COUNTRIES WITH THE LOWEST CAPACITY TO FINANCE IMPORTS

Introduction

Although agriculture generally dominates their economies, many low-income developing countries have been net food importers for a long time. Furthermore, over the last two decades the food trade balance has tended to deteriorate in many of them. Neither production nor the financial resources to import have kept pace with the growing demand for food. The ability to pay for food imports depends critically on export earnings which in many cases have been inadequate. These problems are particularly acute in the countries reviewed in this section, i.e. in those low-income food-deficit countries (LIFDCs) with the lowest capacity to finance food imports (FDCs). This group includes 31 countries and is a subgroup of the FAO-defined LIFDC group which currently comprises 88 countries.

The excessive food import dependence of many poor countries has always been prominent in the development debate, but the recent conclusion of the Uruguay Round of GATT negotiations has drawn even greater attention to the issue. Trade liberalization is expected to lead to higher prices for agricultural products in international markets. In addition, several of these countries will increasingly have to pay world market prices as export subsidies in their favour are reduced. This may provide an opportunity for increasing agricultural output and rural employment in the importing countries, as long as higher prices are allowed to reach the farmers. However, any longer-term benefits on the side of domestic production, exports and import substitution opportunities have to be weighed against the immediate problems of paying more to cover food import needs and possibly of higher prices to consumers.

Many FDCs are large recipients of food aid and other emergency relief arrangements. They have also benefited from external financial assistance and other forms of non-export-generated inflows. However, a longer-term solution is required, bearing in mind that the prospects for external assistance are not encouraging and that food aid resources, already declining in recent years, may decline further as a result of the decreases in food stocks that are expected to follow the Uruguay Round agreement. This review aims at providing quantitative information on some of the determinants of the problem, which can be helpful references for the design of appropriate policies for the long term.

The evolution and structure of food imports

The 31 FDCs considered in this review were selected from among the 88 LIFDCs on the criterion that their food imports absorbed one-quarter or more of their total export earnings during 1988-90.

Table 2 provides some basic information on FDCs. Most countries in this group are small in terms of population – only ten of them have more than 10 million inhabitants. However, their combined population rose from 270 million in 1972 to 400 million in 1991, implying generally high rates of population growth. These are also, by definition, low-income countries with per caput GNP less than US$1 000 in 1991. For some of them (Mozambique, Guinea-Bissau, Somalia, Sierra Leone, Ethiopia and Nepal) per caput GNP was $200 or less.

The magnitude of the food-import financing problem varies considerably among FDCs (Table 3). In 1989-91 the value of food imports as a percentage of total export earnings varied from 24.2 percent (Maldives) to 493.5 percent (Cape Verde). Other countries where total export earnings were insufficient to finance the food import bill included: the Gambia (with a ratio of food imports to exports of 168.8 percent), Lesotho (173.7 percent), Guinea-Bissau (109.9 percent) and Samoa (166.5 percent). In those countries it would appear hard to explain how food imports, let alone less essential imports, can be financed at all. However, explanations generally relate to the availability of non-export sources of financing, such as major net official transfers (that strongly benefited Cape Verde and Guinea-Bissau but also many other FDCs); remittances from expatriates (e.g. Lesotho migrant workers, most of whom are in South Africa); earnings from tourism (such as in Samoa, the Gambia and other FDCs); re-exports not accounted for in official statistics (as in the Gambia); and a strong food aid component of total food imports in many cases.

As well as these extreme situations, there are many other countries that spend a very high percentage of their export earnings on importing food. On average, the FDCs as a whole spend a little more than 50 percent on food imports: 82.4 percent in the countries of the Near East and North Africa; 47.7 in those of sub-Saharan Africa; and about 33 percent in the other two regions.

Perhaps even more worrying is the rate at which these

TABLE 2

Population and current per caput GNP of FDCs

	1972		1991	
	Population	Per caput GNP	Population	Per caput GNP
	('000)	(US$)	('000)	(US$)
Cape Verde	273	150	380	750
Gambia	489	130	958	340
Lesotho	1 110	110	1 812	580
Djibouti	198	...	467	...
Mozambique	9 845	...	16 108	80
Guinea-Bissau	551	160	1 001	200
Somalia	4 559	90	7 805	120
Comoros	279	110	510	510
Sierra Leone	2 760	160	4 243	200
Ethiopia	30 476	70	52 954	120
Burkina Faso	5 848	70	52 954	120
Togo	2 121	150	3 770	410
Senegal	4 405	230	7 624	730
Benin	2 800	140	4 886	380
Rwanda	3 954	80	8 707	250
Mali	5 564	80	8 707	250
Mauritania	1 277	180	2 024	510
Haiti	4 677	100	6 593	380
Nicaragua	2 204	370	3 773	300
Dominican Republic	4 672	430	7 197	940
Samoa	...	...	...	...
Bangladesh	80 000	80	112 000	210
Cambodia	7 114	...	8 774	...
Afghanistan	14 356	...	19 062	...
Nepal	11 890	80	19 401	180
Laos	2 844	...	4 384	250
Sri Lanka	12 861	190	17 247	500
Maldives	127	...	227	...
Egypt	34 253	260	53 571	610
Yemen	6 549	...	12 999	520
Sudan	15 167	230	25 812	...

Source: World Bank. World Tables, 1994; FAO.

TABLE 3

FDCs: selected indicators of food-import size and weight in total trade (by region)

	Value of food imports	Food imports: total imports	Food imports: export earnings	Per caput food imports
	(US$'000)	*(%)*	*(%)*	*(US$)*
1961-63				
Sub-Saharan Africa	136 132	19.0	27.9	2.2
Latin America				
and the Caribbean	29 091	11.7	10.2	3.2
Asia and the Pacific	237 337	24.1	27.6	2.5
Near East				
and North Africa	256 547	19.6	29.9	5.8
TOTAL	659 107	20.2	26.5	3.2
1975-77				
Sub-Saharan Africa	604 016	18.8	32.6	6.7
Latin America				
and the Caribbean	188 456	12.1	13.2	14.9
Asia and the Pacific	652 072	28.2	46.0	4.9
Near East				
and North Africa	1 419 944	22.8	61.9	23.3
TOTAL	2 864 488	21.5	41.0	9.7
1989-91				
Sub-Saharan Africa	1 626 928	20.8	47.7	13.1
Latin America				
and the Caribbean	452 089	15.9	36.7	26.1
Asia and the Pacific	1 197 395	14.9	31.2	6.6
Near East				
and North Africa	3 144 237	25.3	82.4	35.2
TOTAL	6 420 685	20.6	52.2	15.6

Source: FAO.

percentages have grown. In 1961-63, FDCs were spending on average 26 percent of their export earnings on food imports, half the rate of recent years. To a certain extent this trend could be sustained by larger revenues from non-export or unofficial sources, as mentioned above.

An alternative way of assessing the food import issue in FDCs is to examine the share of their food imports in total merchandise imports. This is an important indicator of a country's overall import priorities or needs. A high share of food in total imports implies (apart from its difficulties to finance such food imports) that the country concerned is also deprived of the ability to finance the development process by importing productive inputs. This situation is typical of FDCs. On average, about one-fifth of their total imports are accounted for by food, with this percentage remaining relatively constant over the last 30 years. The comparable figure is about 10 percent for the developing countries as a whole. The severity of this problem varies considerably among the individual countries. In Mauritania and Sierra Leone, for example, over half of total imports are accounted for by food.

Cereals account for about half of the food imports to these countries (Tables 4 and 5). For the group as a whole the share of cereal imports in the total has remained fairly constant during the past 30 years except for in the mid-1970s (following the world food crisis) when the share of cereals rose to 60 percent of food imports. The share has tended to increase in the case of sub-Saharan Africa; has remained unchanged in Latin America and the Caribbean and the Near East and North Africa; and has declined in Asia and the Pacific.

Origin of imports
Table 6 shows the origins of total and food imports for the developing countries as a whole (see also Diversifying markets and intensifying intraregional exchanges, p. 214). Information on the origin of imports was not readily available for the group of FDCs alone, but patterns for this group can be assumed to be fairly similar to those for the developing countries as a whole.

In 1991 food imports originated mainly in the developed market economies (57 percent of the total), the developing countries accounting for only 35 percent and Central and Eastern European countries and the Socialist countries of Asia for 8 percent. Dependence on the developed market economies for food imports was a little higher in 1970 and 1980, but it should be noted that the developing countries depend even more on the developed market economies for non-food imports.

Export structure and agricultural exports
As noted earlier, FDCs are heavily dependent both on food imports and on export earnings from agriculture (Tables 7A and 7B).

In 1990, the share of agricultural exports in total exports exceeded 80 percent in ten of the 26 countries for which data are available. In another five countries the share exceeded 60 percent.

TABLE 4

Share of cereals in food imports (by country)

	1961	1975-77	1989-91
	(........................... % ....)		
Cape Verde	49.0	46.5	48.4
Gambia	50.0	50.1	30.5
Lesotho	2.7	23.1	14.4
Djibouti	54.4	25.0	28.8
Mozambique	37.2	70.9	67.7
Guinea-Bissau	40.5	60.0	73.0
Somalia	45.8	62.9	74.5
Comoros	84.9	65.7	57.5
Sierra Leone	25.3	22.6	54.3
Ethiopia	19.4	61.4	75.5
Burkina Faso	15.8	34.9	48.6
Togo	14.4	14.7	43.6
Senegal	3.2	45.5	47.5
Benin	21.6	38.8	51.8
Rwanda	0.0	10.8	24.1
Mali	7.7	41.6	32.1
Mauritania	40.8	37.1	35.3
Haiti	48.0	64.0	48.3
Nicaragua	43.7	30.5	50.8
Dominican Republic	44.3	64.8	42.2
Samoa	23.3	23.4	18.7
Bangladesh	96.1	93.3	52.6
Cambodia	17.7	88.5	80.4
Afghanistan	33.6	6.4	38.0
Nepal	3.4	0.5	3.7
Laos	88.5	92.3	44.3
Sri Lanka	46.4	85.2	40.5
Maldives	29.7	41.8	54.2
Egypt	66.8	68.7	54.9
Yemen	23.9	31.3	42.3
Sudan	18.2	16.8	56.9

Source: FAO.

TABLE 5

Share of cereals in food imports (by region)

	1961-63	1975-77	1989-91
	(.............................. % ....)		
Sub-Saharan Africa	32.1	43.6	48.4
Latin America and the Caribbean	45.1	56.9	45.8
Asia and the Pacific	63.2	82.1	42.9
Near East and North Africa	52.1	57.8	52.6
TOTAL	51.1	60.3	49.2

Source: FAO.

TABLE 6

Import structure by origin (all products, all food items)

Origin	All products			All food items		
	1970	1980	1991	1970	1980	1991
Developed market economy countries	72.2	62.7	63.5	61.4	62.7	57.1
Developing countries	19.0	29.6	29.2	28.5	27.7	34.9
Central and Eastern European countries	6.9	5.9	1.7	4.6	3.9	1.6
Socialist countries of Asia	1.8	1.8	5.6	5.5	5.6	6.4
World	100.0	100.0	100.0	100.0	100.0	100.0

Source: UNCTAD, Handbook of International Trade and Development Statistics, 1993.

In general, however, this share tended to decline over the past three decades, reflecting to a large extent the poor performances of the agricultural export sector.

In only 11 out of the 26 countries did the exports of manufactures account for more than 20 percent of total export earnings. In three – Afghanistan, Egypt and to a lesser extent Senegal – fuels are an important export item.

In many FDCs agricultural exports are highly concentrated on one or a few agricultural products (Table 8, p. 50). However, among the countries that have shown a distinct trend between 1961 and 1992, a majority of about 60 percent have seen greater commodity diversification and only a minority showed an increase of the dependence on one or a few commodities.

The distinction between agricultural export products that

TABLE 7A

Export structure by main categories (percentage of total value of exports)

Country	All food		Agricultural raw materials	
	1970	1990	1970	1990
Cape Verde	80.6	83.3 [2]	1.9	-
Gambia	99.8	87.3 [6]	0.2	1.6 [6]
Lesotho	...	...	...	...
Djibouti	...	...	...	...
Mozambique	57.2	65.7 [7]	23.1	4.0 [7]
Guinea-Bissau	...	...	...	...
Somalia	85.5	85.6 [3]	8.2	11.1 [3]
Comoros	69.3	71.0 [7]	0.4	1.6 [7]
Sierra Leone	16.4	31.1 [7]	0.7	0.5 [7]
Ethiopia	85.9	77.2 [6]	10.7	16.8 [6]
Burkina Faso	67.9	24.5 [6]	27.6	43.2 [6]
Togo	67.2	22.1 [7]	2.2	16.2 [7]
Senegal	64.8	45.6 [7]	4.1	2.6 [7]
Benin	70.9	61.8 [2]	18.3	25.0 [2]
Rwanda	60.7	79.5	3.2	11.0
Mali	64.8	22.6	23.9	65.8
Mauritania	8.3	64.3 [5]	2.5	0.2 [5]
Haiti	51.7	21.7 [7]	5.8	1.0 [7]
Nicaragua	56.8	73.4 [4]	23.8	13.8 [4]
Dominican Republic	87.8	22.0	0.1	0.5
Samoa	94.4	89.1 [7]	1.0	3.4 [7]
Bangladesh	9.8 [1]	15.0 [7]	26.4 [1]	7.7 [7]
Cambodia	...	...	...	...
Afghanistan	36.1	23.9 [6]	35.8	16.0 [6]
Nepal	28.6 [1]	22.1 [7]	39.8 [1]	11.6 [7]
Laos	5.5	30.9 [2]	27.6	38.6 [2]
Sri Lanka	72.6	34.0	25.3	8.6
Maldives	...	...	...	...
Egypt	21.3	8.9 [7]	46.3	11.4 [7]
Yemen	82.7	50.0 [4]	7.6	6.2 [4]
Sudan	24.6	38.7	74.6	58.4

[1] Data collected in 1975.
[2] Data collected in 1980.
[3] Data collected in 1985.
[4] Data collected in 1986.
[5] Data collected in 1987.
[6] Data collected in 1988.
[7] Data collected in 1989.

TABLE 7B

Export structure by main categories (percentage of total value of exports)

Country	Fuels		Ores and metals		Manufactured	
	1970	1990	1970	1990	1970	1990
Cape Verde	-	-	11.0	2.8 [6]	6.5	11.1 [6]
Gambia	-	-	-	-	-	10.2 [6]
Lesotho	...	...	...	...	...	...
Djibouti	...	...	...	...	...	...
Mozambique	8.1	0.1 [7]	2.1	12.1 [7]	9.5	17.5 [7]
Guinea-Bissau	...	...	...	...	...	...
Somalia	-	0.2 [3]	0.1	0.2 [3]	4.9	1.9 [3]
Comoros	-	-	-	0.8 [7]	30.2	26.6 [7]
Sierra Leone	2.6	3.5 [7]	18.9	43.4 [7]	60.8	20.6 [7]
Ethiopia	1.2	3.0 [6]	0.6	0.2 [6]	1.6	2.7 [6]
Burkina Faso	-	-	0.1	0.2 [6]	4.4	7.3 [6]
Togo	-	-	24.9	53.4 [7]	5.7	7.1 [7]
Senegal	2.9	18.6 [7]	9.3	7.0 [7]	18.8	25.9 [7]
Benin	0.2	4.2 [2]	0.1	1.1 [2]	10.6	3.4 [2]
Rwanda	-	-	35.0	1.4	-	1.5
Mali	0.1	0.1	0.7	0.1	9.6	6.8
Mauritania	0.1	3.9 [5]	88.3	31.2 [5]	0.8	0.4 [5]
Haiti	-	-	16.9	1.0 [7]	23.7	71.9 [7]
Nicaragua	0.1	1.0 [4]	3.2	1.3 [4]	16.0	7.3 [4]
Dominican Republic	-	-	7.5	1.5	3.6	70.4
Samoa	-	-	-	-	1.3	-
Bangladesh	-	1.2 [7]	-	-	63.6 [1]	75.2 [7]
Cambodia	...	...	...	...	...	...
Afghanistan	16.9	42.9 [6]	-	-	10.9	17.1 [6]
Nepal	-	-	-	-	37.7 [1]	65.8 [7]
Laos	-	-	36.1	22.5 [2]	30.8	7.6 [2]
Sri Lanka	-	6.2	0.7	1.5	1.4	49.3
Maldives	...	...	...	...	...	...
Egypt	4.8 3	0.5 [7]	0.6	10.2 [7]	27.1	39.0 [7]
Yemen	-	6.2 [4]	9.5	1.4 [4]	0.1	33.6 [4]
Sudan	0.4	0.4	0.4	0.3	0.1	1.3

Source: UNCTAD, *Handbook of International Trade and Development Statistics, 1993.*

TABLE 8

Share of main agricultural export commodities in total agricultural exports

Country	1961	1970	1980	1992	Product
Cape Verde	...	...	...	...	...
Gambia	85.5	47.9	54.7	23.2	Groundnuts
Lesotho	50.5	63.8	35.1	26.9	Cattle, wool
Djibouti	...	...	...	...	...
Mozambique	28.7	20.3	34.8	...	Cotton, cashew
Guinea-Bissau	33.2	70.0	29.2	38.4	Groundnuts, cashew nuts
Somalia	49.2	29.2	27.8	20.4	Bananas, sheep, goats
Comoros	59.9	45.8	81.2	93.9	Vanilla, cloves
Sierra Leone	50.8	43.0	45.7	17.2	Palm kernels, coffee
Ethiopia	58.6	64.4	69.6	55.2	Coffee
Burkina Faso	57.8	23.2	49.8	70.8	Cotton, cattle
Togo	35.3	60.4	50.2	62.9	Cocoa beans, cotton
Senegal	43.6	46.0	28.0	...	Groundnut oil
Benin	15.7	19.9	26.0	71.6	Palm oil, cocoa beans, cotton
Rwanda	85.6	87.5	66.8	58.4	Coffee
Mali	28.5	44.3	41.6	60.0	Cattle, cotton
Mauritania	50.9	33.0	46.9	74.3	Cattle, shellfish (fresh, frozen and cured)
Haiti	52.7	63.9	80.5	37.7	Coffee
Nicaragua	32.7	24.1	44.1	23.6	Coffee, cotton
Dominican Republic	46.6	55.7	55.6	40.6	Sugar
Samoa	...	...	...	...	...
Bangladesh	84.5	73.1	58.7	33.3	Jute
Cambodia	32.6	16.8	97.6	69.0	Rubber dry, industrial roundwood (non-coniferous)
Afghanistan	24.1	18.2	41.7	41.9	Raisins, fur, skins
Nepal	18.1	...	19.7	33.7	Sugar cane, jute, lentils
Laos	32.7	84.6	66.6	41.0	Nutmeg, sawnwood, coffee
Sri Lanka	67.4	58.2	54.9	50.9	Tea
Maldives	100.0	100.0	69.7	...	Copra, finfish
Egypt	81.4	66.3	62.5	12.8	Cotton
Yemen	22.1	23.9	33.7	17.4	Coffee, cotton, water melons
Sudan	52.4	62.5	42.6	31.9	Cotton
ALL COUNTRIES	**49.3**	**49.9**	**50.5**	**44.3**	

Source: FAO, Country tables, various years, Economic and Social Policy Department, Rome.

compete with products in the developed countries and those that do not has significant policy implications. This distinction provides a broad indication of the extent to which FDCs as a group can expect to capture a larger share of developed country markets through successful price competition; or whether they have to depend mainly on the demand for their "non-competing" agricultural exports. In other words, countries that specialize in non-competing products need to compete among themselves to capture developed country markets, which in many cases are already saturated or have limited long-term potential. On the other hand, markets for several competing products are more dynamic and can be expected to benefit from the trade liberalization and reductions in support consecutive to the Uruguay Round.

The identification of these different types of product is difficult and to a certain extent arbitrary. Here we adopt the definition of "broadly non-competing" products as used by Riedel[4] to refer to those products for which the developing country share of world exports exceeds 80 percent. The products are cocoa, coffee, tea, bananas, spices, copra, groundnuts, palm oil, coconut oil, jute, natural rubber, sisal and silk.

Table 9 shows the widely varying degrees of dependence on non-competing products in FDCs. For some countries, non-competing products account for over 90 percent of total agricultural exports (for example, in island states with very narrow resource bases, such as the Comoros and Cape Verde, and in coffee-dependent Rwanda), while for others the share is insignificant (for example, in the cotton exporters Egypt, Mali and the Sudan). However, a large majority of these countries have recorded a move towards "competing" exports. This tendency, and the somewhat reduced dependence on a few major export products observed above, suggests that opportunities for export diversification are being exploited even by particularly poor and resource-deprived countries. A more diversified export structure should provide opportunities for expanding and stabilizing FDCs' export earnings from agriculture. The fact that this has not occurred and that agricultural export performances have remained generally disappointing in FDCs (Table 10) reflect, in particular, the poor initial conditions from which improvements have been achieved in many of these countries as well as the general market conditions and policy environment that govern agricultural trade (see Part III,

---

[4] J. Riedel. 1984. Trade as the engine of growth in the developing countries, revisited. *Economic Journal*, 94 (373): 56-73.

TABLE 9

Broadly non-competing agricultural exports as a percentage of total agricultural exports

	1961	1991
Cape Verde	80.1	95.3
Gambia	85.1	46.4
Lesotho	0.0	0.0
Djibouti	...	...
Mozambique	30.8	15.2
Guinea-Bissau	71.2	1.2
Somalia	50.8	8.7
Comoros	100.0	100.0
Sierra Leone	25.5	87.5
Ethiopia	62.8	56.9
Burkina Faso	0.0	0.4
Togo	80.2	26.4
Senegal	43.0	7.6
Benin	67.5	2.6
Rwanda	85.9	92.7
Mali	30.3	0.1
Mauritania	0.0	0.0
Haiti	72.3	49.8
Nicaragua	37.4	42.9
Dominican Republic	32.1	24.1
Samoa	98.1	26.7
Bangladesh	72.2	87.5
Cambodia	2.9	0.0
Afghanistan	0.0	0.0
Nepal	3.3	7.0
Laos	61.0	35.1
Sri Lanka	94.0	85.0
Maldives	100.0	0.0
Egypt	0.7	3.7
Yemen	28.0	22.8
Sudan	9.3	2.2

Source: FAO.

p. 199). Whatever headway in efficiency or diversification these countries may be able to achieve, its effective translation into competitive gains will depend crucially on progress in trade liberalization and improved access to developed countries' markets.

TABLE 10

Selected FDCs: indicators of agricultural export performance

	Export volume, volume, annual rate of change		Net barter terms of agricultural trade	Purchasing power of agricultural exports
	1971-1980	1981-1990	1992-1993	1992-1993
	(.............. % ....)		(..... 1979-81 = 100 .....)	
Afghanistan	5.2	-11.6	107	20
Bangladesh	1.7	0.4	71	56
Sri Lanka	1.8	2.2	54	48
Egypt	-4.8	-1.9	30	37
Ethiopia	0.8	1.0	87	31
Mauritania	-1.4	-3.6	125	78
Mozambique	-5.4	-8.5	73	16
Sierra Leone	-2.2	-2.9	31	12
Sudan	4.4	3.3	50	57
Dominican Republic	-1.7	-4.3	59	36
Nicaragua	5.6	-0.1	56	27

Note: Net barter agricultural terms of trade are agricultural export prices deflated by import prices of manufactures and crude petroleum; the purchasing power of agricultural exports is calculated by deflating export values by import prices. Thus, the difference between the two indices is accounted for by changes in export volumes. For instance, Afghanistan improved agricultural terms of trade by 7 percent between 1979-81 and 1992-93; but the decline in export volumes caused the purchasing capacity of agricultural exports to fall by 80 percent during this period. Source: FAO.

Sustainability of high food-import dependence

The fact that FDCs are predominantly agriculture-based economies facing particular difficulties to finance the most essential of imports – food – indicates serious general development problems. The problems of food-import dependence are worsening in these countries. This implies increasing costs for FDCs' treasuries and also in terms of external dependence in general, of development opportunities missed because of the need to limit imports of productive capital goods and of a precarious base for food security.

A recent study conducted for FAO attempted to quantify the impact of the factors affecting food imports in these countries.[5] The

---

[5] G. Zanias. *Food imports and export performance in low-income food-deficit countries with the lowest capacity to finance imports.* Forthcoming as an FAO Economic and Social Development Paper. Rome. FAO.

results of this study are revealing, as much for what they do not show as for what they do. They confirm the importance of changes in import prices, purchasing capacity of exports and, more than any other factor, domestic production performances, in determining food imports. The results, however, did not always conform to expectations or, in spite of the use of sophisticated econometric techniques, did so leaving margins of uncertainty. In addition, such important factors as changes in per caput incomes and foreign exchange reserves did not appear to influence food imports. These sometimes puzzling or inconclusive results indicate the existence of other factors and influences that require further case-by-case investigation, but they also point to another general conclusion. It has been observed that many FDCs purchase far more food than their export sector can afford. This is so because the external account gap is covered primarily through financial or food assistance, remittances and other, more or less reliable, sources of income.[6] Thus, it is hardly surprising that in many cases food imports should not depend on export performances, in the short term at least. Large but irregular flows of resources from non-export origins may also help to explain why food imports should not appear to react much to such fundamentals as changes in import prices, domestic income or international reserves.

Such situations present obvious risks. The sustainability of non-trade forms of financing can be questioned to the extent that they largely depend on discretionary donor dispositions or other similarly uncertain sources of financing. If allowed to continue, the combination of high and growing dependence on food imports and precarious or unreliable sources of financing may create explosive situations.

The variable that appears to have the greatest impact on food imports in FDCs is domestic food production. This unsurprising finding has important implications. On the one hand, it suggests that these countries have found the resources to import more food

---

[6] IMF data indicate that strong dependence on food imports in these countries is only one aspect of the major imbalances in their overall current accounts. Their balance of trade and services has shown a chronic deficit, estimated at about US$17 billion in recent years. This has been only partially covered by positive net current transfers of about $14 billion. Being heavily indebted (their external debt currently represents over 450 percent of their annual export earnings), these countries have benefited, however, from various debt alleviation measures that have kept debt service payments at relatively low levels.

in periods of domestic production shortfalls, even though international market conditions or other variables affecting import decisions may have been negative. This is, again, largely related to the availability of external assistance in various forms. On the other hand, positive changes in domestic supply conditions resulted in commensurate reductions in food purchases, underlining the importance of domestic agriculture in alleviating external welfare and import dependence.

Agricultural specialization has not enabled FDCs to develop a strong agricultural export base or expand their domestic food supply adequately. Yet, for many FDCs there are currently few alternatives to agriculture-based development, and it is likely to be a long time before these countries are able to diversify their overall economic structures significantly and gain competitiveness in other economic sectors. Conversely, several FDCs may have a considerable potential for developing agriculture efficiently and thus reducing import dependence and/or enhancing export revenues. The observed move towards diversification of agricultural exports in many FDCs is an encouraging feature in this context. The most effective way of achieving food security, financial autonomy and maximization of developmental opportunities may, therefore, still be to enhance the productive potential of domestic agriculture.

POLICY REFORM AND THE CONSUMER

Since the early 1980s, policy reforms initiated in many countries have been biased in favour of greater market orientation and a more open economy. Such reforms have had a substantial impact on food consumers, by directly and indirectly affecting the factors that determine food demand, as well as on food producers because of changes in agricultural policies and policy measures. The following discussion examines how and why these policy reforms have come about, and the effects they are expected to have had on consumers.

Most, although certainly not all, analyses of the effects of policy reform in the economic literature have attempted to quantify the impacts of the agricultural market and trade liberalization on the producer and on the net welfare of the country as a whole. Rather less attention has been given to the taxpayer and particularly little to the consumer. As a result, this review presents a conceptual overview that is supported to the extent possible by the limited empirical findings available.

Food consumers in the policy process

Why should the food consumer have received comparatively so little attention? In the first place because, to the extent that macroeconomists analyse the impacts of macropolicy measures on real sectors of the economy, including agriculture, they tend to be concerned with whether the country as a whole gains or loses. It is often not politically astute to expose the gains (far less the losses) of individual groups and, indeed, the necessary data are often not available in the quantity and quality required to perform such analyses. Furthermore, much of the economic analysis is driven by or directed towards ministries of agriculture and trade which, by and large, consider their clientele to be respectively agricultural producers and exporters (including agricultural exporters).

Another reason is that although – or perhaps because – every person in society is a food consumer, food consumers for the most part are not generally organized to bring systematic political pressure to bear on policies that run counter to their best interests. An increasing number of countries have consumer associations that focus on providing better information to consumers, directing their lobbying power accordingly. At the same time, many of the higher-income countries have seen the formation of consumer advocacy groups around specific issues such as tighter meat and slaughterhouse inspection, banning the use of growth hormones, increasing the nutritional levels in feeding programmes or the more general issue of food safety. Given that, as income increases the proportion of household income spent on food declines and consumption patterns shift in favour of preferred higher value items in terms of both perceived quality (for example, paying a premium for meat and eggs produced in more "humane" production systems) and quantity, the interests of different income groups diverge and, arguably, consumer groups tend to reflect disproportionately the concerns of the better-off and more politically articulate consumers.

In contrast, the issues that have, usually informally, united consumers (especially urban consumers) in the lower-income countries have been food shortages, high food prices and sudden large increases in food prices. Consumers' concerns have been manifested in demonstrations or sometimes riots and governments have occasionally even fallen as a result. Many developing countries have therefore had policies to subsidize food prices for urban consumers. Since the ministries of agriculture and trade tend to be the focus of any consumer unrest, who better at least to demonstrate concern about the impacts of the policies they promulgate on all affected groups, including the consumer?

Whither policy reform?
In the developing countries, government policies have led to pervasive price distortions and hence misallocation of resources. Vollrath reports that empirical findings indicate that "the trade,

macroeconomic and sector-specific pricing policies adopted in the developing countries since the early 1950s have given rise to the following incentive biases: against the production of tradable goods and in favour of non-tradables; within the tradable goods sector, against exports compared with import-competing goods; within the export sector, against agricultural products compared with manufactured goods; and within agriculture, against export compared with food crops".[7] The correction of these policy distortions has necessitated painful adjustments.

Pressures for policy reform during the past 15 years have four main sources. First, a large number of countries that had taken on very high levels of external debt in the 1970s suddenly found, in the early 1980s, that their economic circumstances were reversed and they could no longer sustain their heavy debt burdens. Belt-tightening and policy reform became the order of the day. Such structural adjustment usually called for: the reduction of government spending; the reduction of government intervention in or its complete withdrawal from agricultural input and output markets; the phasing-out of subsidies; the privatization of the functions of former parastatals; and the devaluation of overvalued exchange rates, i.e. in general, "getting the prices right".

Second, beginning in the first half of the 1980s, a number of countries, particularly in the developed world, found that the budgetary costs of supporting their farmers in the style to which they had become accustomed had become untenable. Much of the policy reform that has taken place in these countries has been prompted by the desire to limit government budget exposure. Reform has consisted of more precise definition and directing of aid to beneficiary groups, lower support levels, decoupling support payments from current production and reducing the presence of the government.

Third, the late 1980s and early 1990s saw the breakdown of the command and control economies of Central and Eastern Europe and the republics of the former USSR and the beginning of a difficult and painful process of transition towards more open market-oriented economies. In the early stages, the transition process disrupted traditional trading patterns, drastically reduced real per caput incomes, reduced demand and disrupted production, processing and distribution. It is only recently that some countries of Central and Eastern Europe have begun to recover from this

---

[7] **T.L. Vollrath. 1994. The role of agriculture and its prerequisites in economic development.** *Food Policy*, **19(5): 469-478.**

initial plunge in economic well-being. As part of the transition process, even the most basic legal and economic institutions had to be created to allow and encourage the private sector to operate as part of a functioning market economy.

Finally, even countries that do not fall into any of the above categories have been caught up in the general moves to reduce the presence of government in those areas where the private sector can perform better and more efficiently and to liberalize markets and trade.

The last 15 years have seen a serious questioning of the very role of government in a market-driven economy. From this questioning and from necessity, policy reform in the direction of open market-orientation has taken place to varying degrees in almost every country. An important outcome is that food prices are increasingly being determined by market forces, i.e. by the interaction of the relationship between demand and supply.

The effects of policy reform on food consumers depend, therefore, on the extent to which the policy measures abandoned and those adopted affect the determinants of demand and of consumer supply. It is, however, difficult to predict the probable outcomes of changes in individual variables because the complex of policy reforms under structural adjustment programmes, in the transition economies and as a result of the GATT agreement (and any combination of the above), have a variety of effects on both supply and demand functions. The overall outcome for consumer prices and total quantity purchased will depend on the direction and magnitude of the shifts in the demand and supply curves and also on the price elasticities of demand and supply.

In addition, the adjustment period following the introduction of major policy reforms can be long. To free prices so that they can be determined by market forces means the "marketization" of all aspects of the production and marketing system. Experience has shown that, initially, liberalization and privatization of the processing and distribution sectors often result in serious slowdowns of production and little competitive challenge. The reason for the former is that the withdrawal of the state from these parts of the marketing chain can rarely be substituted immediately by hitherto underdeveloped private institutions. The lack of competitive challenge comes when a government or parastatal monopoly is replaced by a private one – such a change in ownership merely changes the recipient of monopoly profits. The outcome is that during the adjustment period the transmission of price signals through the marketing chain is severely hindered in both directions. In other words, the signals about consumer demand that are sent at the retail level are not being properly transmitted through the intermediate levels of processing, distribution and wholesaling to farmers so that they can alter their production decisions accordingly. Neither are the signals about the supply of agricultural and food products, whether they originate with the farmer or elsewhere in the marketing system, being adequately sent through the marketing chain to the consumer. Consequently, the pressures to reduce consumer prices and respond to changing consumer demand through increases in the efficiency and effectiveness of marketing may well, in the short to medium term, have no effect on the retail price increases caused by subsidy removal. Many governments have yet to put appropriate policies in place to address these problems.

In fact, the whole question of consumer supply – i.e. the relationship between quantities of different food items supplied at the retail level and retail prices – is particularly complex because it depends on a whole range of variables among which policy measures tend to figure prominently. Macroeconomic policies (especially those relating to the exchange rate and exchange controls), trade policies, fiscal policies, agricultural support measures (and the way in which they are implemented) and any other policies that affect the development of the food processing and distribution industries all affect consumer supply (i.e. supply at the retail level). Furthermore, the extent to which the retail supply of food depends on the supply of domestically produced agricultural and processed products is extremely variable both across countries and within the same country at different times and for different items. This degree of complexity means that, even if one could be reasonably sure about the effects of specific policy reforms on the domestic agricultural supply function, the relationship between farmgate and consumer supply is too dependent on such a wide range of other policy measures to be determined *a priori*.

Food consumption and the demand for food

Farmers produce food because consumers purchase it. This may seem obvious, but it is a perspective that tends to be overlooked. High priority is given to all aspects of food and agricultural production while relatively little attention is paid to the final users. Part of the reason probably lies in a frequent failure to distinguish between consumption and demand.

Consumption refers only to a physical process and can therefore be measured in physical units. In contrast, demand is an economic concept; a demand function describes the relationship between the price of a commodity and the quantity demanded at each price, *all other things being equal*. Changes in consumption can be caused either by *movements along* a given demand curve – a response to changing prices – or by *shifts in* a demand curve, i.e. at any given price a different quantity is now demanded because of such factors as changing income levels (see Box 2). The demand for food at the consumer level leads, by way of the demand for processed foods and added "marketing" services (primary and secondary processing, packaging and distribution), to a derived demand for agricultural products at the farm level – and that is the demand function faced by the farmer, or would be if government policies did not distort the market-signalling mechanism.

A number of the policy reforms that have been implemented have directly affected the total demand for food and the composition of the food basket purchased, through their effects on household incomes and food prices, both absolute and relative. Structural adjustment programmes of the traditional type have generally led to decreasing real wages in the short to medium term, often accompanied by higher unemployment and therefore fewer wage-earners per household. This phenomenon has also occurred in the countries in transition from centrally planned to market economies. The declines in real household income have been substantial and the speed of recovery can be very slow.

A number of policy reforms are likely to affect consumer prices of food items. The removal of food subsidies increases food prices. In some countries, only imported staple foods, largely purchased by urban consumers, were subsidized. In other countries, the effective consumer food subsidy arose from massive subsidies to the agricultural sector and the removal of these subsidies has increased the prices of all food items for rural and urban consumers. Overvalued exchange rates impose a tax on exports and subsidize imports. Correcting an overvalued exchange rate will cause the price of tradable goods to rise relative to the price of non-tradables. Exports become cheaper in the foreign currency so quantity demanded in the export market will increase, putting upward pressure on the domestic price of the export good. Similarly, the domestic price of import goods will rise, thus curtailing the domestic quantity demanded of imported items. Thus the prices of tradable food items will rise whether they are exportable or imports. Some countries have used direct agricultural export taxes to curtail exports and to maintain lower domestic agricultural prices, thereby, provided these lower prices are passed on, lowering consumer prices. Removal of such export taxes will increase consumer food prices. In contrast, a reduction in import tariffs and relaxations of import controls will tend to exert a downward pressure on prices.

A fall in monetary and real incomes shifts the demand curve so

BOX 2
FACTORS AFFECTING THE DEMAND FOR FOOD

The demand for a food commodity is a function of several variables: the price of the item in question, the prices of complementary and substitutable items, income, demographic variables and tastes or preferences. In the short to medium term, the major determinants are prices and incomes and these are the most likely to be immediately affected by changes in government policies. In this context, it should be noted that a change in the price of a commodity has two effects, the income effect and the substitution effect. The substitution effect is such that a negative change in the price of the commodity *always* leads to a positive change in the quantity demanded. The income effect, however, depends on whether the commodity is "normal" or not. If it is normal, the positive change in income implicit in the fall of the commodity's price will lead to a positive change in the quantity demanded and therefore reinforce the substitution effect. If the commodity is "inferior", the income effect will be negative and therefore partially offset the substitution effect since it will work in the opposite direction. However, for an inferior good, the overall effect is still that a price fall (or rise) will lead to an increase (or decrease) in the quantity demanded. In contrast, the effect of a change in income, with no change in the price of the commodity, depends on whether the good is normal – in which case an increase in income increases the quantity demanded – or inferior – an increase in income decreases the quantity demanded.

The household's demand for different food items also depends on a variety of demographic factors, including the number and age of household members and the age of the principal food purchaser. The age of household members affects demand in two ways. First, children and elderly people eat less on average. Second, children have different consumption patterns from adults. The effects of age of the principal food purchaser might purely be a reflection of changing needs over a lifetime, irrespective of when that lifetime began, but there could also be a "vintage" effect, which refers to the changing tastes of each generation of food purchasers. In addition, the size of the household may exert an independent effect on demand – the "household scale effect".

Tastes or preferences include such factors as seasonal variations in consumption patterns for reasons other than seasonal price variability, religious and social taboos and lack of familiarity with particular foods.

Associated with demand functions are a number of different "elasticity" measures, each of which shows the responsiveness of demand to changes in a particular variable. An elasticity coefficient can be interpreted as the percentage change in quantity demanded in response to a 1 percent change in the relevant variable *all other things being equal*. The most important elasticity coefficients are:
• Own-price elasticity of demand: the change in quantity demanded is proportionate to the change in own-price.

• Cross-price elasticity of demand: the change in quantity demanded is proportionate to the change in price of another commodity.

The cross-price elasticity can be positive or negative, depending on whether the two commodities are substitutes or complements:

• Income elasticity of demand: the change in quantity demanded is proportionate to the change in income.

There are two measures of income elasticity: the income elasticity of expenditure on the commodity and the income elasticity of quantity purchased. Strictly speaking, these measures should be identical if the commodity is precisely defined since they are calculated with all the other variables assumed constant. However, this is rarely the case in practice. Take, for example, rice. Evidence from countries in West Africa and Asia suggests that the local varieties of rice command a premium price over imported varieties. Thus the total expenditure on rice could increase as real incomes rise without necessarily increasing the total quantity purchased. Conversely, the total quantity purchased could increase without an increase in total expenditure as households suffering a decline in real incomes substitute the cheaper commodity for the more expensive.

that at any given price less food is now purchased. For those countries that had been subsidizing urban or indeed all consumer prices, the removal of such subsidies and other policy reforms that lead to increased food prices also reduce the quantity purchased. Both declines in real income and changes in relative prices (not only between different food items but also between food and non-food items) lead to changes in the composition of the household food basket.

The empirical evidence strongly suggests that, in countries of any income level, lower-income households have higher price and income elasticities of demand for food, which means that the poorer groups will be more severely affected in terms of the total quantity of food purchased and the nutritional quality.[8] The impact will be exacerbated if lower-income households face higher unit food prices than do higher-income households. This can occur if, for example, the household has insufficient income reserves to be able to buy in bulk or if transport costs to cheaper retail outlets are high. The consumer responds to reduced incomes and higher prices by trying to maintain food intake through increasing the proportion of household income spent on food and altering consumption patterns in favour of relatively cheaper commodities. In addition, attempts will be made to augment supplies through interhousehold transfers (e.g. obtaining food from rural relatives) and where possible increasing own production in the urban and peri-urban areas, which can in certain circumstances lead to environmental and health problems.

Policy reform and food prices

How great an impact policy reform has on consumer prices depends critically on the economic and crop-specific situation at the time of price liberalization and on the speed with which reforms are implemented. Reusse[9] noted that the countries that had implemented major reforms in terms of desubsidization, deregulation and exchange-rate adjustment in the period 1985-87 had done so in favourable circumstances, "characterized by declining dollar and interest rates, falling petroleum prices and low

---

[8] See, for example, C. Waterfield. 1985. Disaggregating food consumption parameters. *Food Policy,* November 1985, 337-351; and B. Senauer. 1990. Household behaviour and nutrition in developing countries. *Food Policy,* October 1990, 408-417.

[9] E. Reusse. 1987. Liberalization and agricultural marketing. *Food Policy,* November 1987, 299-317.

international price levels for staple foods, especially grains and livestock products, together with good domestic crop results. The combination of these factors kept the immediate effect on urban consumer prices moderate." Whether countries undergoing reform since 1987 have done so in relatively less favourable conditions is a question that can only be answered by carrying out comparative analytical studies. Certainly the effects of policy reforms in the countries in transition from centrally planned economies have had a substantial negative impact on consumer prices, but in those countries the effective consumer subsidy arose from heavy subsidies to agriculture as a whole rather than by specific subsidies on imported staples.

To the extent that policy reforms in certain countries have succeeded in their objective of shifting the burden of agricultural support from the consumer to the taxpayer, one would expect lower-income consumers to have benefited more than higher-income groups from any resulting price falls because of the progressivity of income tax. However, if the costs are partly being met through the imposition of a value-added tax on food, the effect is highly regressive and hits hardest the poorest sections of the community. It is highly questionable how far consumer prices have actually fallen in response to such policy reforms. There seems to be a degree of "stickiness" in retail food prices – except, perhaps, for highly seasonal fresh produce such as fruit and vegetables – which may reflect the use of market power by processors, distributors or retailers. Furthermore, the proportion of the farmgate price of an agricultural commodity in the retail price of a food item is lower the more value is added in the marketing system. For example, in the United States the value of the wheat in a loaf of bread that costs US$1.20 is about 6 cents ($0.06). The recent reductions in support prices of changes in the Common Agricultural Policy of the EC have yet to be felt through noticeable changes in consumer prices in the member states. The effects of entry for new member countries will depend on the level and form of existing agricultural support. Finland and Austria, for example, which had much higher levels of agricultural protection, expected to see quite substantial reductions in consumer prices as a result of EU membership. On the other hand, the consumers of the Central and Eastern European economies in transition have already had to adjust to the removal or reduction of food subsidies: EU membership for them will lead to yet higher food prices on entry and, in addition, food may be subject to value-added tax.[10]

The inclination of governments to focus attention on their vociferous urban consumer constituency has tended to obscure the effects of policy reform on the agricultural household as food consumer as well as food producer. A large proportion of the population in most developing countries, including many of the poor and malnourished, resides in semi-subsistence farm households. The way in which such households respond to changes in food prices is rather less straightforward. A widely used tool of empirical analysis is an agricultural household model that integrates the farm family's production and consumption decisions. When a food commodity is produced partly for consumption and partly for sale, the price increase could have a positive impact on farm profits and hence household income so that the effect of price increases is completely offset. Thus if the profit effect is large and the income elasticity of demand for the commodity high, a price increase could lead the farm household to consume more of the product.

> The implication for nutrition is that higher food prices may actually
> lead to an improvement in the nutrition of farm household members,
> because of the effects of profits on income. Even if the consumption of
> the commodity for which the price has increased declines, the
> increased profits and income can be used to buy increased amounts of
> other foodstuffs, the result being an improvement in nutrient intake....
> Lower food prices raise the welfare and probably the nutrition of urban
> households, at least in the short run. However, higher prices may
> improve the welfare and nutrition of agricultural households, and
> possibly even of rural non-farm families whose income depends on
> agriculture, such as agricultural labourers.[11]

Protecting vulnerable groups of consumers
In order to alleviate the negative impacts of policy reforms, including the removal of general food subsidies, on the poorest and most vulnerable sections of society, a number of governments have tried to direct support more effectively to poorer consumers. Broadly speaking, support can be directed to a specific geographical area or income level or by using a "self-targeting" commodity (discussed below). However, major problems with such support systems – be they through subsidies such as food stamps or through some form of rationing – are increased administrative and information costs and incentives to abuse the system. In a poorly designed system, the budgetary costs of support could be as high as

---

[10] **The level of value-added tax on food varies greatly from country to country in the EU, from a high of 25 percent in Denmark to a low of zero in the United Kingdom.**
[11] **Senauer, op. cit., footnote 8, p. 63.**

a general subsidy or, if substantially lower, could well mean that an unacceptably high proportion of the target group is not being assisted. Whether this is in fact true or not requires rigorous assessment on a case-by-case basis which, by and large, seems not to have been carried out.

There is a further serious problem with such support schemes and that is the very weak information base on which decisions about how to design them are being made. This is far more complex than the recurrent complaint by analysts about the scarcity of reliable data in developing countries. Problems have been identified with the methodologies used and also with the assumptions about the sort of data that are needed to yield results that are accurate enough to be of real use to policy-makers.

Recent work in Kenya and the Philippines[12] investigated the reliability of food quantity information collected from household expenditure surveys. The conclusions are that the food expenditure data on which most demand analysis has rested systematically overestimate the income elasticities for food staples. There are two main reasons for this upward bias. First, food quantities or food expenditures are not measured independently of income if, as is often the case, total expenditures are used as the proxy for incomes. (Indeed, for very low-income consumers whose total expenditure on food is typically as much as two-thirds of total income, this is intuitively a reasonable approach.) Second, food transfers from high-income to low-income households are underrecorded. Such transfers occur, for example, as guest and hired worker meals.

The policy consequences of what might at first sight appear to be a minor technical question are profound. For food staples projections of aggregate demand that are based on assumptions of aggregate income growth and use such upwardly biased income elasticities will overstate the actual requirements. Furthermore, the benefits of various income-generating policies on household food security have consequently also been overstated. It is therefore probable that insufficient policy emphasis has been given to intrahousehold issues, micronutrient consumption and non-nutrient health issues. The use of 24-hour food recall data that detail food intake rather than availability seems likely to give unbiased estimates of food demand and hence provide better information to policy-makers.

---

[12] H. Bouis, L. Haddad and E. Kennedy. 1992. Does it matter how we survey demand for food? *Food Policy*, October 1992, 349-360.

Intrahousehold issues undoubtedly require further attention if vulnerable groups are to receive effective protection. One issue is the allocation of food among the family members, which, if inappropriate, can exacerbate the effects of an inadequate household food supply or leave some individuals malnourished even when the total food availability is apparently adequate. Studies show substantial variations of intrahousehold food allocation from country to country. In some cases, the allocation pattern discriminates against women and girls, while in others the bias is in favour of adults over children. In yet others, there is both a sex and age bias, with the male household head receiving a disproportionate share. If this type of bias is detected from studies of intrahousehold food allocation patterns, it might be possible to use the information to design special intervention programmes aimed at protecting the vulnerable groups of consumers so identified. Such special intervention programmes could include supplementary feeding to certain groups, such as pregnant and lactating women and small children, or the provision of school meals or milk either to all children of school age or perhaps just at girls' schools.

A related issue is the decision-making process within the household which is often correlated with the generation of income. The evidence suggests that the more control women have over income, the better is the nutritional status, particularly of children. Thus concern has been expressed about policy measures and reforms that encourage the commercialization of smallholder agriculture and the production of cash crops because men tend to take control over the income so generated whereas in traditional agriculture, especially in Africa, women have exerted a great deal of control over the food produced for home consumption as well as the cash from any sales. This would tend to suggest that even if the benefits of income-generating policies on household food security have been overstated in general, policy measures that can assist women to gain control over some cash income are likely to be of some benefit in improving child nutrition and health. Possible policy measures to this end could include programmes to support the partial commercialization of activities that are more likely to be carried out by women, such as soap-making and kitchen gardening, subject always to there being an adequate demand for such products.

Increasing attention is being given to introducing "self-targeting" subsidies and it is in this area that inadequate information can have potentially serious consequences. The idea behind the self-targeting subsidy is that the subsidy should be attached to a commodity that is consumed disproportionately or solely by low-income groups. In order to identify an appropriate candidate for self-targeting, it is necessary to disaggregate food consumption parameters to obtain estimates of own-price, cross-price and income elasticities for the different commodities and for different income groups. Presumably, the disaggregation ought also to differentiate between urban and rural consumers as they have greatly differing consumption patterns. Of particular interest has been the identification of "inferior" food items. In this context, the word inferior is a technical term that refers to a commodity for which the quantity consumed falls as income increases and which is therefore purchased mostly by lower-income groups. Subsidizing such a commodity would cause its consumption to rise, thereby improving the calorific intake of the poorest consumers and, because the fall in the price of a commodity also has the effect of increasing the consumer's income, the subsidy would enable more of other, preferred food items to be purchased.

A review of attempts to disaggregate food consumption parameters as a basis for designing directed nutritional interventions was carried out in 1985.[13] The findings demonstrate a clear need to improve and standardize survey techniques and then to standardize methodologies and models. The conclusion is that the disaggregation approach could provide useful information to policy-makers, allowing them to design nutrition programmes that would more effectively direct a government's limited resources to the poor. One might also expect that such information could better identify who is really "poor". However, the approach would not necessarily lead to the identification of a suitable candidate for a self-targeting subsidy.

> After all the expense and effort of determining disaggregated consumption parameters, it is possible that no ideal commodity may be found. For example, in Brazil no commodity was found that is eaten by the poor and not by the rich. Although some commodities, such as low-quality rice, were found to make better vehicles than others, targeting nutritional subsidies in Brazil is far from ideal.[14]

If a commodity is identified but is insufficiently inferior, then the costs of the subsidy could turn out to be extremely high. The point is also made that even if a suitable inferior commodity can be identified, subsidizing it will not by itself solve all of a country's nutritional problems. Thus a self-targeting scheme based on one commodity could at best form part of a larger strategy that could

---

[13] Waterfield, op. cit., footnote 8, p. 63.
[14] Ibid.

include a whole variety of additional measures, such as special intervention programmes, buffer stock schemes and food stamps (or some other form of income transfer), to improve household food security and nutrition.

Zambia attempted to introduce a self-targeting subsidy for maize in late 1986 by subsidizing only the relatively inferior roller meal. At the same time, breakfast meal, which was the preferred form, was to be sold at an economic price, which involved a price increase of 120 percent. The scheme went badly wrong, leading to civil disturbances, and had to be abandoned. It has been argued that the problems lay not with the scheme itself so much as in the manner of its introduction.

> It appears to have been instituted without sufficient attention to problems of supply and the relative demands for the different grades of mealie-meal which would ensue in the context of the new price structure. As a result the rapid disappearance of roller meal from the retail outlets, and the sharp rise in the price of breakfast meal, meant that the majority of consumers were faced with a de facto overnight abolition of the maize-meal subsidy, with no opportunity to adapt their consumption patterns.[15]

Given this turn of events, Zambia adopted a different approach by first introducing a rationing programme restricted to urban consumers and later supplying coupons only to eligible households, eligibility being determined by household income level for those in formal employment while, for those not in formal employment, the number of dependants for whom coupons can be claimed was limited.

The degree to which any country has ever really been successful at directing support has been called into question. A review in 1988[16] looked at ten countries with large food subsidy programmes that had been attempting major policy reform. It found that, in the eight years since 1980, none had been able to increase the degree to which food subsidies were directed to the absolute poor; in addition, there were no indications that the efficiency of the programmes had been improved either. However, seven years on, a thorough analysis of the results in some of the countries that have experimented more or less successfully with directed consumer subsidy schemes could provide useful guidance in designing

---

[15] R. Pearce. 1991. Urban food subsidies in the context of adjustment. *Food Policy,* December 1991, 436-450.
[16] P. Pinstrup-Andersen. 1988. Macroeconomic adjustment and human nutrition. *Food Policy,* February 1988, 37-46.

systems that are both more efficient and more effective under the conditions in which policy reform is now being implemented.

In conclusion

Policy reforms affect consumers directly because they have an impact on the factors that affect food demand, which in the short to medium term are largely the absolute and relative prices of different food items and household incomes. Whatever the problems with data and methodology, there is substantial evidence that in any country the lower-income groups are more sensitive to changes in these variables and that the very poor (however poverty is defined) are particularly vulnerable in the short and medium term to changes that are expected to be of benefit to them in the long term. However, the true responses of the most vulnerable groups of consumers to changes in household incomes and food prices are very far from being intuitively obvious. By carefully analysing consumer behaviour that reflects the differing patterns of demand response in lower-income households, governments will be able to design and implement policy interventions that can go a long way towards protecting those most affected by broader policy reforms. What such policy interventions should be depends on a wide range of factors, including how much a particular government can afford. So far no final conclusions have been reached with discussions being able to indicate only those areas where policy measures might be used without jeopardizing the ultimate objectives of the reform programme. Another point to be made is that, while protecting the lowest income groups may justifyably be a high priority in policy terms, governments should recognize that "vulnerable" groups of consumers are not necessarily restricted only to the poorest households. Factors that are not easy to deal with in the framework of consumer demand analysis, such as intrahousehold allocation of food resources and decision-making power, need much more study, as do the differences between urban and rural consumers and the consumption responses of households that are simultaneously food consumers and food producers.

Malnutrition is not only a problem for the poor, although they are undoubtedly most at risk. Changes in tastes, in preferences for different food items and in the food basket purchased have normally been evolutionary rather than revolutionary. However, it may be that radical policy reforms change *relative* food prices, as well as reduce incomes, so quickly and drastically that the resulting disruption of traditional consumption patterns gives governments sufficient cause for concern to justify intervention.

Identifying issues and setting out a conceptual framework is only the first step, however. Countries that are undergoing or planning to undergo major policy reform need to improve their knowledge and understanding of the effects of such reform on consumers, especially on vulnerable groups, whose prior identification must not be taken for granted. "The generation of such information should be pursued in two ways: *i)* analyses to improve current understanding of how specific policies frequently found in adjustment programmes and combinations of such policies affect incomes, food consumption, nutritional status and health of specific groups of low-income people; and *ii)* continuous monitoring and surveillance of changes in the welfare of various groups of low-income people using indicators such as nutritional status, mortality, household food sufficiency, incomes and prices during periods of adjustment."[17] International agencies such as FAO and UNICEF, in collaboration with research institutes and universities, could play an important role in assisting governments to generate and analyse the necessary information.

[17] **Pinstrup-Andersen, op. cit., footnote 16, p. 69.**

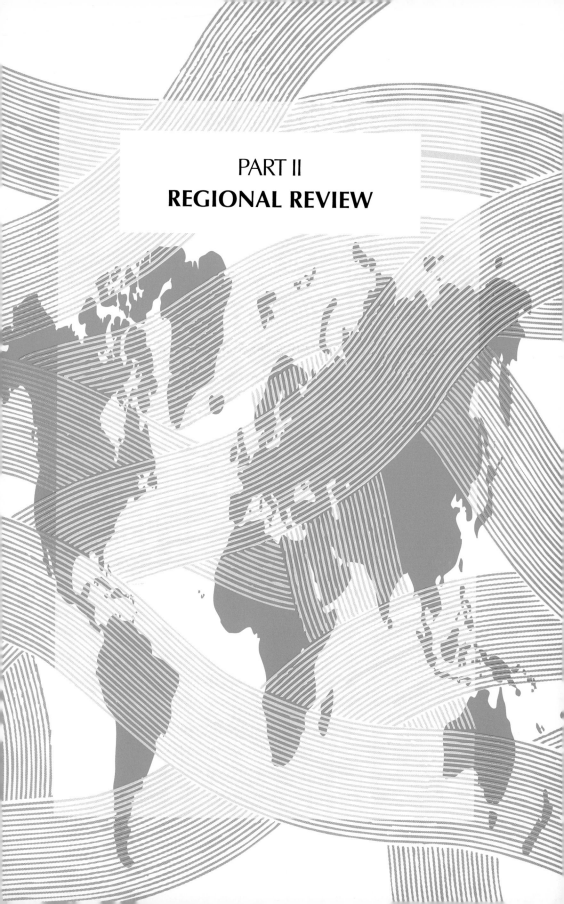

PART II
REGIONAL REVIEW

REGIONAL REVIEW
I. Developing country regions

SUB-SAHARAN AFRICA

REGIONAL OVERVIEW
Economic developments

Economic growth in sub-Saharan Africa is estimated to have accelerated from barely 0.5 percent in 1993 to about 2 percent in 1994. However, economic expansion in 1994 still remained well below population growth, bringing the region's cumulative decline in per caput income to 15 percent over the past 20 years (World Bank estimates).

Nevertheless, for many countries in the region the short-term economic outlook is more positive than it has been for a long time. Favourable factors include a better external environment, stronger agricultural commodity prices, the easing of some war situations, particularly in southern Africa, the positive effects of devaluation of the CFA franc, some progress in stabilization and economic liberalization and the increasing integration of South Africa into the regional economies (see following section). The World Bank projects that output will increase by 3.8 percent per year in the 1995 to 2000 period, although it recognizes that these projections may be optimistic. The realization of such positive forecasts will depend to a large extent on three factors that relate to economic and political management: first, the ability to use current windfalls from stronger commodity prices productively, while resisting pressure for increasing consumption beyond sustainable levels; second, the political determination to pursue reform while both external constraints and internal resistance from interest groups become less demanding; and third, the ability to achieve greater political and social stability. The region will have to face the fact that the high commodity price bonanza must come to an end and external assistance may be significantly reduced in the years to come.

Figure 6

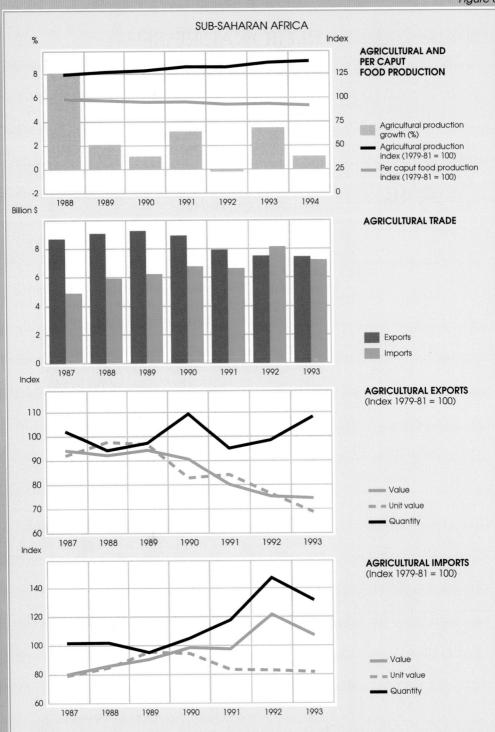

SUB-SAHARAN AFRICA

AGRICULTURAL AND PER CAPUT FOOD PRODUCTION

- Agricultural production growth (%)
- Agricultural production index (1979-81 = 100)
- Per caput food production index (1979-81 = 100)

AGRICULTURAL TRADE

- Exports
- Imports

AGRICULTURAL EXPORTS
(Index 1979-81 = 100)

- Value
- Unit value
- Quantity

AGRICULTURAL IMPORTS
(Index 1979-81 = 100)

- Value
- Unit value
- Quantity

Source: FAO

SUB-SAHARAN AFRICA

Agricultural performances

In the agricultural sector, which typically contributes one-third of GDP and employs more than two-thirds of the economically active population, the last 25 years have been characterized by steadily declining per caput production. From a peak in 1975, per caput agricultural production had by 1993 declined by 20 percent, with a brief interruption of the downward tendency only during the second half of the 1980s. The pattern for food production has been almost identical, but with the decline in per caput terms over the same period reaching 23 percent. After a modest recovery in 1993, the downward trend in per caput production volumes was resumed in 1994, as agricultural production expanded only by an estimated 1.1 percent, implying a 2 percent drop in per caput terms.

Prospects for 1995 appear mixed across the different subregions. The current food supply situation appears to be generally satisfactory in western and central Africa, reflecting above-average to record harvests in most countries, although production and distribution in Liberia are hampered by civil strife.

However, a massive cereal deficit is forecast for southern Africa in 1995/96 as a result of expected drought-reduced harvests in many countries, including Botswana, Lesotho, Namibia, South Africa and parts of Swaziland, Zimbabwe, Malawi, Mozambique and Zambia. Cereal import requirements in the subregion are expected to rise dramatically and local emergency interventions will be necessary for drought victims. In East Africa large-scale emergency assistance will also be needed throughout 1995, despite some good harvests. Food production in Burundi and Rwanda has failed to recover fully from the effects of civil strife. Large numbers of internally displaced persons in both countries continue to require emergency food assistance. In Somalia the departure of United Nations Operations in Somalia (UNOSOM) may lead to renewed food problems if the security situation deteriorates.

Agricultural trade

The economies of many countries in the region benefited significantly from the new opportunities provided by recent developments in commodity markets. The gains from improved terms of trade that

SUB-SAHARAN AFRICA

resulted from the increase in non-oil commodity prices in 1994-95 relative to 1993 are estimated to average 4 percent of GDP among the 20 largest gainers – 13 of them being sub-Saharan countries.[1] The largest gains in net terms of trade as a percentage of GDP are estimated to be in Côte d'Ivoire (12 percent) followed by Uganda and Ghana (close to 7 percent) and Chad, Cameroon and Zaire (around 4 to 5 percent). Agricultural producers and exporters, and the economy as a whole, may be expected to benefit greatly from terms of trade gains in the short term (see World Review). However, as mentioned earlier, gradually declining prices for Africa's main agricultural export products are expected.

The CFA devaluation

The export sectors and overall economies of the 14 CFA zone member countries also benefited from the devaluation of the CFA franc in early 1994 and the international financial assistance that accompanied this operation.[2] One and a half years later the prognosis appears positive, in spite of the social and economic management problems caused by the initial price shock, and uncertainties on the success of the operation in the longer term. The devaluation initially resulted in sharp and sudden increases in the prices of imported goods, including food staples, which caused a wave of strikes and demonstrations in several countries. Stringent fiscal and monetary policies brought annual inflation rates down to around 20 to 40 percent over the following months. These were well below the hyperinflation rates many had predicted. Signs have emerged recently, however, of increased inflation and difficulties in maintaining budgetary discipline in some countries. In addition, the negative social impact of the devaluation continues to be felt. A meeting sponsored by the World Health Organization (WHO) and Unesco in February 1995 concluded that, in the 14 countries concerned, living standards in urban areas had fallen and access to health care and resources for schools had been seriously affected.

On the other hand, the devaluation contributed to a strong expansion of export earnings and a reduction of external deficits. This provided a welcome respite to stressed economies, although it is recognized that much remains to be done to consolidate competitiveness and current account balancing. Agricultural exporters

[1] World Bank. 1995. *Global economic prospects and the developing countries.* Washington, DC.
[2] A preliminary review of the CFA devaluation was presented in *The State of Food and Agriculture 1994.* Rome, FAO.

SUB-SAHARAN AFRICA

benefited significantly from the devaluation, which coincided with a period of notable world market price increases for several of their main commodity exports. For instance, Côte d'Ivoire, which had been suffering economic recession since the mid-1980s, increased its economic activity by close to 2 percent in 1994 and is expected to expand it by a further 5 percent in 1995, largely because of booming export performances. Cocoa exports were the main source of incremental gain, but other commodities also contributed significantly to the overall improvement. Economic growth is also expected to accelerate in Senegal, from 1.8 percent in 1994 to 3.5 percent in 1995, a significant contributing factor being groundnut exports that benefited from the devaluation and the strongest market prices since 1990. Other countries' export sectors showed mixed degrees of success. After an initial surge, Burkina Faso's agricultural sales, with the exception of cotton, lost dynamism.

As regards the policy response to the effects of devaluation on the food sector, a variety of consumer relief measures were provided in the form of price controls, trade regulations and social safety nets.

Price controls. The first policy response of most governments following the devaluation was a tighter control or freezing of prices. This led to shortages and disruptions and prices were raised or allowed to rise, albeit often not continuously. Cameroon provides an example of the difficulties of adjusting price management to a fluid situation. On 19 January the government raised the prices of bread and wheat flour by 85 percent; three days later it cancelled that decision and announced a six-month price freeze; and this decision was itself reversed in late January, when the prices of wheat and wheat-flour were raised, but by only 30 to 40 percent over their predevaluation levels and well below what had been decided on 19 January. Although bread prices were kept at predevaluation levels, bakers were permitted to reduce bread weight. In June 1994, the government lifted price controls on five staples, including rice and flour.

Similar problems were encountered in Mali. Here the prices of a range of basic foods were initially frozen, but soon afterwards were raised on 34 essential commodities, including cereals. As hoarding and

shortages continued, traders were permitted to raise prices moderately.

In the Congo the problems created by sharp food price increases consecutive to the devaluation were aggravated by disruptions in railway transportation caused by civil unrest. To alleviate the resulting shortages the official prices of bread and flour were frozen until early March. A price ceiling was also announced for wheat-flour.

Prices were also initially frozen in the Niger and Togo, but controls were relaxed soon afterwards.

Changes in external trade regulations. Several governments responded to the initial crisis by reducing import duties on food and other essential items. In Cameroon, import duties on wheat and rice were suspended from 17 February until 30 June and were set at 5 percent thereafter. In the Congo, the government suspended taxes on imported basic commodities. Côte d'Ivoire had imported significant volumes of rice and built up stocks before the devaluation and this helped to counter the negative effects on urban consumers. After the devaluation, which doubled cost, insurance and freight (c.i.f.) prices of imported rice, customs tariffs were reduced on most imported food and beverage products, including two grades of rice that are widely consumed in urban areas. In Senegal, in February, import duties on all products were reduced from 15 percent *ad valorem* to 10 percent, while those on rice and wheat were suspended altogether. In addition, imported rice and wheat were exempted from certain taxes. Import duties were also sharply reduced in the Niger and Gabon.

Safety net programmes. Most governments announced some form of safety net programme for the poor, at least as a transitional measure. These efforts were backed by international assistance, directly or indirectly intended for social relief. In particular, the Government of France earmarked 300 million French francs (US$51 million) for the CFA franc countries' "social funds".

Country measures included the introduction in Chad of food and nutrition projects and intensive public works programmes. In Cameroon, a special programme was introduced to create employment through public works and the maintenance of infrastructures. In the

Comoros, the budget for the social sectors was increased and a community development support fund was established. Wages, salaries and pensions were raised in several countries, notably Côte d'Ivoire, Mali and the Niger. In Gabon, the 1994 budget made provisions for temporary subsidies of basic consumer goods such as bread. In Côte d'Ivoire consumer subsidies, intended as temporary measures to reduce the impact of devaluation-induced price increases, were expected to remain in place until at least October 1995.

Agricultural policies
The policy environment for agriculture in sub-Saharan Africa has remained dominated by the general targets of economic liberalization, market-oriented reforms and divestment. Measures to liberalize the sector have often been partial and fragmented, however, and have alternated with new or old forms of government market intervention. While in some cases such discontinuity was caused by the demands of social problems and economic and market circumstances, in others it was mainly the result of recurring crises and political difficulty in maintaining a consistent framework for reform. Liberalizing what were, and in some cases still are, heavily regulated markets presents particularly difficult problems in the region. While social problems allow only narrow margins for manoeuvring, the efficiency of operations is constrained by financial, administrative and infrastructural limitations. The following country examples illustrate recent attempts at overcoming such constraints.

In the area of market intervention an agreement between *Côte d'Ivoire* and the World Bank led to a redefinition of the role of the state board in charge of the marketing of agricultural products. Under the agreement, the government will reduce the role of the state in the marketing of these commodities and allow private exporters and growers to play a greater role.

In *Kenya*, the National Cereals and Produce Board was unable to pay for wheat and maize deliveries and encouraged farmers to look for alternative markets. Instead of direct producer price support, the government strategy aims at supporting the rural community through improving rural access roads and providing marketing information, research and extension services – a strategy now widely adopted in

82

the region. The privatization of the coffee industry is expected to be gradual in order that the continuing quality of the product can be ensured in internal markets. The reforms already in place include the licensing of private coffee millers and the holding of auctions in US dollars.

In *Senegal,* the government virtually stopped supplying subsidized fertilizers and only offered limited credit to farmers. While price controls on high-quality rice were removed, the government remained actively involved in cotton, rice and peanut production and marketing. An agricultural development policy declaration was issued in April 1994 outlining plans for price liberalization and privatization. This programme is to be implemented under a structural adjustment loan provided by France, Germany, the European Development Fund and the United States. It is expected to liberalize rice markets further and to stimulate more privatization. In particular, an agreement was reached to privatize the national groundnut processing agency, but the modalities remain under discussion.

In *Ethiopia,* a law was promulgated to improve the management of public enterprises and to eliminate the monopoly and power of some official marketing and trade corporations. Since April 1992, the government has allowed private companies to market and distribute seeds and fertilizers.

In the area of international trade, increasing external openness continued to be a general policy objective. However, many countries found it difficult to advance trade liberalization and there were numerous cases of the halting, reversal or relaxation of such policies. In *Kenya,* all imports of maize and wheat, except those for humanitarian purposes, were suspended in mid-1994 for six months. The ban on maize imports was lifted in late 1994 when variable duties were imposed instead. These measures were intended to curb maize imports, which had reached major proportions after the severe and protracted drought, and to protect local farmers from a potential crisis caused by the liberalization of maize marketing. The financial and market problems linked to excessive import dependence led the government to formalize a food policy strategy with the main objective of raising food self-sufficiency. Various policies, including trade measures, were adopted to this end. Among these were: the elimination of income

taxes for maize producers; the encouragement of fertilizer imports through priority allocation of foreign exchange and subsidies, with a view to reversing the downward trend in fertilizer consumption; subsidized credit plans for small farmers; increased farm credit; and higher price protection for domestic staple cereal production through, *inter alia,* import duties.

In early 1994, the Government of *Nigeria* imposed a ban on imports of maize, barley and rice. The measure was reversed in early 1995 for rice, but imports of this commodity were subjected to a 100 percent customs duty.

At the end of 1994 the authorities of the copper belt in *Zambia,* banned the export of maize out of the area, because of erratic supplies. A shortfall of 270 000 tonnes of maize was expected in 1995, the country's maize consumption being 212 000 tonnes per month.

Acute food shortages caused by drought led the Government of *Tanzania* to encourage the local business community to import food as a way of averting famine. The government also banned food exports in late 1994, as the country was experiencing a grain drain, estimated at 95 000 tonnes per year, caused by smuggling to neighbouring countries.

Sierra Leone, once a net exporter of rice, experienced deteriorating supply conditions largely related to civil unrest and rebel activity, and progressively emerged as a net importer of this staple. To encourage domestic production, the government recently introduced a 15 percent duty on imported rice and removed a 10 percent turnover tax on domestic rice.

SUB-SAHARAN AFRICA

[3] In a report prepared by the South African Government for GATT it is stated that "...South Africa, despite its modern sector, is largely a third world country. As such, it is grappling with the problems faced by most of these countries, such as a high rate of population growth, rising unemployment, declining standards of living, inadequate literacy rates, a process of rapid urbanization and increasing demands for socio-economic uplifted programmes." GATT. 1993. *South Africa: trade policy review*, Vol. II. Geneva.

[4] Data from AGROSTAT that do not include data from the TBVC areas. There is a lack of data on the economically active population in the homelands, and data from different sources tend to differ, often substantially, but it is safe to assume that, in general, there has been a decreasing trend in the number of people employed in agriculture, although agricultural employment may have increased in individual years. See, for instance, C.J. van Rooyen, J.F. Kristen, J. van Zyl and N. Vink. 1995. *Structural adjustment, policy reform and agricultural performance in South Africa.* University of Pretoria. (Unpublished working paper)

THE REPUBLIC OF SOUTH AFRICA

In 1994, South African general elections with universal franchise were the culmination of the democratization of political and other institutions from the old apartheid system. South Africa's return to the community of nations is a major event not only for the country itself, but for the entire southern Africa subregion. It will mean the transition from a climate of conflict, enmity and mutual suspicion to one of peace, political stability and economic cooperation and will benefit all countries in the region.

South Africa's annual per caput income of US$2 800 places it in the upper-middle income group of nations. In addition, the country has a number of developed country characteristics such as good infrastructure, technologically advanced industry and a well-established financial system. The relatively high average income and other characteristics can be misleading, however, as they mask large disparities in income distribution and in access to infrastructure and amenities between the white minority and an impoverished black population whose living standards are more characteristic of poor developing countries.[3] This report analyses the agricultural and rural development issues currently faced by policy-makers in the new South Africa as the country becomes a full member of the world community.

Topology, population and climate

The Republic of South Africa spans 3 000 km from the South Atlantic to the Indian Ocean and covers an area of 1.221 million km². The major part of the country has an elevation of between 1 200 and 1 800 m. South Africa is situated within the temperate zone. It has an average rainfall of 511 mm per annum, but has wide interyear and interregional differences with rainfall diminishing towards the west. This diversity of local climates limits the negative effects of severe droughts and offers some protection against general crop failures.

In 1993, total population was estimated at 39.8 million, of which 50 percent is located in rural areas. About 12.8 percent of the economically active population was employed in agriculture.[4] This percentage has been declining continuously from a peak of 33.3 percent in 1969. Before the abolition of the apartheid or "separate development" system, about

SUB-SAHARAN AFRICA

8 million people were resident in one of the four "independent" homelands of Transkei, Bophuthatswana, Venda and the Ciskei (otherwise known as TBVC states).

Agriculture: general characteristics

South Africa's agricultural sector is characterized by extreme dualism. The white-dominated commercial sector, consisting of large, capital-intensive farms, coexists with an impoverished black-dominated smallholder sector which produces mainly for subsistence.

Agriculture's share of GDP was about 5 percent in the early 1990s having followed a declining trend (albeit with some variations) from 12.4 percent in 1960 to 7 percent in 1980. Agricultural growth has been variable. Growth was slow in the 1960s and 1980s (1.6 and 1.4 percent average annual growth respectively) and high in the 1970s (5.8 percent). With a population growth of 2.6 percent, per caput agricultural GDP was negative during the 1960s and 1980s. Agriculture is highly important as a source of employment and subsistence and as a supplier to a vibrant processing sector.

South Africa is self-sufficient or nearly so in all major agricultural commodity categories, with the exception of meat and oilseeds. Thus, the self-sufficiency index is 134 for field crops, 152 for horticultural crops and 97 for animal products.[5]

About 95 percent of the total gross value of agricultural production is generated in the white-controlled commercial sector. Field crops dominate total agricultural production value although their share has diminished from 47 percent in 1970 and 1980 to less than 35 percent in 1990. Horticultural crops have been growing by 2.8 percent per annum in value terms between 1960 and 1990 and reached 21 percent of the total in the early 1990s. The share of animal products in total gross value has also increased from 36 percent and 37 percent in 1970 and 1980 respectively to 45 percent in 1990. Maize is the main field crop (64 percent of the total value of field crops); it occupies more land than any other crop in South Africa (44 percent of the total land devoted to field crops) and constitutes 75 percent of total grain production. Wheat (22 percent of total field crop area), oats (10 percent), sorghum and barley are the other major field crops.[6] The growth in volume of horticultural products over the last two decades is

[5] Data for 1989/90. Indices calculated in N.T. Christodoulou and N. Vink. 1990. *The potential for black smallholder farmers' participation in the South African agricultural economy.* Paper presented at the Conference on Land Reform and Agricultural Development, Norwick Park Initiative, UK.

[6] Although in terms of area oats seem to be a major crop, only part of the area is harvested. In terms of value, barley and sorghum are more important commodities.

partly the result of the growth in exports that followed the lifting of international sanctions in 1989 and the devaluation of the rand. The large increase in the volume of livestock products (50 percent between the 1970s and the 1990s) is caused mainly by the spectacular performance of the poultry sector.[7]

It is estimated that in 1990, 28.9 percent of the total gross value of agricultural production in the homelands (or 3.1 percent of total GDP of the homelands) was marketed, the rest being produced for subsistence.[8] Field crops and livestock dominate the value of production in roughly equal shares. Remittances from migrants and pensions constitute a higher share of total income in the homelands than do income earnings derived from agriculture.

Agriculture in South Africa's development strategy
The duality that prevails in agriculture in South Africa reflects the contrast in the socio-economic conditions in the country and is a result of past political, economic and social policies within the country's overall development strategy.

Policies directed towards the agricultural sector have to be seen in the light of the strategic objectives of the state at particular periods of time. Before the Second World War, the main objective of agricultural assistance was to bring the incomes of white farmers into line with incomes of other sectors of the economy. For the period after the Second World War, agricultural policy was part of the overall self-sufficiency strategy and aid to the agricultural sector was intensified. The self-sufficiency objective was further strengthened during the 1970s and 1980s as a result of sanctions and boycotts (or threats) imposed on the country by the international community.

The dual nature of South Africa's development status was also reflected in its past policies towards and treatment of the agricultural sector. While many developed countries subsidize agriculture, most developing countries have a history of direct and indirect taxation of agriculture through macroeconomic (fiscal, monetary, exchange rate) and sectoral policies. Agriculture was viewed as a "resource reservoir" – in developing countries its role was to provide surplus food, savings and foreign exchange to support industrialization strategies. In South Africa, both

[7] For more details on the performance of various crops see World Bank. 1994. *South African agriculture: structure, performance and options for the future.* Informal Discussion Paper No. 6. Washington, DC, World Bank, South African Department.

[8] Figures calculated from data in World Bank, ibid. See also C.J. van Rooyen. J. van Zyl and T.I. Fényes. 1987. A comparison of the contribution and relative performance of agriculture in southern Africa. *Development South Africa,* 4(2). Reliable data for the homelands are lacking because of the subsistence and non-market nature of production.

elements (taxation and subsidization) have been present at the same time.

Historical evidence demonstrates that there has been a policy of squeezing (in terms of opportunities for growth) the African smallholder sector with the aim of channelling labour from agriculture to the mines, factories and white settler farms. At the same time, policies provided heavy subsidization of the predominantly white large-scale agricultural sector with the dual objective of achieving self-sufficiency in the major commodity groups and of supporting the incomes of white farmers. A brief overview of the role of agriculture in the development process is necessary in order to understand better the present situation and the problems faced by policy-makers in the country.[9]

Historical evidence at the end of the nineteenth century shows a dynamic, viable African agricultural sector dominated by family farms, open to the adoption of new technologies and meeting the increasing demand for agricultural goods from mining, manufacturing and urban centres. African family farming had the support of land companies and large landowners who were extracting rents from tenant farmers. These family farms were successfully competing with settler farmers in both domestic and foreign markets.

The evolution in the twentieth century of the present structure of the South African agricultural sector can be divided into three broad periods: the period between 1913 and 1948 when the basic elements of the present dualistic structure were established; the period between 1948 and the mid-1980s during which, as a result of policy choices and incentives, the large commercial sector became increasingly capital intensive; and the current period starting in 1985 when a number of reforms in the sector were initiated.

The period between 1913 and 1948. With the establishment of the Union of South Africa in 1910, a series of policies were put into place in support of white commercial farming and against black agriculture. A number of land-allocation laws created a segregation of white and black farmers. The Natives' Land Act of 1913 (effective from 1916) segregated Africans and Europeans on a territorial basis restricting Africans to native

[9] For a more detailed but still concise review of the evolution of the agrarian structure in South Africa see World Bank, op. cit., footnote 7. On the land issue in particular see H.P. Binswanger and K. Deininger. 1993. South African land policy: the legacy of history and current options. *World Development*, 21(9); see also van Rooyen, van Zyl and Fényes, op. cit., footnote 8.

reserves. The reserves were allocated about 7.8 percent of the total land area increasing to 13.7 percent with the Native Trust and Land Act of 1936.[10] For Africans no land acquisitions or other land transactions were permitted outside the reserves. Several related government acts restricted the ability of farm workers to change employment and prevented African farmers from joining marketing cooperatives or farmers' unions. These measures severely curtailed African farmers' access to markets, credit and farm services.

As a result of the measures, Africans could practise subsistence farming in the homelands only while various pre-existing forms of tenancy (e.g. sharecropping) diminished drastically over time. Participating in the labour markets became increasingly the only way for African farmers to earn an income. At the same time, a number of policies and provisions aided the establishment of white farms and allocated lands to white farmers. Favourable procedures were established for leasing and purchasing land; institutions were set up (a land bank and agricultural cooperatives) to facilitate access to credit and other services for white commercial farmers; and the Agricultural Marketing Act of 1947 created marketing schemes and the boards to control them.[11]

The period from 1948 to 1985. The race-based geographical segregation policy was intensified after 1948. Legislation in 1951 and 1959 established eight national units (self-governing homelands or *bantustans*). Their boundaries coincided with the reserve boundaries created by the land acts. The area of the homelands was set at 17 million hectares in 1954. Controls were imposed on the migration of Africans into the white-controlled areas. Between 1960 and the early 1980s, about 3.5 million people (predominantly Africans) were resettled (through such measures as the eviction of black tenants and redundant workers from white farms, intracity removals, homeland consolidation and urban relocation from white areas to the homelands). The concern about increasing poverty and land degradation in the homelands resulted in the establishment of "betterment schemes" aimed at improving conditions. In the 1970s and early 1980s, such schemes were supplemented by large centrally managed agricultural development projects. The latter often experienced

[10] Discriminating practices had started earlier than 1910, in the form of a number of levies and fees imposed on African farmers, such as higher taxes for Africans as opposed to those for white farmers and twice as many taxes on share-croppers and rent-paying squatters as on labour-tenants.
[11] There is an analysis of the role of marketing boards later in this section.

financial losses while failing to promote viable smallholder farming. Projects have had only limited success in achieving broad-based rural development in the homelands while their welfare objectives have been restricted to employment generation in rural areas.

While the options and opportunities of black agriculture in the homelands were being curtailed, white agriculture was promoted. Up until the 1960s, the incentives given to white farmers (especially in terms of assistance in acquiring and enlarging landholdings) favoured an expansive mode of agricultural production in which land, machinery and labour inputs were largely complementary. Over the period, farmers responded to the low cost of both land and labour by acquiring more land and hiring more labour.

A shift towards mechanization, especially the mechanical harvesting of field crops, began in the 1960s and intensified in the 1970s, as a result of policy-induced incentives (mainly subsidized interest rates) making a capital intensive mode of production more profitable. During that period, mechanization and labour inputs were substitutes and the typical farm model in South Africa was established: large farms using capital-intensive technology and great amounts of intermediate inputs.

The substitution of capital for labour seems paradoxical in view of the strong labour market segmentation that caused agricultural wages to be as low as 30 percent of the wages in manufacturing and mining. The segmentation of labour markets was the result of several "Pass Laws" that made the movement of black labour between farms and from agriculture to other sectors either impossible or extremely costly. This apparent paradox is explained by looking at the policy-induced incentives for capital-intensive farming. Real interest rates (*ex post*) on loans to farmers by the land bank and farm cooperatives remained largely negative for most of the decade of the 1970s. Preferential tax treatment included the introduction in 1970 of a 100 percent capital write-off in the year of purchase. Agriculture was also assisted by input subsidies, including subsidies on fertilizers and chemicals, subsidies for irrigation investment and subsidized water provision for irrigation.

SUB-SAHARAN AFRICA

The marketing system and its role in shaping the structure of agriculture: the prereform period

South Africa's marketing system is a product of the 1937 and 1968 Marketing Acts that established marketing schemes and boards.[12] Marketing schemes, on the basis of the type of market control they can exercise, are of four major categories:

- *Single-channel fixed price schemes* (maize and winter grains) in which the board exercises statutory monopoly powers and provides pre-announced prices.
- *Single-channel pool schemes* (deciduous fruits) in which the board has statutory monopoly power; producers market their products through a pool conducted by the boards and receive pooled prices based on market realizations.
- *Surplus-removal or price support schemes* (meat, grain sorghum) in which the board intervenes to maintain minimum prices.
- *Supervisory schemes* (canning fruit, cotton) where the board has supervisory functions and a mediating role between producers and consumers.

While the boards had a number of powers at their disposal they used only a few: the imposition of special levies to finance operations and administrative costs; the authority to buy a product at an approved price; the enforcement of single-channel marketing (i.e. solely through the board and its agents); power to fix the product price; and control of imports and exports.[13]

Before the latest reforms (see section on Current issues and future prospects, p. 97) almost two-thirds of the gross value of agricultural production was subject to marketing schemes with varying levels of intervention while an additional 10 percent was marketed under "special legislation", which provided conditions similar to those of marketing boards. Quantitative controls were applied to most agricultural imports while the beef and wine industries were subjected to production quotas to control supply.[14]

Similar marketing arrangements (i.e. marketing boards with statutory powers) were followed by the semi-independent *bantustans* although lack of information makes it difficult to assess how effective these marketing arrangements were in controlling trade and

[12] **For more details on the history and functioning of the boards and the marketing system in general see LAPC. 1993.** *Agricultural marketing and pricing in a democratic South Africa.* Land and Agricultural Policy Centre Policy Paper No. 2. Johannesburg, September 1993; Food Studies Group. *Agricultural marketing and pricing in South Africa.* Draft prepared for the World Bank; also World Bank, op. cit., footnote 7, p. 86, Chapter 4.

[13] For details see *Report of the Committee of Inquiry into the Marketing Act,* prepared by the Kassier Committee of Inquiry into the Marketing Act, December 1992. The Committee was established in 1992 to conduct an inquiry into the marketing of agricultural products. See also World Bank, op. cit., footnote 7, p. 86.

[14] LAPC, op. cit., footnote 12.

SUB-SAHARAN AFRICA

providing appropriate marketing services. A major difference between the marketing systems in the Republic of South Africa (RSA) and in the *bantustans* was that, while in the former producers played a major role in the institutions that controlled and implemented the various schemes, in the latter small-scale producers had very limited power to intervene in the management of control institutions.[15]

For major crops, such as maize, wheat and winter cereals, the marketing structure had a big impact on prices. Prices set by the board at producer and consumer levels usually exceeded the world price, resulting in welfare transfers from consumers and/or taxpayers to producers. A panterritorial price scheme for producers aggravated the negative effects on price efficiency. Occasional surpluses of maize were exported at a loss, but losses were covered by stabilization levies. For wheat, domestic prices were set above world prices (between 11 and 46 percent higher in the 1980 to 1987 period) and imports were subjected to strict controls on quantity to protect the domestic price.

The complicated marketing regulations and controls and the extensive use of tariffs and quantitative restrictions resulted in a predominantly inward looking agricultural sector largely isolated from foreign market competition. The enforcement of single-channel marketing deterred entry and competition in the sector, while a system of licences (such as the meat scheme's quota control scheme) promoted concentration on processing and distribution systems.

Prereform policies and their economic and social effects

A review of the performance of the agricultural sector in South Africa up to the mid-1980s shows that, despite the country's limited agricultural resource base, agriculture had achieved an impressive production performance in almost all major products and was producing surpluses in some. Thus, the long-standing objective of self-sufficiency was largely met. The diversity of the country's resource endowment, which allows the production of a variety of commodities, contributed to this success, as did the high level of technological sophistication and managerial skills of South African farmers.

---

[15] See LAPC, op. cit., footnote 12.

SUB-SAHARAN AFRICA

In spite of these achievements in agricultural production and self-sufficiency, the structure and pattern of growth of the sector, which was to a large extent shaped by policy action, turned out to be unsustainable from both the strict economic and the social efficiency viewpoints.

A major problem has been the inequality of access to resources and support services between large commercial farmers and those in the homelands. Land distribution data show that 86 percent of agricultural land is held by 55 000 predominantly white large-scale commercial farmers and supports a rural population of 5.3 million. On the other hand, 13.1 million black residents in the homelands live on the remaining 14 percent of agricultural land.[16] Likewise, the ratio of government spending in the modern sector to the homeland sector was 4:1 in the 1980s, down from 14:1 in the 1950s and 179:1 before the Second World War. Large commercial farmers obtained 96.7 percent of the transfer payments in the budget.[17]

Inequalities in the distribution of resources have been caused by policies, regulations and restrictions rather than by a natural outcome of a market-based process in which land concentration would result from economies of scale in production. Certainly, for some South African agricultural activities extensive operations are efficient (for instance, for livestock raising in dry areas) even in the absence of policy, but this is not the case for a number of others.

Apart from the serious social implications of past policies, their cost in terms of economic efficiency, although difficult to calculate precisely, has probably been substantial. Such policies hampered the dynamism that African farming had at the beginning of the century. Restrictions on free exchange in the land and labour markets eliminated the possibility of mutually beneficial, profit-maximizing arrangements between landlords and potential tenants or labourers. In combination with policies on interest rates and the tax treatment of capital, restrictions in market activity pushed the agricultural sector towards a capital-intensive structure and away from labour, the abundant resource in the country.

The high capital intensity of production in the presence of high unemployment is found not only in agriculture but is a characteristic of the whole

[16] This is different from saying that 13.1 million make a living off 14 percent of the land. Agriculture in the homelands is the source of about 20 percent of total income, while the larger part comes from the remittances of family members working in the farms, factories and mines outside the homelands and from pensions. Some of the inequality in land distributions can be attributed to high population growth in the homelands. Quality of land also plays a role. For instance, the white farm land located in Karoo and Kalahari has very little population-carrying capacity. On the other hand, some of the farmland in the high rainfall areas of the homelands is on hillsides and highly degradable. Even after these qualifications are made, however, inequality in land distribution is still extreme.

[17] World Bank, op. cit., footnote 7, p. 86.

SUB-SAHARAN AFRICA

economic structure, resulting from the inward-looking import-substitution policies of the country. Some of those policies towards non-agricultural sectors (such as tariffs and quotas) were detrimental not only to overall productivity in the country but also to the profitability of farming as they restricted agriculture to high-cost domestic sources of input supply.

Eventually, inefficiencies in resource allocation led to stagnating productivity in agriculture. Substantial transfers of resources from consumers, directly in the form of higher prices or as taxpayers in the form of transfers of public funds, were needed to keep parts of the commercial agricultural sector alive in the face of declining profitability in the 1970s.

The post-1985 period: policy reforms and their impact.
While policy reforms aimed *directly* at agriculture did not start until the early and mid-1980s, the reforms in the financial/banking sector of the late 1970s and the devaluation of the rand had a significant impact on the agricultural sector. The imposition of more stringent reserve requirements on the commercial banks and the concomitant increase in the interest rate made it impossible for the land bank to continue subsidizing the interest rate on farm loans.[18] The devaluation of the rand increased the cost of agricultural inputs, which have a large import component, while the increase in interest rates increased the debt burden of an already overextended commercial farm sector.

Policy reforms affecting the agricultural sector (in the wider sense) were initiated in the early 1980s within a climate of fiscal austerity and economic liberalization which, in turn, was the result of budgetary considerations and the realization that the inward-looking development model was counterproductive for overall factor productivity, economic growth and employment generation.[19] For agriculture, in addition to fiscal considerations (a significant motive underlying the reforms), a number of other factors created pressure for policy change:[20] the realization that overall productivity (total factor productivity) for controlled major subsectors (such as maize) was growing only slightly or remained stagnant while that of uncontrolled sectors (horticulture, poultry meat) was increasing; pressures from commercial farmers and industrial interests that were not served by the controlled system

---

[18] See N. Vink. 1993. Entrepreneurs and the political economy of reform in South Africa. *Agrekon,* 32(4); see also van Rooyen, van Zyl and Fényes, op. cit., footnote 8, p. 86.

[19] For data on overall GDP performance see below.

[20] Van Rooyen, van Zyl and Fényes, op. cit., footnote 8, p. 86.

as well as some successful legal cases against the control boards; the flourishing of parallel trade in some commodities that undermined the effectiveness of controls; and, last but not least, pressures and agreements during the GATT negotiations for tariffication and abolition of quantitative controls on imports. The main objectives of agricultural policy have made a major shift from food self-sufficiency to household-level food security.

As a result of fiscal pressures, budgetary allocations in support of farmers were reduced by more than 50 percent in real terms after 1987. Direct producer price subsidies (e.g. to maize producers) were eliminated. Government subsidies to several sectors, including wheat, maize and the dairy industry, were halted. Price controls on bread and flour were abolished in 1991. There was a reduction in administered prices to producers and a move away from cost-plus to more market-determined prices. Since 1987, there has been a marked decline in real producer prices of key commodities such as maize and wheat. The tax code has also been reformed and capital equipment now has a three-year write-off period rather than only one year.

The South African marketing system has been substantially changed. The Kassier Committee of Inquiry into the Marketing Act, appointed by the Minister of Agriculture in June 1992, produced a report strongly opposed to the system of statutory controls. The reform of marketing schemes, some of which had begun in the early and mid-1980s, intensified after the publication of the report which recommended widespread deregulation of the marketing system. Thus, six out of a total of 21 marketing schemes have been abolished (bananas, chicory, rooibos tea, eggs, potatoes and dry beans) while others have been reformed away from single-channel marketing (e.g. leaf tobacco, ostrich products, maize and lucerne hay). For the main cereals, the ban on erecting silos and the registration of millers and confectioners have been repealed. Grain sorghum and groundnut marketing schemes were reformed by surplus-removal schemes. For red meat, in addition to the abolition of movement limitations, the restrictive registration of producers, abattoirs, butchers, dealers, processors and importers was also repealed.

In the homelands, the "top-down" rural development policy favouring estate farms was abolished in favour of

SUB-SAHARAN AFRICA

an approach that emphasized service provision to farmers (infrastructure, extension and research services and improved credit access). In 1991, the Land Acts were abolished.

The short-term effects of the change in policies are difficult to disentangle from the effects of the general economic trends in the country and from the effects of other exogenous factors. During the 1980s and early 1990s, apart from over the period 1986 to 1988, growth rates of real GDP declined in South Africa. A continuous decline in overall productivity growth (total factor productivity growth was -0.5 percent per year between 1973 and 1984 and -1.1 percent between 1981 and 1988), despite an increasing investment:GDP ratio, contributed to a negative per caput GDP growth after 1982. The situation deteriorated with the imposition of financial sanctions in 1985 and the political turmoil and uncertainty in the country. GDP growth was -0.6 percent in 1990 and 1991 and -2.1 in 1992 caused, in part, by the severe drought in the country.

The policy changes in agriculture accelerated a cost-price squeeze that had started in the early 1970s. While the liberalization of output markets caused declines in real output prices, there was no commensurate decline in the prices of agricultural inputs. This was partly the result of high import protection for farm machinery and implement manufacturing and monopolies within those industries.

The fall in profitability of the farm sector has had severe implications on many farmers' ability to repay debts while the real costs of borrowing increase. Several years of negative real interest rates for the farm sector provided a strong incentive for debt accumulation. Real farm debt reached its highest level in 1985 and has decreased since as the conditions for borrowing have deteriorated and the borrowing ability of a number of farmers has declined along with profitability. Short-term borrowing has been substituted for long-term indebtedness and the ratio of short- to long-term debt has increased substantially. A survey on the financial situation of farmers, published in 1985 by the South African Agricultural Union, showed that 49 percent of the farmers were financially sound at the end of 1983, but the percentage was expected to fall to below 39 percent at the end of 1984.[21] In addition, 22.4 percent

---

[21] Van Rooyen, van Zyl and Fényes, op. cit., footnote 8, p. 86.

SUB-SAHARAN AFRICA

of farmers had debt burdens at "critical" levels in 1983 and this percentage was expected to have grown to 33 percent in 1984. Debt difficulties were not uniformly distributed among agricultural subsectors. Summer crops were affected the most (52 percent of farms were beyond the critical level) while winter crops were less affected (22.6 percent of farms).

Despite declining farm profitability, unsustainable debt problems and sharp reductions in farm incomes, massive farm failures have been avoided thanks to a number of government programmes providing substantial amounts of aid to farmers under financial assistance schemes. Substantial financial help was provided to the sector to help farmers face the consequences of the 1991/92 catastrophic drought. Financial assistance schemes have kept farm insolvencies at low levels in relation to the number that would otherwise have occurred. Nevertheless, an increase in insolvencies was observed, from an average of 80 in the 1960s and 1970s to 141 in 1985, 317 in 1987 and 267 in 1990. The expectation of continuing public financial assistance to prevent insolvencies along with the fear of collapsing land prices encouraged the financial sector to continue its provision of short-term credit to farmers to keep them on their farms.[22] While public financial assistance was successful in keeping farmers (especially grain farmers who had the majority of arrears) on the land by preventing foreclosures, it slowed down necessary adjustments in the structure of the farm sector, input mix and possible relocations in production. In that sense, such assistance had the opposite effects to the "structural adjustment" measures taken since the 1980s.

There are signs of some improvements in efficiency that resulted from the shift in policies. The capital intensity of production fell and employment in agriculture rose. Cropping patterns shifted away from maize, for which the area planted decreased by 12.5 percent between 1981 and 1988. Similar trends have been observed for wheat, grain sorghum, sunflower seed, soybeans and cotton. Increases have been observed in the production and export of more profitable (and more labour-intensive) horticultural products. There is also evidence of an increasing number of input substitutions in response to price signals.[23] Studies reveal that between 1983 and 1991

[22] World Bank, op. cit., footnote 7, p. 86.

[23] J. Sartorius von Bach and J. van Zyl. 1992. Comment: returns to size and structure of agriculture – a suggested interpretation. *Development South Africa*, 9(1).

SUB-SAHARAN AFRICA

total factor productivity (TFP) in agriculture grew by 4.63 percent a year outpacing a 3.11 percent decline in the terms of trade. This is a significant improvement over the period 1973 to 1983 for which TFP increased by only 0.27 percent annually. Improved capacity utilization (e.g. a longer replacement period for tractors) may account for much of the difference.[24]

South African agriculture: current issues and future prospects

The changes in policy towards the agricultural sector that were implemented mainly during the 1980s and early 1990s are a step towards establishing a more flexible and efficient sector. Pricing and marketing reforms, supplemented by reforms that reduce the concentration in input markets, processing and distribution, reduce the gap between producer and consumer prices of food and have widespread benefits.

Although the evidence shows that the structure of an agricultural sector that is dependent on large, heavily capitalized farms practising monoculture may be unsustainable without government support for some crops and in some agroclimatic conditions, sweeping generalizations regarding the efficiency of large-scale farms cannot be made. The diversity of agroclimatic conditions in South Africa can support enterprises with varying optimal scales of operations, degrees of capitalization, etc. Freer input and output markets and the abolition of restrictive policy measures will be the major determinants of an efficient farm structure for different commodities and enterprises. Where large-scale, capital-intensive farms prove unviable, policies and programmes can be put in place to speed up the market process of land redistribution and help poor rural people acquire land. In such cases, policy interventions in favour of land redistribution will promote both efficiency and equity objectives.

Land redistribution options

Land reform in South Africa is necessary for reasons that go beyond improved efficiency, and its implementation (or lack thereof) will have important social and political consequences with significant implications for economic development. The demise of the black farming sector in the homelands and its low productivity is, to a large extent, the result of land

[24] J. van Zyl, H.D. van Schalk-wyk and C. Thirtle. 1993. En-trepreneurship and the bottom line: how much of agriculture's profits are due to changes in price, how much to productiv-ity. *Agrekon,* 32(4).

SUB-SAHARAN AFRICA

allocation decisions and a lack of access to credit, adequate infrastructure and other agricultural services. International experience shows that failure to address effectively inequities in access to resources and the concomitant poverty and marginalization of disenfranchised social groups may result in social unrest, capital flight and economic decline.[25]

There are two parts to the process of land reform currently being discussed in South Africa. First, land restoration, i.e. the administrative or adjudicative process by which land is allocated to individuals or communities unjustly evicted as a result of racially based land legislation policies and, second, land redistribution, i.e. the process through which selected groups of individuals are provided with access to land and the necessary means for its effective use. The extent to which land is redistributed, the criteria by which beneficiaries are selected, the means of acquiring the land for redistribution and the provision of the support services necessary for effective land-use are at the centre of the rural restructuring debate in South Africa.

To the extent that a land reform programme will address welfare objectives, policy-makers face the task of reconciling the historical claims of black farmers for access to land while at the same time maintaining a dynamic agricultural sector and expanding the benefits of agricultural growth to rural communities and non-agricultural sectors. Welfare and efficiency objectives will have to be reconciled in cases of individuals who qualify for land or assistance under welfare criteria but do not have adequate farming or other land-use experience.

For a successful land reform programme, the actual transfer of land to beneficiaries is considered only the first step towards a rural restructuring effort. Communities should have access to the financial, physical and human capital necessary to make effective and productive use of the reallocated land. The type and amount of assistance to be provided to the emerging farmers and farming communities and the administrative modalities for doing so are important policy issues to be resolved in designing the land redistribution scheme. Thus, the problem of rural restructuring is one of access to and redistribution of resources of which land is the most important but certainly not the only one.

[25] In this report we hope only to present the nature and basic elements of the land reform programme in South Africa and not a detailed account of all options available, their merits and drawbacks. For more information on such issues see LAPC. 1994. *Proceedings of the Land Redistribution Options Conference,* 12 to 15 October 1993. Johannesburg, Land and Agriculture Policy Centre; see also Binswanger and Deininger, op. cit., footnote 9, p. 87. In the same volume a special section is included on Experience with agricultural policy: some lessons for South Africa.

SUB-SAHARAN AFRICA

Recent policy reforms that reduce support to the large commercial sector may aid the land reform process to the extent that they will result in land sales on the part of those large-scale farms unable to survive in an unprotected environment. Relying on only such measures will not be sufficient to achieve the objectives of the land reform programme. In an uncertain political-economic environment such as the one currently in South Africa, land is valued more highly than its productive worth so large landowners will be reluctant to sell land even though they may be receiving lower policy-related support. In addition, the financial position of disenfranchised groups will not permit them to participate actively in the land market and, as a result, the welfare and equity objectives of the land reform programme will only be partially met.

Experience shows that for land-reform-based rural development to be successful, it is imperative that land tenure rights and arrangements be protected by law or constitutional act. Such legislative acts secure private ownership and sanction various forms of tenure, such as private titles and communal arrangements, which are the prevalent form of landownership in the homelands. Local communities are given ample powers to manage their internal land affairs while at the same time guaranteeing a minimum set of democratic rights to their members.[26] A clear legal framework for land rights will remove uncertainty about landownership and, as such, promote investment and environmental conservation.

From the above discussion it becomes clear that rural restructuring and revival goes beyond land redistribution to encompass a series of supportive policies and programmes.[27] Although the extent and precise form of the redistribution programme are still under discussion, there is a consensus that, given international experience, a market-based reform that takes into account the realities in South Africa, rather than a state-controlled land reform, is the most appropriate form of land redistribution.[28] Past experiences with the Trust Land Transfer programme in South Africa and with the resettlement programme in Zimbabwe show that such state-controlled land transfers can be lengthy, costly and unproductive, tend to increase land prices and can be the source of land degradation if carried out before proper farming systems

---

[26] Binswanger and Deininger, op. cit., footnote 9, p. 87; M. Lipton and M. Lipton. 1993. *Creating rural livelihoods: some lessons for South Africa from experiences elsewhere. World Development*, 21(9).

[27] The Government's Reconstruction and Development Programme (RDP) considers land reform as "the central and driving force of a rural development programme". RDP identifies restitution of land to victims of forced removal, redistribution of land to landless people and tenure reform as the three key elements of the land reform programme. A Land Claims Court and Commission has been established to process claims. A review of present tenure practices is under way and a two-year pilot programme for redistribution is being implemented in each province of the country, to be expanded as progress is achieved. See RSA Department of Land Affairs. 1994. *Land Reform Pilot Programme: a project of the Reconstruction and Development Programme.*

[28] Under a state-controlled programme the state buys the land and redistributes it to the eligible beneficiaries.

SUB-SAHARAN AFRICA

can be adopted.[29] Innovative approaches to a market-based land reform need to be explored. For instance, funding can be provided to employees in large white commercial farms so that they can acquire equity and associated ownership and decision-making powers in such enterprises.

For the welfare objectives of the land reform programme to be met, a basic grant element could be incorporated to aid eligible groups or individuals to acquire a core land component (e.g. a housing site). A matching grant scheme will attract individuals or groups who are likely to make the most productive use of the purchased land.

The country's relatively limited agricultural resource base limits the options for and the extent of land redistribution.[30] Thus, given land restoration, the potential of land allocation by opening new lands or redistributing existing ones under state control is limited. As a result, land redistribution by and in itself cannot fully address the rural (and urban) poverty problem in South Africa even if the problem of the provision of access to credit and other services is successfully solved.[31] Improved access to services (including credit) and infrastructure in the homelands is expected to cause significant agricultural expansion. Given small-scale agriculture's strong linkages to other non-farming sectors (i.e. upstream and downstream agroindustry) such an expansion will stimulate employment. The limited resource base and its fragility pose an effective limit on such growth, however, and may have negative environmental impacts. Thus it is necessary that land redistribution be accompanied by programmes to provide rural (and urban) safety nets and access to social and economic infrastructure.

Concluding remarks

The prospects for the resumption of economic growth in South Africa are positive. A positive per caput GDP growth in 1994 reverses the negative trend that started in 1982. The recent unification of the exchange rate and partial liberalization of the capital account proved to be a success, and demonstrated the confidence of international investors in the country's economy and the credibility of the government's prudent macroeconomic management policies. At the same time, the country is strengthening cooperation with its neighbours by

[29] See M. Missiaen. 1995. *South Africa policy profile.* United States Department of Agriculture, Economic Research Service. (Unpublished paper)

[30] Less than 16 percent of the land in white farming areas is arable, while the figure is 12 percent for the homelands. Missiaen, ibid.

[31] Model simulation by the World Bank indicates that if 30 percent of land is transferred from large to small farms, 1 million rural jobs will be generated over five years. See World Bank. Summary: options for land reform and rural restructuring in *Proceedings of the Land Redistribution Options Conference,* op. cit., footnote 25, p. 98.

SUB-SAHARAN AFRICA

becoming a member of the Southern African Development Community (SADC) and by renegotiating the treaty on the Southern Africa Customs Union (SACU) towards establishing a more democratic decision-making process and a fairer distribution of benefits.

A number of difficult obstacles still lie ahead. The government is seeking to balance the demands of the previously disenfranchised black majority for better living conditions and employment opportunities with the need for fiscal austerity and increased liberalization of the economy so that productivity can be increased. Short-term measures to alleviate poverty are needed. The data show that the demand for such policies is more acute in rural areas. It has been estimated that 16.4 million South Africans (45 percent of the total population) had incomes below the minimum subsistence level in 1989, 93 percent of these people were black and approximately 80 percent lived in rural areas. Around 2.3 million South Africans (87 percent of them black), including children under 12 and pregnant and lactating mothers, can be defined as malnourished.[32] Hence the urgency for an agriculture-based rural development, including land redistribution and the abolition of policies that inhibit the increased use of labour.

[32] See LAPC. 1993. *Food security and food policy.* Land and Agricultural Policy Centre Briefing No. 1. Johannesburg.

ASIA AND THE PACIFIC

REGIONAL OVERVIEW
Economic developments

Asia and the Pacific continued to outperform all other regions in 1994, recording an economic growth rate of 8.2 percent. GDP growth rates of 7 percent or more were achieved by nine countries, including the most populous ones: the People's Republic of China, India, Indonesia, the Republic of Korea, Pakistan and the Philippines. Prospects for 1995 and 1996 are also encouraging. The Asian Development Bank (AsDB) estimates the average regional growth rate to be 7.5 percent over the next two years.

The region's exports increased at a strong pace, growing by 11 percent in 1993 and nearly 17 percent in 1994. Factors that encourage export growth include the recovery in some Organisation for Economic Cooperation and Development (OECD) countries (especially the United States), substantial investments in information and electronics industries throughout the region in general and a rapid increase in foreign investment in South Asia in particular.

Trade within Asia and the Pacific continued to grow at a faster rate than trade with the rest of the world, while both formal and informal economic cooperation and integration efforts increased. In particular, countries are attempting to learn lessons from the positive experiences of the growth triangles in order to encourage further subregional economic integration.[33] The recent depreciation of the US dollar relative to the Japanese yen is the one unsettling factor. Since many Asian and Pacific countries hold large portions of their debt in yen, their dollar-based export earnings will not go as far in repayment of that debt as in previous years.

China's economy grew by 11.8 percent in 1994, down slightly from its astonishing performance of 13.4 percent in 1993. China accelerated its economic reforms in 1994, taking steps to unify the official and market exchange rates, strengthen the central bank and reorganize commercial banks. The unification of the exchange rate resulted in an effective devaluation of 50 percent, contributing to the country's 30 percent increase in exports in 1994. The government is

[33] For a discussion of Asia's growth triangles see Asian regional review in *The State of Food and Agriculture 1993*. Rome, FAO.

Figure 7

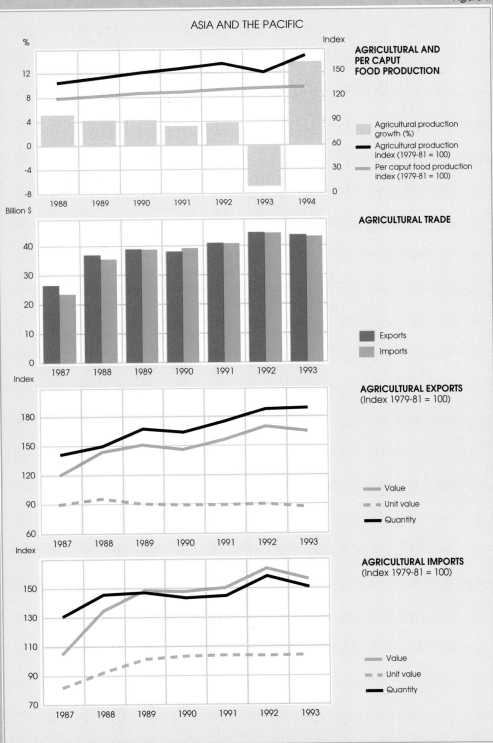

ASIA AND THE PACIFIC

AGRICULTURAL AND PER CAPUT FOOD PRODUCTION

Agricultural production growth (%)
Agricultural production index (1979-81 = 100)
Per caput food production index (1979-81 = 100)

AGRICULTURAL TRADE

Exports
Imports

AGRICULTURAL EXPORTS (Index 1979-81 = 100)

Value
Unit value
Quantity

AGRICULTURAL IMPORTS (Index 1979-81 = 100)

Value
Unit value
Quantity

Source: FAO

ASIA AND THE PACIFIC

continuing its overall strategy of phasing out subsidies to farmers, urban consumers and state-owned enterprises.

In the region's second-largest developing economy, India, growth increased from 4.3 percent in 1993 to 5.3 percent in 1994. The stabilization programme and market-oriented reforms that India began in 1991 are credited with much of the country's recent success in increasing private investment, domestic savings and foreign capital inflows. Other South Asian countries have also achieved some success in stabilization and reform efforts. With a growth rate of 7 percent, Nepal had its best economic performance of the past decade and, in Bangladesh, overall economic growth increased by 4.6 percent in 1994 with the manufacturing sector growing by 13 percent.

The consistently strong economies of Southeast Asia, Indonesia, Malaysia and Thailand strengthened economic performance in all sectors in 1994. In contrast to past years, the Philippines also shared in the subregion's strong growth. The industrial sector led the economic recovery in the Philippines, with industrial growth increasing to 6.1 percent in 1994, compared with 1.6 percent in 1993. In addition to the Uruguay Round, the agricultural sectors of the Southeast Asian countries will be affected by the Association of Southeast Asian Nations (ASEAN) Free Trade Agreement in coming years, as negotiators decided to include agricultural commodities in the agreement's planned tariff reductions.

Average GDP growth in the Pacific Islands fell from 11.8 percent in 1993 to 1.4 percent in 1994 and exports fell slightly. Papua New Guinea accounted for most of the reduction in subregional growth and exports. However, this drastic drop in economic growth is mainly the result of national accounting methods and does not reflect a severe slowdown in economic activity. In 1993, the economic impact from newly developed oil fields was responsible for raising the industrial growth rate to 35 percent, but without this influence growth in the industrial sector fell by more than 4 percent in 1994. Among the other islands, Fiji (3.2 percent) and Tonga (4.7 percent) improved their growth performance during 1993 and the Solomon Islands maintained its previous year's growth rate at about 4 percent.

Agricultural performance and issues

In 1994, agricultural production in the Asia and Pacific region increased by 2.5 percent. The region's total cereal production, however, was lower by more than 5 million tonnes, primarily because of weather-related problems in China. Overall, regional agricultural performance remains strong – between 1990 and 1994, agricultural production increased by 13 percent and per caput food production by 7 percent. Table 11 presents agricultural GDP growth rates for 1992 to 1994 and estimates for 1995.

In *China* unfavourable weather held agricultural growth to 3.5 percent in 1994. Floods or droughts affected more than 50 million hectares of cropland. Nevertheless, the country's 1994 total cereal production of 397 million tonnes was down only slightly from the record 1993 harvest level of 406 million tonnes. Cotton production increased by more than 13 percent, oilseed production by 10 percent and fruit production by 15 percent. Similarly, meat production increased by 12 percent, dairy production by 6 percent and fisheries by 15 percent.

China's agricultural policy-makers are concerned that the combination of relatively low procurement prices for cereals, large increases in fertilizer and other input prices and expanding economic opportunities in non-farming activities are leading to lower levels of private investment in agriculture and a reduction in the area planted to cereals. Moreover, the disparity between rural and urban incomes is widening, contributing to rural-urban migration. In 1995, the government plans to address these important issues by improving availability and access to agricultural inputs, strengthening irrigation systems and related infrastructure, increasing investment in mineral fertilizer production and expanding agricultural education, research and extension services.

In *South Asia*, the favourable monsoon rains helped India to produce a record cereal harvest of 212.5 million tonnes in 1994. (A review of India's agricultural sector policies is presented on p. 115.) Sri Lanka's agricultural GDP grew by 3.4 percent; while rice production increased only slightly, 1994 tea output was 4 percent above 1993 levels and 35 percent higher than 1992 production. In October 1994, Sri Lanka's new government reintroduced the fertilizer subsidy

ASIA AND THE PACIFIC

TABLE 11

Growth rates in agricultural GDP

Country	1992	1993	1994	1995[1]
Bangladesh	2.2	1.8	1.8	2.6
Cambodia	1.9	-2.0	1.4	...
China	4.1	4.0	3.5	4.0
India	5.1	2.9	2.4	3.0
Indonesia	6.6	1.4	1.6	4.3
Laos	8.3	2.7	7.6	...
Malaysia	4.3	3.9	0.5	2.3
Mongolia	-3.9	-7.0	7.1	...
Myanmar	10.5	5.1	6.4	...
Nepal	-1.1	-1.4	7.7	-1.0
Pakistan	9.5	-5.3	2.6	2.8
Philippines	0.4	2.1	2.4	3.0
Sri Lanka	-1.6	4.9	3.4	2.6
Thailand	4.2	-1.7	2.9	2.9
Viet Nam	7.2	3.8	3.9	3.5

[1] Projections.
Source: AsDB. *Asian Development Outlook 1994.* Manila.

programme. The programme initially subsidized importers and led to a 30 percent reduction in fertilizer prices. However, budgetary pressures eventually forced the government to revise the programme by directing cash subsidies to small farmers.

Pakistan's agricultural sector grew by 2.6 percent in 1994: sugar cane, fisheries, forestry and livestock production improved, while cotton production remained low because of disease and pest problems. Cotton is Pakistan's most important export crop, on average accounting for around 50 percent of agricultural export earnings, but production is down by more than 30 percent from 1991's record levels. In order to increase production and exports, the government removed export taxes and lifted the ban on private sector exports in 1994.

Indonesia's agricultural sector growth increased by only 1.6 percent in 1994: rice production fell by 4 percent because of poor weather; droughts and forest fires affected rubber production and the recent drought has also harmed shrimp production. A government report indicates that 10 percent of the country's shrimp

ASIA AND THE PACIFIC

farms were damaged by industrial pollution in 1994. Concern over the loss of agricultural land to residential and industrial uses prompted the government to ban the conversion of fertile land in Java and Bali. In an effort to improve forestry management, the government also issued a decree that allows the revocation of forest concessions for any one of four offences: sale or storage of illegally cut timber; abandonment of a concession for two consecutive years; transfer of forest concession rights to third parties without prior consent; and violation of existing forest conservation laws.

In *Viet Nam* floods affected some 200 000 hectares of rice land in both the northern and the southern parts of the country, but agricultural sector GDP still increased by nearly 4 percent. Recent legal reforms have led to substantial increases of foreign investment in agriculture, agroforestry, fisheries and sugar production. In 1994, the country took a number of steps to integrate its economy further by gaining observer status to GATT (now the World Trade Organization), becoming a full member of the Pacific Economic Cooperation Conference (PECC) and becoming an ASEAN member.

Issues and prospects for regional agriculture

Although the share of agriculture in GDP has declined steadily from 30 percent in the mid-1980s to around 20 percent in recent years, agriculture remains the driving economic force and major employer in many Asian countries. More than 65 percent of the region's inhabitants still live in rural areas and agriculture employs more than half of the economically active population. In general, Asian and Pacific countries have made considerable progress in expanding domestic food production and improving aggregate food supplies. Per caput daily dietary energy supplies (DES) for the region as a whole improved from 2 314 kilocalories in 1980-82 to 2 542 kilocalories by 1990-92.

Moreover, rapidly growing economies, broad-based income growth and expanding export revenues have allowed many countries to strengthen their import capacity to meet changing consumer demand for products such as beef and poultry. For example, the value of meat imports of Asian and Pacific countries has grown by more than 6 percent a year over the past decade. Overall, the Asian and Pacific countries are the world's fastest-growing market for agricultural imports.

ASIA AND THE PACIFIC

The region now accounts for 65 percent of total developing country agricultural imports. Nevertheless, in many countries, including China, India, Indonesia and Thailand, the strong pace of domestic food production has allowed food imports to expand to supply changing food demands and a growing population while the food import dependency ratio remains unchanged.

The region's ability to continue to expand agricultural production and trade in the future will largely depend on its ability to sustain economic growth while responding to growing natural resource and environmental constraints. (Box 3 presents an overview of land degradation problems in the Asia and Pacific region.)

Most Asian and Pacific countries have sustained economic growth by maintaining sound macroeconomic policies that control inflation and fiscal and current account deficits. In addition, countries throughout the region, including the former centrally planned economies, have pursued and progressively strengthened market-oriented structural reforms. These reforms have allowed agricultural sectors to adjust and take advantage of changing internal and external circumstances. The experiences of Asian countries further advanced in the reform process have also demonstrated the importance of careful monitoring and evaluation; attention to the timing and phasing in of new measures; and the development of the institutional capacity necessary for quick corrective actions to strengthen the food security of vulnerable groups affected by the reforms.

It is crucial for the region to continue this process of economic adjustment aimed at improving resource efficiency and encouraging investment in agriculture. A number of recent studies, including one from FAO, estimate that the growth rates of per caput agricultural production in the Asia and Pacific region are likely to decline during the next two decades.[34] This decline is projected to be more pronounced for the East Asian subregion than for South Asia. However, growth in per caput demand is also projected to decline. Cereals demand is expected to grow at about the same rate as production, especially for East Asia, thus self-sufficiency rates are not projected to change much. At these levels of self-sufficiency, net cereal imports in the year 2010

[34] FAO. 1995. *World agriculture: towards 2010.* Chichester, UK, FAO-John Wiley & Sons.

ASIA AND THE PACIFIC

are likely to increase by only 2 million tonnes in the East Asian subregion but may double to 10 million tonnes in South Asia.

Over the long term, FAO expects aggregate cereal self-sufficiency rates to fall from 102 to 97 in South Asia and to stagnate at 96-97 in East Asia in the 20 years ending 2010. This implies a sustained rise in the volume of imported wheat in the tropical countries, rice in the higher-cost producing countries and maize in countries with fast-growing livestock sectors.

In some countries, such as the Republic of Korea, declining production combined with sufficient foreign exchange are likely to raise cereals import dependence, especially for wheat and coarse grains. In some low-income food-deficit countries (LIFDCs) and most of the Pacific Island countries, changing food habits, rising incomes and stagnating production are expected to raise cereal import levels. In other countries, including Indonesia, Malaysia, the Philippines and Sri Lanka, the high costs of stocking food supplies have caused governments to reduce stock levels. As more countries adopt this practice, domestic stocks may play a diminishing role *vis-à-vis* international trade in price and supply stability.

BOX 3
RESOURCE CONSTRAINTS AND AGRICULTURE IN ASIA AND THE PACIFIC

The Asian and Pacific countries must confront the related resource issues of land degradation and increasing water scarcity to sustain agricultural and food production growth. A significant proportion of Asia's land in crop production is fragile; this includes arid and rain-fed semi-arid areas, areas with unreliable rainfall and areas with steep slopes and/or poor soils. It is these areas where environmental degradation and rural poverty tend to be most severe.

FAO estimates that the uncropped cultivable area in South Asia (0.051 hectares per person) will be halved in 20 years, while that of East Asia (excluding China) will drop by a third to 0.103 hectares per person. These estimates show that the region has the least potential for cultivated area expansion of any other region in the world except for the Near East and North Africa. The limited cultivable area for expansion and the continuing conversion of fertile agricultural land to non-agricultural uses mean that production increases have to come mainly from yield increases.

Yield increases will be difficult to accomplish, however, given the quickening pace of land degradation and water scarcity. The most damaging factors are soil erosion, nutrient mining, salinization of soils and loss and contamination of water. The extent and intensity of land degradation and water scarcity have been difficult to measure, but indications of the magnitude of the problem can be obtained from just two recent United Nations Environment Programme (UNEP) estimates for Asia:

• Per caput water availability, which fell by half in the 30 years ending 1980, might fall by another 35 percent by the year 2000.
• Deforestation, overgrazing and mismanagement of arable land caused water and wind erosion and physical and chemical degradation on 452 million hectares or 40 percent of the world's total degraded soils.

The drag on yield growth caused by unsustainable farming systems has become a pervasive problem in areas where the vicious circle of poverty and environmental degradation has been established. Dwindling per caput resources lead to further intensification of resource use and encroachment on to fragile areas which, in turn, leads to greater impoverishment. Resource degradation problems are extensive enough in the region to justify priority status and a strategy involving: shifting technology from hardware solutions to more knowledge- and information-based ones; establishing well-defined property or user rights for public and private resources; ensuring people's participation and decentralized resource management; and including direct and indirect environmental costs in agricultural commodity pricing.

INDIA

Economic review

India, which embarked on a programme of structural reforms in June 1991 after four decades of planning, is currently attracting significant attention throughout the world. Its large economy and population, vast natural resources and, above all, its highly educated, skilled and scientific labour force mean that India is destined to play a major role in the community of nations.

With a per caput income of about US$310 in 1994, India is one of the world's low-income countries. Unlike those of most East Asian countries, the economy in India was characterized by slow growth during most of the period since the Second World War. It was only during the 1980s that the GDP growth rate accelerated to 5.4 percent and per caput income grew by 3.3 percent per annum. This decade of high growth was followed in 1990 by one of the severest foreign exchange crises in the history of the country. In response, India initiated radical stabilization measures and a structural adjustment programme in June 1991.

Soon after independence, India adopted the path of planned development where the public sector was to play a dominant role in fostering growth at both the central and state levels. The First Five-Year Plan, which was launched in 1950-51, was based on the Harrod-Domar model and primarily concentrated on raising the level of investment in irrigation, power and other infrastructure for accelerating growth. The development strategy was changed radically in 1956 with the initiation of the Nehru-Mahalanobis model of industrial development that emphasized the development of heavy industry under the public sector. Domestic industry was protected from foreign competition through high tariff walls, exchange-rate management, controls and licences. This strategy of import substitution and heavy-industry promotion has been criticized for having created a non-competitive, inefficient, capital-intensive and high-cost industrial structure. It is further argued that this policy discriminated against labour-intensive tradable agriculture and resulted in unwarranted export pessimism because of excessive concern about self-sufficiency. The criticism, however, must be balanced against the fact that during this period India built a large infrastructure not only in heavy and machine goods

industries, but also in the areas of power, irrigation, credit, higher education, scientific research and training.

The mid-1960s and early 1970s were characterized by serious economic problems. First, because of wars with neighbours, large resources were diverted towards defence, resulting in a sharp decline in public investment that adversely affected the growth of the economy. Second, the foreign exchange situation forced India to devalue its currency in 1966. Finally, food production failed to keep pace with demand and the country became increasingly dependent on food imports under the United States Government's PL 480. The situation became critical in the mid-1960s with the failure of two consecutive crops in 1964/65 and 1965/66 and the country had to import large quantities of foodgrains under PL 480.

In the late 1960s, agricultural growth revived with the adoption of green revolution technology in some regions. Coincidentally, the manufacturing sector which had seen a notable deceleration in growth from 1964-65 to 1975-76, began registering far higher growth from 1977 to 1978.

During the 1980s, the Indian economy witnessed an unprecedented growth rate of 5.4 percent per annum. The 1980s was also a period when limited liberalization measures were initiated and steps were taken to modernize some of the most important industries, such as cement, steel, aluminium and power generation equipment.

The genesis and causes of the 1990 crisis

From 1950 to 1980, while the Indian economy was growing at a relatively slow rate of 3.6 percent, domestic investment exceeded domestic savings by only a small margin. The gap could be bridged through foreign borrowing on a small scale.[35] However, during the period 1979 to 1990, when the growth rate of GDP accelerated to 5.4 percent, the gap between savings and investment widened substantially. The need to finance large capital expenditures and imports of machinery and raw materials, including oil, necessitated heavy borrowing from abroad. The result was a cumulative increase in foreign debt and in repayment liability. Foreign debt increased from US$23.5 billion in 1980 to $63.40 billion in 1991. In 1991, nearly 28 percent of

[35] The gap between the domestic rate of investment and the domestic rate of savings is reflected in imports exceeding exports and is financed through foreign borrowing.

total export revenues went to service the debt. The most important reason for the internal savings rate falling increasingly short of investment requirements was the expanding fiscal deficit of the government which had risen from an average of 6.3 percent of GDP during the Seventh Five-Year Plan to 8.2 percent by 1990-91.

Large fiscal deficits arose for a number of reasons: exorbitant expenditures were incurred by the central government's subsidies of fertilizers, food and exports and by the state governments' of power, transport and irrigation. The inefficient functioning of many of the central and state public sector enterprises further burdened the government budget.

Finally, in addition to the current account deficit, mounting capital account expenditures by the government and public enterprises had to be financed through public borrowing. By 1990, internal debt liabilities had increased to 53 percent of GDP compared with 35 percent in 1980, and interest payments accounted for as much as 24 percent of total government expenditure. In addition, the sources of foreign borrowing underwent some important changes, as soft International Development Association (IDA) and government-to-government loans dried up and high-cost commercial loans from the banks and non-resident Indians had to fill the gap.

As long as the international credibility of India was high, loans were forthcoming and the country could go on living on foreign borrowing. However, the combination of a number of factors, including the sharp rise in import prices of oil and the downgrading of India's credit rating, led to a loss of confidence that resulted in the drying up of short-term credit along with a net outflow of non-resident Indian deposits. Thus, in spite of borrowing from the International Monetary Fund (IMF), the foreign exchange reserves declined.

It was against this background that the new economic policy was introduced. The multilateral agencies such as IMF and the World Bank insisted that the policy-makers undertake structural reforms before they agreed to salvage the country from the foreign exchange crisis.

The main components of new economic policy
The aim of the new policy was to bring about a realignment of domestic demand with available resources and to initiate changes in supply and

production structures with a view to eliminating the external imbalance. The economy was to be liberalized and gradually integrated with the world economy by the dismantling of tariff walls, the protection of foreign direct investment and upgrading the technology of production in various fields. The broad thrusts of the programmes were financial stability, outward-looking policies and deregulation of domestic markets.

The reforms consisted of two components. The short-term immediate stabilization measures focused on correcting the disequilibrium in the foreign exchange market through demand reduction, reforms in trade policy, a reduction in the fiscal deficit and the dismantling of barriers to the free flow of capital. External competitiveness was to be improved through a large nominal depreciation of the exchange rate.

The medium-term structural adjustment programme introduced reforms in fiscal, exchange rate, trade and industrial policy as well as policies concerning the public sector, the financial sector and the capital market. These reforms included elements such as deregulation of prices and investments, changes in the structure of taxation and public expenditure, moderation in wage increases, privatization of public enterprises and greater integration with the world economy.

The adjustment policies introduced were not specific to the agricultural sector, but concerned the entire economy. Nevertheless, keeping in view the importance and predominance of the agricultural sector in the Indian economy, in terms of both income generation and employment and its intimate relationship with other sectors of the economy through input-output and consumption linkages, the macroeconomic and other changes implied in the stabilization and structural adjustment programme had a significant impact on the sector.

A general review of agricultural development since independence helps to provide the necessary basis for understanding the full implications of structural reform for the agricultural sector of India.

Agricultural policy in India during the planning era
Prior to the liberalization of the Indian economy of June 1991, agricultural policy was governed by a planning framework. The entire gamut of macroeconomic

policies, notably trade, fiscal and monetary policies, was designed to serve planning objectives. The plans for the agricultural sector, including its financing and production targets, were all decided through a series of governmental processes at the state and central levels.

The nature and role of planning for the Indian agricultural sector was primarily determined by the sector's specific characteristic of being under the operation of millions of independent producers. Hence, agricultural planning in India consisted in creating a rural infrastructure combined with providing modern inputs and a framework of incentives for farmers that would enable them to increase output through the adoption of modern technology.

Because food availability emerged as a major concern and constraint to the development process, accelerating agricultural and foodgrains growth with a view to providing food security became the central objective of India's agricultural policy. There were several agricultural components in the first and subsequent five-year plans. The first and most important was the implementation of land reforms during the mid-1950s with the objective of eliminating intermediaries and bringing about a greater degree of equality in land distribution.

The second agricultural component was the undertaking of substantial investment in rural infrastructure. A very high priority was accorded to public investment in irrigation and power (large-, medium- and small-scale) in both the central and the state plans. Simultaneously, policies were introduced to provide cheap institutional credit and other subsidies to the farmers to encourage private investment in irrigation. Large subsidies were also given for charges to users of both irrigation and power and fees were kept significantly below the costs of operation. The main thrust of this effort was to create a macroeconomic environment to encourage private investment by farmers and, thus, stimulate production. Promotional policies, including the Special Food Production Programme and agroclimatic regional planning, land and water development programmes, were aimed at accelerating agricultural development.

Large investments were also undertaken for the development of a research system under the aegis of the

Indian Council of Agricultural Research and the State Agricultural Universities. Simultaneously, a well-designed extension network was instituted for disseminating new technologies to cultivators. The result was a rapid extension of the land area under high-yielding varieties (HYV).

From 1950 until 1967, the Community Development Programme and a network of extension services were the main instruments in transforming traditional agriculture. These were supplemented by programmes to intensify production in a few well-endowed districts during the early 1960s.

The advent of the green revolution in the mid-1960s marked a turning point in the technological "upgrading" of Indian agriculture. The agricultural research and extension system received special attention during this period since Mexican wheat and International Rice Research Institute (IRRI) rice varieties had to be adapted to Indian conditions and made acceptable to farmers through extension and training.

Initially, new technology was confined to wheat production in the northwestern states of India. In the early 1970s, however, new varieties of rice were successfully introduced and the rice revolution spread not only in Punjab and Haryana but also to many other parts of India including the southern coastal areas. The focus of agricultural policy became the modernization of agriculture through extending seed-fertilizer technology to different parts of the country. Measures were also taken to involve small and marginal farmers in the production process by providing them with new inputs, including seeds, fertilizers and credit at subsidized rates.

Administered prices were the third area of policy during the planning era. In the context of pervading food shortages up until the mid-1950s, agricultural price policy had aimed at serving the main planning objective of keeping foodgrain prices low in the interest of food security. With the founding of the Agricultural Price Commission in 1965, price policy also provided incentives to farmers to increase production by establishing remunerative prices and assuring minimum support prices. The objective of the price policy was to reconcile two opposing interests – that of the farmers for fair remuneration and that of the consumers for reasonable prices.

The fourth important component of policy was the establishment of a comprehensive management system for the procurement, storage and public distribution of foodgrains to provide food to consumers at reasonable prices. During periods of scarcity, minimum support and procurement price operations were combined with compulsory procurement, levies on millers, zonal restrictions and other measures to enable the distribution of foodgrains (at subsidized rates) through the public distribution system (PDS). Sufficient food stocks were kept for running the PDS and also to help to stabilize prices through open market operations.

The fifth component was tightly controlled trade and exchange rate policies. In the case of agriculture, except for a few traditional commercial crops, the sector was insulated from world markets through the almost total control of exports and imports. The estimated surplus over domestic consumption requirements determined the quantities to be exported and vice versa for imports. Foodgrains, sugar and edible oils were imported in times of scarcity to prevent domestic prices of essential commodities from rising and to impart a measure of stability to domestic prices in the interest of both producers and consumers. Foreign trade in most agricultural goods was subject to quota or other restrictions such as minimum price requirements.

Finally, financial policy attempted to mobilize resources for public sector expenditure and for public investment. A system was created to extend cooperative and institutional credit to the rural sector, thus facilitating private investment in infrastructure and encouraging the adoption of new technology.

The planning strategy and agriculture
This overall policy package achieved many of the government's objectives. The land reforms were modest but succeeded in making owner-operators the dominant mode of cultivation. However, the legislation regarding land ceilings failed to a large degree. Policies also succeeded in accelerating the growth of agriculture and foodgrains production. As compared to a paltry growth rate of less than 0.25 percent per annum from 1904 to 1944, agricultural output grew by 2.7 percent and foodgrains production by 2.9 percent per annum during the 1949 to 1990 period. The introduction of HYVs

ASIA AND THE PACIFIC

during the mid-1960s resulted in a phenomenal increase in the growth rates of wheat and later rice production. Wheat output recorded an annual growth rate of 5.1 percent from 1967 to 1990, while the growth rate in rice production accelerated to 4.1 percent per annum between 1980 and 1990.

In addition, new technologies which were confined to wheat in the irrigated areas of Punjab, Haryana and western Uttar Pradesh during the first phase (1967 to 1975), began spreading to other areas. With a breakthrough in rice, the new technology gradually spread to the irrigated coastal regions of Andhra Pradesh, Tamil Nadu and Karnataka. During the 1980s, new technology spread to the highly populated eastern states of Bihar, Orissa, West Bengal and Assam, resulting in a significant increase in rice production.

Finally, and most important, accelerated growth in foodgrains production resulted in a greater degree of food security for a rapidly rising population and in a reduction of dependence on food imports. By the end of the 1970s, India had become marginally self-sufficient in foodgrains. The steady growth in foodgrains production, over time, increased both physical and economic access to them. The availability of cereals (measured in terms of kilocalories per caput per day) increased by more than 20 percent from 1960 to 1990.

Access to food for the poorer sectors of the population improved as the rapid growth in productivity lowered the real price of wheat and rice. During the 1980s, while the adjusted wholesale prices of all commodities recorded an annual compound growth rate of 6.9 percent per annum, the wholesale prices of wheat and rice rose at an annual rate of only 4.1 percent and 6.5 percent, respectively. The gains from productivity increases were shared by both producers and consumers. Hence, even though the intersectoral barter terms of trade became adverse for wheat and rice growers, their income terms of trade remained favourable because of yield and profitability increases.

Access to food for the poor increased because the proportion of per caput income required to buy food declined over time. While the index of per caput income increased by 545 percent from 1970 to 1990, the price index of food increased by only 280 percent. Finally, access to food for the poor increased because of anti-poverty programmes such as the Integrated Rural

Development Programme, the Rural Landless Employment Guarantee Programme, the National Rural Employment Programme and, later on, the Jawahar Rozgar Yojana. Effective mechanisms were developed for the relief of food scarcities and for resolving the problems of extremely severe droughts through the initiation of special employment programmes.

The planning policies in the context of the structural adjustment programme

While studies recognize India's policy achievements in higher growth and increasing food security to its rising population, the huge fertilizer, irrigation, electricity, credit and consumer food subsidies eventually became unsustainable. At the same time, external trade policies, domestic regulation of agriculture and related policy distortions heavily discriminated against agriculture relative to manufacturing. Moreover, land reform failed to bring about an equitable distribution of land and, as a consequence, very large inequalities continue to exist in the countryside. Finally, the new technologies that were encouraged by the policies and regulations were more appropriate for the richly endowed irrigated regions of India.

Regional inequalities in productivity and income have remained high and in some cases have tended to increase. Agriculturists in general, and small and marginal farmers and landless labourers in particular, remain extremely poor in the less well-endowed regions. The incidence of rural and urban poverty is very high. According to the latest planning commission estimates, in 1987-88, 39 percent of the population in rural areas and 40 percent in urban areas of India were living below the poverty line. As many as 83 million children in India were malnourished in 1991.

Until recently, while many critics focused their attention on these limitations, the general thrust of agricultural policy within the framework of planning had not been seriously questioned. However, after the new economic policy was introduced in 1991, all aspects of planning and associated macroeconomic policy have come under serious discussion:

- The inward-looking, import substitution development strategy, whcih was aimed at rapid industrialization, shifted resources from tradable

agriculture to industry by turning the terms of trade against agriculture.

- The overvaluation of the exchange rate subsidized imports and adversely affected all exports, especially agricultural exports.
- Most sector-specific policies at all stages of production, consumption and marketing of agricultural produce, worked against agriculture. For example, the price policy was in practice designed primarily to help the consumers. Farmers were generally given low administered prices in the name of helping the urban poor even when they had to pay higher prices for domestically produced inputs because of the protection given to local industry. In addition, a major proportion of the costs of the inefficient functioning of parastatal organizations, such as the Food Corporation of India, were borne by farmers.

In India, large subsidies given on agricultural inputs have led to resource misallocation. One study estimates the various subsidies given to the agricultural sector for fertilizers, irrigation and electricity to be in the order of 90.9 billion rupees (Rs) per year during the 1980s.[36] These subsidies placed an unsustainable burden on state and central finances, reducing the government's capacity to undertake large investments. Even then, these subsidies failed to compensate the farmers for the negative impact of lower administered output prices, discrimination against agriculture because of overvalued currency and higher input prices caused by the excessive protection given to industry.

Accordingly, it is argued that many components of economic reforms, such as devaluation of the rupee, drastic reduction of customs duties and reduction of protection to industry, are likely to end discrimination against tradable agriculture. Furthermore, trade liberalization would lead to increased exports from tradable agriculture, which is at a distinct comparative advantage since devaluation and trade reforms.

The impact of macroeconomic reforms on the agricultural sector

India's new economic policy was launched in June 1991. The government began to liberalize the economy by reforming trade, financial, tax and investment

[36] G. Ashok. 1989. Input subsidies in Indian agriculture – a statistical analysis. *Economic and Political Weekly*, XXIV(25).

ASIA AND THE PACIFIC

---

[37] **The Kulak Lobby is the wealthy farmers' lobby. In India, rich farmers are fairly well organized. The more important of their organizations include Bhartiya Kisan Union (Indian Farmers' Union) in the northern part of India and Krishak Samaj (Farmers' Society) in the south. In addition to these organizations, many political parties have, for a long time, supported the demand for higher output prices. Many of the organizations that until the mid 1960s were opposed to any rise in foodgrain prices, have since openly backed rises in output prices as a way of winning the support of a large section of medium-income and rich rural people.**

policies. Public enterprises were restructured and the budget controlled more closely. Specific policy reforms included floating the rupee, abolishing most industrial licensing, removing import licensing, reducing tariffs and relaxing foreign investment regulations. Although it is too early to assess their full impact, it is important to look at some of the short- and medium-term consequences of these reforms for the agricultural sector.

The short-term stabilization measures included sharp cuts in public spending and fiscal austerity. Consequently, there was a large cut not only in current expenditures but also in public investment. The severe demand restriction resulted in economic growth decelerating from 5.4 percent in 1990-91 to only 0.9 percent in 1991-92, but the economy revived subsequently and the growth rate of GDP rose to 4.3 percent during 1992-93 and 1993-94. It is expected to accelerate to 5.3 percent during 1994-95.

The growth rate in agriculture, which was 3.8 percent in 1990, dropped to -2.3 percent in 1991, but revived to 5.1 percent in 1992, 2.9 percent in 1993 and 2.4 percent in 1994. However, the vagaries of monsoons make it very difficult to establish a link between economic reforms and the growth rate in agriculture over a short period of time.

The fiscal adjustments that had the most significant effect on agriculture were the reductions of public investment in irrigation, power and other rural infrastructure, including agricultural research, roads and communications.

The devaluation of the rupee, reductions in tariff barriers and removal of protection to industry (through quotas and licensing) were expected to help end discrimination against agriculture and enable it to obtain more inputs at lower international prices.

The withdrawal of subsidies on fertilizers, electricity and irrigation was an important component in reducing the fiscal deficit. The most important capital input in agriculture is fertilizer. While most of the nitrogenous (N) fertilizers are produced indigenously, most potassium and phosphatic fertilizers are imported. The subsidy to nitrogenous fertilizers was partially withdrawn in 1991. Soon after raising the price of urea by 35 percent, the government reduced it by 5 percent under pressure from the Kulak Lobby.[37] Later, on the

recommendation of the Joint Parliamentary Committee on Fertilizer Pricing, the price of urea was reduced by a further 10 percent effective 25 August 1992. The phosphatic (P) and potassic (K) fertilizers were no longer controlled in 1992 and their prices registered a sharp rise as demand increased. To enable indigenous fertilizer producers to compete with importers, the import duty on phosphoric acid was abolished. An adverse consequence of the disproportionate rise in the prices of P and K has been the highly unbalanced use of fertilizers. As against an overall N:P:K ratio of 4:2:1 aggregated for the country, the consumption ratios were 9:3:3 prior to the reforms. In order to restore some balance, the government once again raised the price of urea, by 20 percent, with effect from 10 June 1994. Fertilizer consumption increased to 12.4 million tonnes in 1993-94 and is expected to register a sharp increase to 14.1 million tonnes in 1994-95, mainly as a result of increased demand from the eastern states.

State governments are also giving large subsidies for power and irrigation use. In some cases, these subsidies are so large that states are unable to finance long-term investment in irrigation and power production. This is one important cause of the decline of public investment in agriculture.

A substantial nominal devaluation of the rupee in June-July 1991 made exports of many agricultural commodities more competitive. Thus, exports of rice, wheat, cotton, fruit and vegetables, fish and fish products and meat received a significant boost. Agricultural and agroprocessing industry exports increased from US$3.338 billion in 1991-92 to $4.151 billion in 1993-94.

Despite recommendations for a complete overhaul of the rural credit structure, the abolition of subsidized credit and the closure of regional rural banks, the structure has not been changed in any radical manner since liberalization.[38]

Procurement price adjustments aimed at increasing incentives to producers constitute an important component of the reform package. Prices had to be increased to compensate farmers for increases in the price of inputs such as fertilizers and electricity. Earlier concerns to follow the traditional policy of keeping food prices low as a critically important anti-poverty measure have been swept away by the need for giving

[38] The government established the Narsimham Committee in 1991 to recommend reforms of the monetary system.

ASIA AND THE PACIFIC

greater incentives and increased profitability to producers. However, given the technical and institutional constraints to agricultural production, Indian experts have generally questioned the efficacy of using higher agricultural prices alone to bring about faster agricultural growth. Various studies on short- and long-term price elasticities demonstrate that output responds more readily to infrastructure (especially irrigation) than it does to prices.[39]

In the case of wheat, for example, the procurement, minimum support price was raised from Rs225 in April 1990 to Rs350 per quintal in January 1994 while its price was raised from Rs234 to Rs330 per quintal during the same time. In the case of paddy, the procurement price was raised from Rs205 in 1990/91 to Rs340 per quintal in 1994/95. The release price of rice was raised from Rs377 to Rs537 per quintal in April 1994. The price rises of these cereals have created a peculiar situation as the release price for wheat and rice from the public distribution system (PDS) have become even higher than the market price. Consequently, the offtake from public stocks has declined sharply, leading to a large buildup of food stocks to more than 30 million tonnes. As a result of these hikes in administrative prices, Indian rice has become uncompetitive in the international market and wheat exports have also become unfeasible.[40] Moreover, the sharp increases in foodgrain prices and release prices from the "fair price shops" has had a negative impact on food security for the poor in India. Recent reports indicate that the extent of poverty has increased over the last three years.

Liberalization of Indian agriculture and policy issues
Providing food security continues to be the central objective of India's agricultural policy. With a large and growing population of 844 million and an expected acceleration in per caput income over the next decade, the demand for foodgrains is likely to grow at a rapid rate. Policy-makers recognize that accelerating growth in foodgrains production is an essential prerequisite for meeting the rising food demand.

Higher agricultural growth requires both public and private investment in irrigation and other rural infrastructure. However, the rate of investment in agriculture has declined since the early 1980s. An important reason has been that in most states a large

[39] G. Bhalla, ed. 1994. *Economic liberalization and Indian agriculture.* New Delhi, New United Press.
[40] Government of India. 1995. *Economic survey 1994-95.* New Delhi, Government Press, p. 80.

ASIA AND THE PACIFIC

proportion of the government budget is required for huge subsidies on power, transport and water and on the inefficient functioning of both power and irrigation systems. In addition, policy-makers are considering decentralizing and privatizing irrigation projects (with explicit subsidies to be provided for socially important schemes), leasing distribution systems to panchayats[41] and forming irrigation cooperatives to establish and collect water charges and to manage and maintain distribution channels.

Private investment in agriculture is likely to increase if public investment grows to allow farmers to adopt yield-raising technology and if farmers have the incentives of remunerative prices.

The reforms and agricultural exports

There is a general agreement among economists and policy-makers that India has export potential in some agricultural products. In addition to traditional commodities, such as tea and coffee, exports of many new commodities, including fish products, rice, fruits and processed food, have shown a rapid increase. Some studies argue that there is major scope for increasing exports of foodgrains such as rice and wheat. In the short term, however, the competitiveness of several agricultural commodities is gradually being eroded because of high inflation attributed to the new economic policy.

The extent to which India should free its trade in foodgrains, oils and sugar, as a consequence of becoming a signatory to GATT, is an issue that has generated a great deal of debate. The main argument in favour suggests that India would stand to gain immensely from complete trade liberalization and that even the interest of food security would be served in a much more efficient and less costly way if, instead of relying on huge food stocks, imports and exports of foodgrains were used as a way of countering domestic supply fluctuations.

The opposite point of view argues that India should not free its trade immediately and that its demand for foodgrains should be met through domestic production instead. This view suggests that, because food production is the predominant means of living for a large percentage of the country's workforce whose fortunes depend on the growth rate of output and

---

[41] Panchayats are the duly elected and traditional governing bodies at the village level. Recently, the government has, through a constitutional amendment, conferred many statutory rights on local bodies, including the panchayats.

productivity in the foodgrains sector, India should be insulated from international price changes. This group argues that free trade is likely to accentuate the variability in domestic market prices in the short term as a result of large fluctuations in the international prices of agricultural commodities. This would expose market prices to great risk and uncertainty. These fluctuations would adversely affect food security for the poor.

The practical approach to trade liberalization suggests that the new liberal climate should make it possible to dispense with many coercive instruments such as compulsory procurement, zonal restrictions and limits on stocks, and to make more effective use of markets at both the national and international levels. Important measures include: reducing the costs of procurement and storage through the better functioning of the Food Corporation of India and the association of private trade with procurement operations; correcting many of the existing deficiencies in the PDS through gradually directing assistance only to the poor in both rural and urban areas, removing its urban bias and extending it to most of the rural areas and strengthening the coverage in poor states such as Bihar and Orissa; introducing a more cost-effective strategy for the management of food stocks, which should take into account likely food demands, the extent of fluctuations in domestic output and prices; allowing the Food Corporation of India to enter the international future markets with a view to reducing buffer stocks and cutting down on costs and subsidies; and developing regional cooperation.

Concluding remarks
In the wake of the macroeconomic reforms, it is possible for the agricultural sector to derive large benefits not only by catering to increasing domestic demand, but also by making use of the export possibilities brought by increased access to foreign markets. Globalization of Indian agriculture offers both opportunities and challenges to policy-makers. Opportunities exist for deriving large benefits through substantial increase in agricultural exports, especially exports of high-value labour-intensive agricultural products. This can become possible, however, only if the agricultural sector is able to generate larger surpluses through increased public and private investment in rural infrastructure, in research and

ASIA AND THE PACIFIC

development, new technology and in marketing. The challenges lie not only in modernizing small-scale agriculture and in making it efficient and competitive, but also in involving the mass of rural people including small and marginal farmers and landless agricultural labourers, in all parts of India, in the development process.

LATIN AMERICA AND THE CARIBBEAN

REGIONAL OVERVIEW
In the past it has often been argued that countries in the Latin American and Caribbean region do not have agricultural policies but only, or primarily, intervene in the sector to adjust for events in the macroeconomic sphere. Whatever the validity of this argument, the subordinate role of agricultural policies has become increasingly obvious in recent years as market forces, rather than government intervention, have been allowed increasingly to determine resource allocation and price formation. This process has been common to a large majority of countries throughout the world, but has been particularly marked in several countries in the region. However, the expected benefits of the widely adopted market-oriented approach appear still to be bypassing regional agriculture. The overall economic improvement in recent years has contrasted with generally poor performances in the agricultural sector, thus fuelling the debate as to whether the pace and modalities of liberalization should be reconsidered so as to extend its benefits to disfavoured, particularly rural, areas. Furthermore, the recent turbulence in financial markets has introduced new uncertainties on the general economic and agricultural outlook for several countries in the region. These events have roused another debate on the limits of an economic policy that combines external openness with exchange rate management as an anti-inflationary anchor.

This section briefly reviews the main features of the current economic and agricultural situation in the region and traces some of the implications for agricultural policies and performances in individual countries.

Economic developments
The economic situation in Latin America and the Caribbean in 1994 and the first quarter of 1995 was generally characterized by moderate growth, slowing inflation and pronounced financial and current account imbalances financed by large, but declining, capital inflows.

Regional economic growth in 1994 was estimated at 3.7 percent, up from an average of 3.2 percent during 1991-93.[42] General factors behind the accelerated growth included economic recovery in the industrial countries, continued expansion of domestic investment and further progress in stabilization and structural reform. A notable

---

[42] Economic estimates in this section are from the Economic Commission for Latin America and the Caribbean (ECLAC).

Figure 8

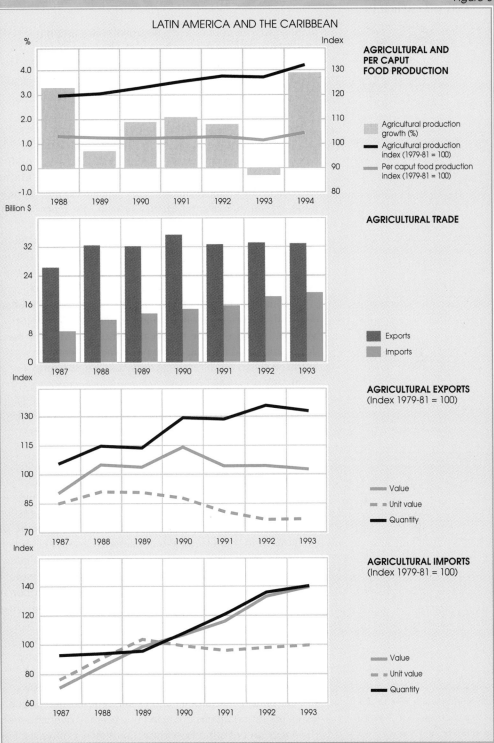

LATIN AMERICA AND THE CARIBBEAN

AGRICULTURAL AND PER CAPUT FOOD PRODUCTION

- Agricultural production growth (%)
- Agricultural production index (1979-81 = 100)
- Per caput food production index (1979-81 = 100)

AGRICULTURAL TRADE

- Exports
- Imports

AGRICULTURAL EXPORTS
(Index 1979-81 = 100)

- Value
- Unit value
- Quantity

AGRICULTURAL IMPORTS
(Index 1979-81 = 100)

- Value
- Unit value
- Quantity

Source: FAO

feature was the convergence of growth rates among countries in the region (perhaps reflecting the greater convergence in policies); a majority of countries achieved moderate growth rates and only a few recorded declines. The inflation rate fell to 16 percent (excluding Brazil), the lowest in many years. Brazil also achieved significant progress on the price front, with monthly inflation rates falling from almost 47 percent in June to 0.6 percent in December. Regional exports expanded by 14.3 percent in value, well above the 5 percent growth rate in 1992-93; this was the result in particular of the dynamism of intraregional trade and an increase, for the first time in five years, in non-fuel commodity prices. With imports rising even faster, however, the current account deficit increased from US$46 billion to $49.7 billion. The financing of such a deficit was rendered possible by capital inflows that, while lower than those of 1992 and 1993, still amounted to $57 billion.

The financial crisis in Mexico in December 1994 has had destabilizing financial and economic effects not only for Mexico, but also for the region as a whole. In Mexico, the devaluation and floating of the peso since December was followed by an inflationary upsurge and a tightening of fiscal and monetary policies. As a result, the country's short-term outlook is for a severe economic recession (GDP is expected to fall by about 3 percent in 1995), although the current restrictive stabilization measures are seen to be transitory in nature.

The events in Mexico had negative effects on financial markets throughout the region and worldwide. Capital inflows slowed down and stockmarkets fell, accentuating a process already under way following rising interest rates in the United States. Several countries faced heavy pressure on exchange and interest rates, while also experiencing higher debt repayment costs as a result of increasing interest rates in the creditor countries. Prospects for a strengthening of economic growth in the developed countries, and further pressure on exchange rates, suggest that such problems may accentuate in the coming years.

The situation raised again the issue of the role of foreign capital in the region's economies. *The State of Food and Agriculture 1994* discussed the difficult problems of economic management that are posed by capital inflows and the undesirable side-effects of such inflows, including losses in competitiveness caused by currency overvaluation. The Mexican crisis has now raised another set of issues. For Mexico itself, it has spurred concerns on its heavy socio-

economic costs and the capacity of both the country and the international financial community to restore stabilization and market confidence fully in the near future. For the rest of Latin America and the Caribbean, concerns have been voiced on the possible extension of the crisis to other countries and even on a major and generalized disruption of the ongoing recovery process. Such fears do not appear to be founded, however. Unlike the situation that led to the debt crisis of the 1980s, recent flows were largely in the form of bond issues and direct investment (rather than floating-rate bank loans) and were directed towards the private, rather than the public sector. In addition, the recent record of stabilization and reform in several countries across the region appears to have created enough market confidence to make a general reversal in private flows unlikely. However, recent events underlined the potential risks of accumulating foreign liability beyond sustainable levels, and the importance of maintaining the confidence of financial markets through credible and consistent macroeconomic policies and transparency of financial markets.

Agricultural performances

The recent record of agricultural production suggests that there are continuing difficulties in overcoming the crisis of the sector that began in the early 1980s. This protracted crisis is illustrated by the fact that regional per caput agricultural production has never again reached the levels of 1981 – although the poor performances concerned mainly the non-food agricultural sector. After the relatively favourable 1987-88 biennium, when production recovered from particularly poor performances, regional agriculture entered a renewed period of sluggish growth. From 1989 to 1993, per caput agricultural production declined by 2 to 3 percent overall. Although preliminary information for 1994 points to a substantial increase in agricultural production (4.1 percent, or 2.2 percent in per caput terms), per caput production would remain slightly below the peak level of 1981. Favourable production estimates for 1994 largely reflect a significant expansion in agricultural production in Brazil (6.7 percent) and Argentina (8.5 percent), although in the latter the increase to a large extent represents a recovery from the 5.8 percent drop recorded in 1993. On the other hand, many countries recorded lacklustre or poor performances. Among the largest producers, agricultural production is estimated to have increased by as little as

LATIN AMERICA AND THE CARIBBEAN

1.3 percent in Mexico, while in Colombia it may have declined by 3 percent.

The record of regional agricultural trade since the beginning of the 1980s has also been generally disappointing. Much of this period was characterized by extremely depressed prices for the region's main export commodities and deteriorating agricultural terms of trade. Agricultural exports in US-dollar terms barely increased during 1980-93 in spite of an average annual increase in export volumes of 2 percent. As the increase in merchandise import prices largely outpaced that in agricultural export value, the purchasing capacity of the region's agricultural exports fell by about one-quarter during the same 13-year period. Trade performances improved more recently, however. Available information for 1994-95 indicates that the strengthening in commodity prices may have enabled significant increases in export revenues in many countries, despite competitive losses from currency overvaluation in several of them.

Economic developments and the implications for agriculture

The recent economic and financial events outlined above are having a major impact on domestic and international conditions for agricultural development. In *Mexico,* the peso devaluation significantly altered the price relationships between domestic and imported products. Higher prices of imported grain resulted in competitive gains for domestic producers, more direct purchases to local producers by the milling and livestock industries and fewer purchases of imported grain from government stocks. On the other hand, the livestock and feeding industries, which use large quantities of feedgrain imported from the United States, were losers from the devaluation. This was particularly so for livestock producers who used dollar-denominated loans under the GSM-102 credit guarantee programme for which repayments were due at the new exchange rate.

In *Venezuela,* another country hit by severe financial difficulties and economic recession, the strong devaluation of the bolívar and foreign currency control resulted, *inter alia,* in lower food imports and the suspension of the GSM-102 credit guarantee programme. At the same time, farmers suffered from drastic cuts on subsidized credit and price support measures. The recession has also resulted in shifts in consumption patterns. Meat consumption fell, leading to reduced demand for feed and smaller herds and flocks;

while demand shifted from bread-wheat to less expensive maize and rice products.

In *Brazil*, the remarkable success of the new stabilization programme in reducing inflation combined with the increase in consumer purchasing capacity (per caput GDP rose by close to 3 percent in 1994 and may rise at a similar rate in 1995) are likely to benefit significantly agriculture on the demand side. Agricultural prices were an important factor in reducing inflation, thanks to an exceptional crop year. On the supply side, however, the Brazilian subsidized credit and price support programmes were constrained by macroeconomic stabilization measures. In the external sector, the establishment of a new band for the real following recent events in international financial markets effectively resulted in a currency devaluation and competitive gains for several key export commodities. For instance, the devaluation was expected to counter the fall in domestic soybean prices; render some competitivenes to the beef industry currently affected by high prices of live cattle; and favour a further expansion of forest product exports, which are expected to reach a new record in 1995. By contrast, the wheat milling industry has expressed concern over the negative effects of higher costs of imported wheat on an already depressed flour market. Economic considerations are also affecting commodity export markets in other ways. The need to hold down prices under the stabilization plan led to consideration being given to diverting some coffee stocks to the internal market.

In *Argentina*, the continuation of a fixed exchange rate regime, a key element in the achievement of price stabilization, has nevertheless created major difficulties for commodity producers. Problems of competitiveness linked to the exchange rate have compounded those arising from declining real prices for key export commodities such as wheat and meat. It has been estimated that, in the three years following introduction of the convertibility plan, the prices of pampa prime land fell by 5 percent; including poorer land, the overall decline was estimated at close to 30 percent. In addition, the agricultural debt was estimated to have risen to US$5 billion, or about 40 percent of the industry's gross product.[43] On the other hand, producers have benefited from revised credit lines by the Banco de la Nación Argentina, elimination of taxes on assets and import duties on capital goods, special loans to (pre-) finance exports, tax-free rural mortgage rates and a rural modernization programme (*cambio rural*).

[43] *The Economist,* 26 November 1994.

In the context of prudent fiscal, monetary and foreign exchange policies and sustained economic growth, *Colombia* has pursued its economic opening policy (*apertura*) implemented in 1991. However, this policy, which introduced across-the-board reductions in credit and export and other subsidies and import liberalization, has been criticized by farmers' associations for having depressed agriculture. Indeed, agricultural production between 1991 and 1993 rose by only 0.8 percent per year, agricultural exports declined by 2.7 percent per year, in spite of an expansion in export volumes, and the volume of agricultural imports rose by one-third – the latter reportedly undermining domestic production. It is difficult to assess the weight of *apertura* in such performances (other factors, such as long periods of drought in 1992 and 1993, the relative appreciation of the currency and low international prices of coffee and other export commodities, also played a role). In any case, the problems faced by agriculture led to the introduction of support measures to improve the efficiency of the sector. A new agricultural law was introduced in late 1993 that included provisions for minimum guaranteed prices, commodity stabilization funds, compensation to growers affected by subsidized imports and subsidized credit loans for farm investment. Early policy announcements from the new administration that took office in August 1994 suggest a supportive approach towards agriculture. In particular, a programme of "absorption agreements" was announced in which processor industries, such as feed manufacturers and oilseed crushers, agree to purchase all domestically produced commodities at specified prices.

In spite of its unquestionable economic success, *Chile* has also faced problems in its agricultural sector. In 1993 agricultural output increased by about 5 percent (compared with 5.6 percent for the economy as a whole), but agricultural exports fell by 4.5 percent, after many years of expansion. Production rose further by 5.6 percent in 1994, but the agricultural trade surplus, which was already reduced in 1993, narrowed further, reflecting in particular mediocre fruit export performances and rising imports. Agricultural producers and exporters have faced difficulties from rising costs (particularly of labour), an appreciation of the peso *vis-à-vis* the US dollar and competition from imports for several traditional crops. In line with its market-oriented approach the government has continued to provide only limited support to agriculture. In order to enhance

**LATIN AMERICA
AND THE CARIBBEAN**

exports of fruit, agro-industrial products, wine and other products, the new administration has announced an Export Promotion Fund that began operations on 1 January 1995 with an initial capital of US$10 million.

CENTRAL AMERICA
Introduction and overview

After over a decade during which the Central American region [44] was racked by civil strife, the 1990s brought relative peace and tranquillity, with the armed conflicts in El Salvador and Nicaragua reaching negotiated settlements and the fighting in Guatemala significantly reduced. Partly as a result of the success of the peace process, average economic growth across the five countries increased from less than 2 percent per annum from 1985 to 1990 to slightly over 3 percent for 1990 to 1994. Costa Rica, the only country of the five that was not involved in armed conflict directly or indirectly, enjoyed the fastest growth rate, at a relatively steady 5 percent per annum for the ten-year period 1984 to 1994. The economy of El Salvador also grew at almost 5 percent per year after 1990, compared with a rate of less than half that during the second half of the 1980s. Considerably less impressive were the recoveries of the other three countries; Guatemala's growth rate rose marginally from 2.9 percent in 1985-90 to 4 percent in 1991-94, while Nicaragua could do no better than reduce its rate of decline, from -3.5 percent per annum to -1.3 percent. In Honduras, the largest and least populated country of the isthmus, the growth rate slowed down slightly in the second period, 2.7 percent compared with the previous 3.2 percent. These growth rates occurred in the context of major steps towards trade liberalization and market deregulation, as discussed below.

After 1990 in particular, the countries implemented stabilization and structural adjustment programmes, with varying degrees of success. Costa Rica began the process in the first half of the 1980s, Guatemala implemented some measures in the middle of the decade, but the other three countries did not initiate comprehensive adjustment programmes until the end of the 1980s or the beginning of the 1990s. For El Salvador and Guatemala, fiscal adjustment played a secondary role in stabilization, because these countries had relatively small budget deficits that were well below 4 percent of GDP. Honduras displayed notable lack of success in reducing its fiscal deficit, which averaged about 7 percent of GDP during 1992-93, virtually the same as for 1985-86. In contrast, Nicaragua achieved spectacular success in reducing the fiscal deficit, from close to 20 percent of GDP during the period 1985 to 1988, to below 4 percent in 1989, a surplus in 1991 and, subsequently, a surplus of about 3 percent. While this reduction in the

[44] This review focuses on the five countries of the Central American Common Market (CACM), namely Costa Rica, El Salvador, Guatemala, Honduras and Nicaragua.

deficit was associated with the elimination of hyperinflation, it brought no respite from falling real GDP and even larger reductions in per caput income. Although Costa Rica has enjoyed the fastest growth rate in the region, its fiscal deficit proved to be a continuing problem in the 1990s (see the section Costa Rica, p. 142).

To the extent that the stabilization measures sought to improve the current trade account, they failed. Over the ten-year period 1985 to 1994, only three trade surpluses were registered by the five countries (Costa Rica, Guatemala and Honduras in 1986) and the regional trade deficit increased continuously after 1988, averaging US$2.5 billion for 1990-94 compared with $1.1 billion for 1985-89. Along with this rapidly increasing trade surplus went a virtual stagnation in agricultural exports. For the five countries taken together, agricultural exports in current prices increased by 7 percent from 1985 to 1986, but in no subsequent year did the total regain the level of 1986. The story of agricultural exports from Central America is a tale of Costa Rica and the rest. In 1993, the agricultural exports of Costa Rica were over 60 percent higher than they had been in 1985 in value terms and 125 percent higher in volume. None of the other Central American countries achieved an increase in export value; indeed, El Salvador, Honduras and Nicaragua showed substantial declines and for Guatemala there was virtually no change.

For El Salvador and Guatemala the decline, in the former case, and stagnation, in the latter, of agricultural export earnings were the result of unfavourable prices, especially for coffee. From 1990 onwards, El Salvador's agricultural exports increased in volume by 14 percent per annum and Guatemala's by 10 percent, yet the growth rates of export earnings for the period were -1.5 and 0.5 percent, respectively. In contrast to the sluggish performance of export earnings, the value of agricultural imports to the region increased dramatically, from US$530 million in 1985 to $1.17 billion in 1993. Owing to a slight decline in import prices, the increase in volume was marginally higher than the increase in value. The large increase in imports to the region resulted in the ratio of agricultural import:export value rising from 1:5 in 1985 (i.e. imports were 20 percent of exports in current prices) to 2:5 in 1993. Indeed, by the early 1990s, El Salvador and Nicaragua were only marginally net exporters of agricultural commodities, and both Guatemala and Honduras seemed to be on a declining trend. It would appear that trade liberalization measures

have tended to stimulate agricultural imports more than agricultural exports. As a consequence, governments have felt pressure to apply selective import-restraint measures, discussed in the National policy reviews, p. 142.

The rise in agricultural imports relative to exports need not in itself be cause for concern on general comparative advantage and efficiency principles. In the specific case of the region, however, the observed shifts in international commodity prices associated with the decline in net agricultural exports do signal cause for concern. In 1993 the ratio of agricultural export prices to import prices for the region as a whole stood 25 percent below the level of 1985. Every country but Honduras showed a statistically significant downward trend in this ratio during the period 1985 to 1993. One of the goals of trade liberalization in Central America has been the fostering of agricultural export diversification into non-traditional products for which world market demand is more income- and price-elastic and more buoyant than it is for coffee, bananas and cotton. However, the weight of these non-traditional products in the total agricultural exports of the region remains modest.

To some extent the absolute and relative decline in agricultural export prices reflects the drop in coffee prices after the collapse of the international coffee agreement. This decline was reversed in late 1994 and into 1995 as the result of frost in Brazil and cooperative action among coffee-exporting countries. However, the recovery of coffee prices may prove to be transitory and is unlikely to stimulate diversification.

Costa Rica has achieved impressive success in agricultural diversification, with non-traditional products increasing export earnings from about US$70 million in 1985 to over $250 million in 1993. Within this category three items, ornamental plants, pineapples and cantaloup, accounted for two-thirds of the total in 1993 (up from 55 percent in 1985). Despite this impressive growth, coffee and bananas accounted for almost 70 percent of Costa Rica's agricultural exports in the 1990s, roughly the same as for Nicaragua and considerably higher than for Guatemala.

Some degree of success in stimulating non-traditional agricultural exports was achieved in Nicaragua, especially for peanuts, beans, melons and onions. These, along with shrimp and lobster, accounted for over one-third of total exports in 1993, although the relatively high percentage was partly the result of total export earnings far below the level of the late 1970s.

LATIN AMERICA
AND THE CARIBBEAN

The lack of export diversification in the region is shown in its most extreme form by El Salvador, for which coffee alone represented over 70 percent of the total export earnings.

The mixed record on agricultural trade was associated with the ambiguous performance of the growth in agricultural production. While the volume of agricultural exports for the region as a whole grew faster from 1990 to 1994 than from 1985 to 1990 (4.8 percent compared with 1.8 percent), the volume of agricultural output grew more slowly in the 1990s for every country except El Salvador (where there was no significant change). During the period 1985 to 1990 all five countries enjoyed growth of agricultural output above or close to the rate of population increase (with Nicaragua and El Salvador lowest at just above 2 percent per annum). For the 1990s no country achieved a 3 percent annual rate of growth and only Costa Rica's rate of 2.5 percent exceeded the population increase. With regard to food production the performance was similar; the average annual growth rate for the region was 2.4 percent for 1985-90 and 1.9 percent for 1990-94. These modest growth rates of agriculture as a whole, food production and exports raise some questions about the effectiveness of liberalization in stimulating agriculture in the region, even for the "success" story of Costa Rica. Increases in world coffee prices improved the trade balances for all five countries in 1995, but this may prove to be a transitory gain (see section International and regional factors, p. 140).

Mediocre food production performances could not be compensated by rises in food imports, as indicated by the low food consumption levels in all countries except for Costa Rica. In the latter, current dietary energy supply (DES) levels are relatively high (about 2 700 kilocalories per day, compared with 2 650 kilocalories for the Latin America and Caribbean region and 2 500 kilocalories for the developing countries as a whole).

In the other four countries, however, calorie intake levels in recent years were barely of the order of 2 250 kilocalories per day. Furthermore, progress has been slow and uneven. While most countries had achieved substantial increases in DES levels until the mid-1980s (more markedly El Salvador and Costa Rica), the general picture since then has been one of stagnation for Costa Rica and decline in El Salvador and Nicaragua. Honduras recorded only very slow increases since the early 1970s.

International and regional factors

In the 1990s, the external economic policy of the Central American governments had three main aspects: attempting to improve the market conditions for traditional exports (coffee and bananas), rejuvenating Central American trade (especially for agricultural products) and changing policy in anticipation of accession to GATT. The governments of the region encountered serious difficulties in establishing a coherent strategy, in part caused by the different levels at which policy dialogue must be pursued for national, regional, hemispheric (i.e. North American Free Trade Agreement [NAFTA]) and world markets.

The most important Central American exports are coffee and bananas. Under the Lomé Convention, the EC established import quotas for various tropical products. The quota for bananas has been of special importance to several small countries in the so-called African, Caribbean and Pacific states (ACP) group. These quotas effectively reduced access to the European banana market for most Latin American countries. Tension over the EC banana quota increased in 1992 when the European Commission announced a reduction in the tariff-free quota for Latin America and a 170 percent duty on imports in excess of the specified limit. In this context, in March 1994 the EC reached a side-agreement with four Latin American countries (Colombia, Costa Rica, Nicaragua and Venezuela) to increase quotas. However, events quickly cast doubt on the sustainability of the agreement, in part because the excluded countries, including Guatemala and Honduras, challenged it in the European Court. While the court sustained the legality of the banana quota system, the four Latin American countries party to the side-agreement began to reconsider their participation. In August 1994, representatives of Latin America's banana-producing countries met in Panama City to establish a common policy. With all the Central American countries except El Salvador (which does not produce bananas) in agreement, the group proposed restricting world supply to push up prices and making a joint submission to the World Trade Organization in protest against EC policy. In addition to the direct impact of restricting access to the European market, the quotas resulted in intensified competition and lower prices elsewhere, especially in the United States.

Notwithstanding the conflict over bananas, the Central American countries made progress on other areas of trade policy with the EC. In the late 1980s, EC policy granted

reduced tariffs to Andean countries for a range of agricultural products, as part of an incentive scheme to discourage the production and trade of illegal drugs. As a result of a joint submission by the Central American governments, the European Commission in 1992 ended the discriminating levies, which affected several regional non-traditional exports (e.g. ornamental plants).

In the case of coffee, regional concern in the 1990s was more over international prices than market access. Following the collapse of the International Coffee Agreement, world prices dropped dramatically. After several years of price decline, the association of coffee-exporting countries (APEC) agreed to withhold 20 percent of stocks from the world market over the period October 1993 to April 1994. With the exception of El Salvador, the Central American governments supported and participated in the stock retention scheme. Improvement of world coffee prices in early 1994 prompted APEC members to release the retained stocks in May 1994. The cooperation among the Central American governments on coffee and bananas suggests potential for policy coordination in other fields.

Perhaps the most ambitious programme of cooperation involved the creation of a regional free-trade zone. A Central American common market was formally established in 1963, and intraregional exports as a proportion of total trade grew rapidly until regional commerce was undermined by the political instability and economic crisis of the late 1970s and 1980s. Intraregional trade during its expanding period largely bypassed agricultural products, except for processed foods. In a development that bodes well for the integration of intraregional commerce, the rejuvenation of the common market has focused on liberalizing agricultural as well as industrial trade. In March 1993, the regional governments agreed to harmonize most agricultural tariffs, with the aim of eliminating them among the five countries. This was followed by the signing of the Central American Free Trade Agreement in October of the same year. Progress on intraregional trade liberalization was greatest among the three northern countries, Honduras, Guatemala and El Salvador.

In spite of these important steps, including an agreement for freer regional trade in basic staples, the existence of alternative routes to trade promotion created tensions that weakened the move towards a coherent regional trade association. Bilateral agreements, Nicaragua with Mexico and Colombia, and Costa Rica with Mexico, cast doubt on

the status of purely regional tariff harmonization. In addition, El Salvador's reduction in tariffs in advance of the agreed schedule and Costa Rica's decision to increase tariffs for revenue purposes, both in early 1995, left regional trade policy driven by unilateral rather than multilateral action. While impressive progress was made towards regional economic cooperation during 1993-94, the ways in which a regional agreement would be reconciled with possible association with NAFTA and bilateral preference schemes remained to be clarified.

Along with moves towards regional integration, the Central American governments took steps towards active participation in GATT and its successor, the World Trade Organization. The main consequence of this for the agricultural sector was a shift from quantitative import controls and other non-tariff barriers to tariffs. With a few exceptions, such as dairy products and pork, governments eliminated the major non-tariff restrictions on agricultural imports and exports. These policy changes, while addressed to all trading partners, could foster regional agricultural trade.

National policy reviews
Costa Rica. Costa Rica was the first Central American country to enter into stabilization and structural adjustment programmes in the era of the Latin American debt crisis. It does not follow, however, that by the 1990s Costa Rica was the most liberalized economy in the region. From the late 1980s, agricultural policy combined protection and aid to targeted sectors with liberalization in other areas. For example, coffee producers received state aid through credits and other measures in response to low world market prices, as did banana growers and the livestock sector. At the same time, most non-tariff barriers affecting imports of agricultural products were converted to tariffs.

As part of a policy to foster greater self-sufficiency in basic staples, a state organization, the National Production Council (CNP), monopolized the import of grains. Yellow maize was removed from the monopoly control of CNP and, from 1992, a majority of maize imports came via the private sector. Wheat and rice imports were privatized in 1994, though further policy action would be required to make the change effective for wheat. Price controls on flour limit the incentive for private-sector imports of wheat, and these were scheduled for elimination in 1995. In order to foster domestic milling, the government maintained a substantial

tariff differential between rough and milled rice. Throughout the 1980s Costa Rica enforced price controls on a broad range of consumer products, but most controls were eliminated in the early 1990s in compliance with World Bank conditionality for an agricultural sector adjustment loan.

More than other countries in the region, Costa Rica pursued the active promotion of non-traditional exports through subsidies to selected firms. At the same time, coffee producers objected to what they considered discriminatory taxation, because they must pay both a production and an export tax. In response, in 1994 the government proposed replacing the two levies with an income tax calculated on net revenue.

Costa Rica could claim to have had the fastest growing and most stable economy in the region over the last ten years (notwithstanding a rate of inflation in the 15 to 25 percent range). However, 1995 brought economic uncertainty as a result of tense negotiations over loan programmes with the World Bank and IMF. Early in the year, the World Bank suspended disbursement of US$100 million, making the release of structural adjustment funds dependent on an agreement between IMF and the government on deficit reduction. Achieving the IMF deficit targets, 3.5 percent of GDP by the end of 1995 and 0.5 percent by the end of 1996, could result in significant interest rate increases. The latter would significantly affect costs of production in the agricultural sector, thus reducing producer incomes and export potential.

El Salvador. During the 1980s the Government of El Salvador, like that of Nicaragua over the same period, intervened extensively in markets in an attempt to contain the effects of civil war. Major liberalization measures were introduced through stabilization and structural adjustment programmes between 1989 and 1991. The major policy changes included restrictive monetary policy, liberalization of the exchange rate, elimination of quantity controls on foreign trade, tariff reduction and an end to state marketing monopolies for sugar and coffee. Further liberalization measures in subsequent years included privatization of commercial banks and the major parastatals involved in export crops (coffee, sugar and cotton).

In a major reversal of previous policy, the government announced in early 1995 that it intended to fix the exchange rate to the US dollar, as a step towards the

"dollarization" of the economy. Whether or not this mechanism succeeds in making El Salvador relatively more attractive to United States foreign investors than its neighbours, it leaves the country out of step with the flexible exchange rate regimes of the rest of Central America.

With regard to agricultural policies, it could be argued that El Salvador went further in liberalization and deregulation than any other country in the region. There is little intervention in grain markets, although a variable import levy was introduced as part of the regional agreement on tariff policy. The government also established a strategic grain reserve to enhance price stability.

Guatemala. As discussed in the section International and regional factors, p. 140, the Government of Guatemala vigorously applied itself to improving market access and prices for coffee and bananas. It is probable that the the government's criticism of the side-agreement on the EC banana market influenced Costa Rica and Nicaragua to reconsider their participation. Structural adjustment measures were initiated in the mid-1980s, although not with the dramatic liberalization impact that occurred in El Salvador or Nicaragua. The mild degree of adjustment resulted from the relatively low level of state intervention in Guatemalan markets.

Along with Costa Rica and El Salvador, the Government of Guatemala introduced changes in the marketing of grains. In addition to applying the regional variable import levy mechanism for yellow maize, rice and sorghum, the government stripped the domestic price stabilization board of important marketing functions. Liberalization of grain trade did not go smoothly; as a result of disagreements with its neighbours over the price band mechanism, Guatemala introduced temporary non-tariff restrictions on grain imports.

The liberalization of agricultural trade has not been equally matched by deregulation in domestic markets. Government bodies continue to set support prices for wheat, sugar and cottonseed, although these are implemented with the consent of producers. Proposals to eliminate domestic regulation and tariff protection for wheat went before the legislature in 1994, but no action was taken.

Honduras. Like Guatemala, Honduras entered the crisis-prone 1980s with a tradition of being a non-interventionist state. What price controls existed in law had little impact in

practice. As a result, policy adjustment tended to focus on macroeconomic policy and tariff reduction. In 1990, the government began a formal, externally supported adjustment programme whose main measures were the elimination of ineffective price controls on consumer goods, reduction in the role of the state marketing institutions, reduced import duties, exchange rate liberalization and contraction of the fiscal deficit. With the purpose of stimulating output, in 1992 the government introduced an agricultural modernization law, the primary focus of which was on reducing state intervention. Since intervention was not great before the law, its impact is likely to be small.

Economic policy in the 1990s lacked a clear focus, both in general and with respect to agriculture. After maintaining a fixed exchange rate during the 1980s, the government shifted policy in the 1990s. However, the auction system begun in mid-1994 increased controls over foreign exchange as much as it liberalized them, since it required documentary evidence that private-sector-held foreign currency derived from either the auction or other formal markets. In trade policy, Honduras reduced tariffs, as noted, but also applied non-tariff measures to block imports of poultry and maize from the United States in 1992 and 1993, and in 1993 it placed restrictions on imports of vegetable oils from other Central American countries.

These shifts in policy, including the reintroduction of consumer price controls for two months in late 1993, suggest that the government had yet to reach a consensus on a general policy framework for the agricultural sector.

Nicaragua. Like El Salvador, Nicaragua had a highly regulated economy throughout the 1980s. During the last two years of the Sandinista government major steps were taken to liberalize domestic markets which, in the context of a war economy, contributed to the subsequent hyperinflation. Once armed conflict ended and military expenditure could be reduced, the fiscal deficit dropped dramatically and relatively low inflation was achieved from 1992 onwards.

The Chomorro government continued the liberalization process with increased vigour, deregulating foreign trade, abolishing state monopolies and privatizing public enterprises. In the context of multilateral conditionality the government eliminated price supports to agricultural producers, stopped credit subsidies and dismantled the remaining controls over consumer prices. As a partial

replacement of the previous price support programme, the government adopted the regional variable import levy scheme for maize, sorghum and rice. While on the one hand these measures made the Nicaraguan economy more liberalized in some ways than those of countries that had begun adjustment earlier, the trade regime included a mixture of free trade elements and ad hoc export promotion measures. These ad hoc measures in part explain the impressive growth (albeit from a very low base) of non-traditional agricultural exports in the 1990s.

NEAR EAST AND NORTH AFRICA

REGIONAL OVERVIEW
Economic and agricultural performance in 1994-95

The conclusion of the Peace Treaty between Israel, the Palestine Liberation Organization (PLO) and Jordan and the ongoing peace negotiations have ushered in a wave of cautious optimism in the Near East and North Africa region. These events are improving the prospects for expanding trade, investment and tourism and for reducing military spending in the region. It is recognized, however, that the greatest peace dividends will be achieved by those countries that have reduced their macroeconomic imbalances through sound economic and financial policies.

Depressed oil prices, combined with a weak dollar and rises in non-oil commodity prices, have seriously hit the region's economies, particularly those of the major fuel exporters. During 1994, oil prices reached their lowest levels in real terms since 1973 and prospects for a significant strengthening in prices do not appear encouraging, at least in the short term. These problems have compelled economic reforms to focus on improving economic efficiency and reducing external debt and fiscal and current account deficits.

The more diversified economies in the region, including those of Egypt, Jordan, Morocco and Tunisia, continued their economic reform programmes with varying success. In Egypt, the macroeconomic environment stabilized as the fiscal deficit was further reduced and inflation better controlled, but growth remains modest. Both Morocco and Tunisia, countries at relatively advanced stages of adjustment, recorded growth rates of around 4 percent. The end of a two-year drought in Morocco had positive impacts on the country's overall economic performance.

In the Syrian Arab Republic, weakened consumer demand and reduced financial in-flows contributed to less buoyant economic activity with GDP growth in 1994 declining to 7 percent from a high of 11 percent the previous year. Turkey faced sluggish economic growth in a context of high inflation, deteriorating fiscal and external deficits and depreciation of the currency. These problems led to the adoption of a stabilization programme in mid-1994.

Figure 9

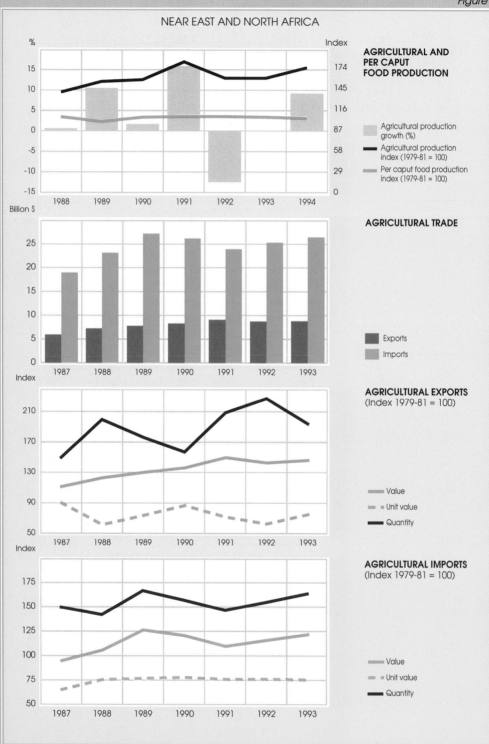

NEAR EAST AND NORTH AFRICA

AGRICULTURAL AND PER CAPUT FOOD PRODUCTION

Agricultural production growth (%)

Agricultural production index (1979-81 = 100)

Per caput food production index (1979-81 = 100)

AGRICULTURAL TRADE

Exports

Imports

AGRICULTURAL EXPORTS
(Index 1979-81 = 100)

Value

Unit value

Quantity

AGRICULTURAL IMPORTS
(Index 1979-81 = 100)

Value

Unit value

Quantity

Source: FAO

NEAR EAST AND NORTH AFRICA

The region's agricultural performance continued to be characterized by pronounced variations over time and among individual countries. Overall, the region's agricultural production increased by 3.3 percent in 1992, 1.5 percent in 1993 and an estimated 1 percent in 1994. High rates of population growth largely outpaced increases in food production in both 1993 and 1994, resulting in reduced levels of per caput food production.

Cereal production has averaged about 91 million tonnes over the past three years (1992 to 1994), 11 percent higher than the previous three-year period, despite a production shortfall in 1994. Poor rains resulted in reduced wheat production in Algeria, Tunisia and Turkey – the decline in the latter being 18 percent – but the overall fall in these countries was partly compensated by a record wheat crop in Morocco (5.5 million tonnes) which came at the end of a severe two-year drought.

As regards recent policy developments, in *Algeria* the transformation of state-owned farms to private farms is changing the historical structure of production in the agricultural sector and improving the efficiency and competitiveness of farm activities. In a major policy shift in April 1994, agricultural policies were liberalized through a reduction in the producer price support for cereals, pulses and other selected crops; higher interest rates; and a reduction in direct and indirect input subsidies.

In *Egypt,* wide-ranging reforms in the agricultural sector have focused on improving resource use and the efficiency of farming activities. Over the past several years, the government has liberalized production and marketing activities of inputs and of most crops. Virtually all subsidies to fertilizers, seeds, feed and pesticides have been eliminated. In 1994, cotton marketing was further liberalized through the opening of a cotton exchange in Alexandria. In 1994, traders were able to purchase cottonseed directly from farms and cooperatives for the first time in more than 30 years.

Egypt's wheat production did decline in 1994, however, after three years of impressive growth. The production decline is attributed to the reduced amounts of irrigated water that resulted from the long winter closure of the High Dam. Water-flows to irrigators are

being reduced in an effort to increase overall water supply to newly reclaimed lands. Cotton exports were valued at US$220 million for the one-year period between August 1993 and July 1994, compared with $90 million the previous year.

The Sudan has embarked on a series of economic policy reforms including floating the Sudanese pound and removing some subsidies on basic goods. Facing severe budgetary constraints and reduced food aid, policy-makers are pursuing a strategy of self-sufficiency in wheat production. The country's cereal production is estimated to have increased by about 55 percent in 1994, drastically reducing import needs. Current government policies are aimed at increasing yields through extension packages that promote the adoption of new technologies. Although recent studies have indicated that new wheat technologies could generate net economic gains exceeding those of cotton, their dissemination among farmers is still low.

In *Saudi Arabia*, the 1994 wheat harvest is expected to be 2.5 million tonnes, down from 3.6 million tonnes in 1993, reflecting further policy measures aimed at limiting excess production. Strict quotas on government wheat purchases from small farmers are helping to reduce production and reach the policy goal of matching wheat production to consumption levels.

Resource use and prospects for agricultural expansion
Although the agricultural potential varies widely among countries, the region's agricultural resource base in general is subject to a number of common, limiting constraints. FAO's 1994 Regional Conference for the Near East (NERC) highlighted the many difficult agricultural production issues facing producers in this region of arid and semi-arid lands.[45] The most pressing constraint is the low and erratic rainfall which severely limits food crop production. Year-to-year variability in crop production is higher in the Near East and North Africa than in any other developing region. For example, the coefficient of variation of cereal production has been over 50 percent in Jordan, Mauritania and Saudi Arabia, while for another ten countries of the region it has been over 25 percent.[46]

Fragmented landholdings and the lack, in rural areas, of adequate physical and institutional structures, such as transport, communication, research and extension

[45] FAO. 1994. FAO Near East Regional Conference. Amman, Jordan, 3-6 July 1994.
[46] The coefficient of variation of production measures the standard deviation of the percentage deviations of annual production levels from trend values.

and marketing infrastructure, are additional constraints in many countries. Another factor that inhibits faster growth and is a threat to sustainable food production is the serious degradation of natural resources including soil erosion, desertification, waterlogging and salinity. The slow growth in food production has also been accentuated by the long-standing political instability between and/or within countries and by social tensions.

In spite of resource constraints and often adverse climatic conditions, untapped potential exists. FAO projects that food output could increase by almost one-third over the 20-year period from 1990 to 2010.[47] As in the past, however, growth in production would be concentrated in a few countries – Egypt, the Islamic Republic of Iran, Morocco and Turkey.

About 70 percent of the projected increase in cereal production over the period would be attributable to yield improvement. This picture runs across the subregions with no significant variations between them, except in the Arabian Peninsula, where Saudi Arabia has already reached average yields of more than 5 tonnes per hectare.

The scope for yield improvement reflects the wide intercountry yield differential that exists at present, with most countries having yields well below those achieved by the better performers. Although many factors are involved, the achievements of the better performers suggest that even with the existing technology of high-yielding varieties, there is still wide scope for increasing yields through effective economic policies, improved land and water management, the appropriate use of modern inputs, good cultural practices and further adaptive research.

The FAO Regional Conference for the Near East also discussed the potential for changes in national cropping patterns through the introduction of new crops such as soybean and sunflower. Countries such as Egypt, the Persian Gulf states, Jordan, the Libyan Arab Jamahiriya and Morocco have already made remarkable advances in controlled environment (or greenhouse) farming of horticultural products for domestic consumption and the export market. Besides generating foreign exchange and seasonal employment opportunities, these farming systems are noted for high productivity, better control over the use of agricultural chemicals and improved water efficiency.

[47] FAO. 1995. *World agriculture: towards 2010.* Chichester, UK, FAO-John Wiley & Sons.

NEAR EAST
AND NORTH AFRICA

Increases in livestock numbers are expected to contribute 35 percent of the growth in meat production over the coming two decades. To raise production in this manner the feed resource base must be enlarged by intensifying range and pasture utilization and using more feed concentrates and agricultural byproducts. Striking a sustainable balance between livestock numbers and the availability of forage and feed is of paramount importance for conserving the natural environment and maintaining livestock production systems in the semi-arid conditions of the region. In some countries in the region, such as Egypt and countries in the West Asia subregion, the potential to expand grazing areas is limited so higher yield per animal is an increasingly important source of growth.

Food consumption and food security

Consumption of food in the region as a whole has been rising rapidly over the last two decades and is projected to continue rising for the foreseeable future. The expected increase in food consumption is the result of a number of factors. Annual population growth rates are among the highest in the world; those registered for the 1970s and 1980s were 2.7 and 3.1 percent respectively, and those expected in the 1990s and from 2000 to 2010 are 2.7 and 2.3 percent. In addition, there is rapid urbanization in the region, with the urban population increasing fourfold from 57 million in 1960 to 210 million in 1990. The urban population has increased from 30 percent of the total population in the early 1960s to 55 percent in 1993. Urbanization implies that most rural migrants, from being net food producers, become net food consumers, while the generally higher levels of income in the urban centres contribute to increasing food demand, as well as to changing the composition of diets.[48]

Overall, in terms of per caput daily dietary energy supplies (DES), the region had an average of 2 898 kilocalories in 1990-92, the highest among developing country regions. FAO estimates put the incidence of chronic undernutrition in the region at 13 percent of the total population, the same level as that of Latin America and the Caribbean, compared with 20 percent for the developing countries as a whole. This comparatively low undernutrition percentage is largely the result of high food availability, but in absolute numbers it

[48] Changes in lifestyle and dietary patterns over the past three decades have led to a shift in morbidity and mortality rates, with diet-related diseases becoming major public health problems now accounting for more than half the mortality rates in the region. In addition to the rapid rise in the total energy intake there has been a steep upward trend in the consumption of animal products, fats and sugars with a decline in that of pulses and nuts. Thus, there is malnutrition of both the poor and the affluent in some countries of the region.

corresponds to about 60 million people. Looking into the future, the incidence of chronic undernutrition is expected to decline further to 9 percent by the year 2010. However, because of the population increase, this 9 percent will correspond to the same total number of people as were undernourished in 1988-90.

Despite this positive outlook at the aggregate, the low-income countries of the region would continue to experience serious food security problems. In 1988-90 the lower-income countries (Djibouti, Mauritania, Somalia, the Sudan and Yemen) had an average food consumption level ranging between 1 764 and 2 447 kilocalories per caput per day, which was well below the average of the region and that of the developing countries as a whole.

Food import dependence
The region depends heavily on imports to meet its food needs. Cereal imports increased from 8.1 million tonnes in 1969-71 to 44.3 million tonnes by 1988-90 and are projected to reach 78.7 million tonnes by the year 2010. Wheat is the largest single cereal commodity imported. Wheat imports of 6.6 million tonnes in 1969-71 (representing 82 percent of cereal imports) increased to 29 million tonnes in 1988-90 and may reach 44 million tonnes by the year 2010. Imports of rice constituted 8 percent of cereal imports, increased from 0.7 million tonnes in 1969-71 to 3.1 million tonnes in 1988-90 and may increase by another 2 million tonnes by the year 2010. Coarse grain imports increased much more quickly than wheat or rice imports, reflecting the rising feed requirements for the expanding livestock sector. Between 1969-71 and 1988-90, coarse grain imports increased 13-fold to 13.3 million tonnes and are projected to reach 20.3 million tonnes by the year 2010.

Imports of other food items, such as livestock products, vegetable oils and sugar, have also grown substantially. Between 1969-71 and 1988-90 meat imports increased ninefold from 121 000 to 1.12 million tonnes and may reach 1.9 million tonnes by 2010; imports of milk increased fivefold from 1.2 million to 6.1 million tonnes and may double to reach 13 million tonnes in 2010. The self-sufficiency ratio of livestock products declined substantially from 99 to 86 percent between 1969-71 and 1988-90 and is projected

NEAR EAST AND NORTH AFRICA

to fall further in the future. A large portion of livestock products imports is accounted for by the high-income oil-producing countries. For example, the value of imports of livestock products in the Arabian Peninsula increased from 16 percent of the total value of livestock products imported into the region in 1969-71 to 27 percent in 1988-90.

A consequence of these large increases in volume of imported foodstuffs is a sharp rise in the foreign exchange expenditures on food imports. The value of total food imports into the region increased more than fourfold from about US$3.6 billion in 1969-71 to about $16.6 billion in 1988-90.[49] Cereals remain the major item of foreign exchange expenditure among the imported foods, accounting for more than 35 percent of the total value of food imports. The import value of livestock products recorded an exceptionally large increase of about 600 percent from US$566 million in 1969-71 to $3.5 billion in 1988-90. The projected large increases in food imports may not constrain the oil-producing countries, but would certainly aggravate the balance of payment difficulties of other countries in the region, especially the low-income food-deficit countries. Indeed, food imports for the region as a whole amount to some 10-12 percent of merchandise exports. However, low-income countries in the region spent a consistently high share (over 25 percent) of their merchandise export earnings on food imports.

---

[49] Note that these figures include the value of food aid.

BOX 4
THE EFFECTS OF THE URUGUAY ROUND ON REGIONAL AGRICULTURE

The effects of trade liberalization on the economies of the region may be negative in the short term. The region is heavily dependent on food imports, so the reduction in subsidies on European agricultural goods (which could amount to as much as 75 percent of the cost of production) is expected to cause greater budgetary outlays on imported food. In 1993, the region imported US$26.4 billion worth of agricultural products and exported only $8.8 billion.

The erosion of preferential trade agreements that favour countries in the region is expected to increase costs in terms of resources being diverted to make agricultural products from the region more competitive with the high-quality produce of the industrialized economies. At present, the EC absorbs 11 percent of the exports of fresh fruits and vegetables of the Maghreb countries. Egypt, Jordan, Lebanon and the Syrian Arab Republic have most favoured nation trade and economic agreements with the EC. The granting of concessions, such as the high entry prices and maximum tariff equivalent granted to the Eastern European economies, will have an adverse impact on the extent of exports from the region.

JORDAN
The role of agriculture

Jordan is a small country, with limited natural resources, especially water. Agriculture contributes around 7 percent of GDP. However, if backward and forward linkages are added, the sector's contribution is estimated to be as high as around one-third. In addition, it employs about 7 percent of the total labour force. Growth in the agricultural sector has been impressive, at an average of 12.5 percent during 1987 to 1991, although this figure dropped to 6.2 percent in the period 1991-93. Despite generally strong growth, agricultural production has been unable to meet domestic consumption needs. With rising standards of living and a population growth rate of 3.4 percent, the demand for food in Jordan has increased rapidly in the last four decades. In 1989, Jordan's food imports bill amounted to US$252.4 million; by 1993, it had increased by more than 87 percent, to $471.3 million.

About 96 percent of Jordan's land receives less than 300 mm of rainfall annually. Most of the cultivable land lies in the highlands, except for 390 000 dunums (39 000 hectares) in the Jordan Valley and the Southern Ghor, which account for 50 percent of the irrigated area of Jordan. The irrigated area in the Jordan Valley represents only 15 percent of the country's cultivated land, but its average share in agricultural production is around 65 percent of vegetables, 60 percent of fruits and 10 percent of field crops.

The major vegetable products, including tomatoes, eggplants, squash, cucumbers, cabbages, cauliflowers and potatoes, are produced for export markets in Saudi Arabia and the other Persian Gulf states and, to a lesser extent, to European countries during the winter. Over the years, the area under fruit trees, mainly olives, has increased whereas the area under major vegetables, other than potatoes and watermelons, has declined. Wheat and barley are irrigated in the desert south of the Jordan Valley and occasionally in the valley itself, as part of a crop rotation.

The sectoral output improved significantly over the last two decades as a result of the wide use of irrigation, modern technological farming systems and increased capital investment. Public and private investment increased the irrigated area by more than 200 percent over the last 20 years. To a great extent, the expansion

of irrigated agriculture compensated for the shrinking per caput area of cultivated land and reduced the risks associated with rain-fed agriculture.

Investment in horticulture in the rain-fed areas and a shift in the cropping pattern from traditional wheat to barley and fruit-trees have led to a 20 percent annual growth in the value of rain-fed agricultural production. The major increase, which has been in fruit-trees and vine crops, is attributable in part to a government support programme implemented in the highlands. The programme provides farmers with subsidized fruit-tree seedlings, food supplies and materials for terracing.

Rangelands, which constitute about 90 percent of Jordan's total agricultural area, are used mainly for keeping sheep and other livestock. The rapid increase in demand for meat and livestock products in the last decade has encouraged barley production, leading to expansion into marginal and submarginal land.

Issues and challenges

Resource conservation. Over the last four decades, Jordan has witnessed an increasing demand for water and land resources caused by population pressure and growing numbers of urban and industrial users. These factors are negatively affecting the country's capacity to produce food.

Rapid investment in irrigation in the Jordan Valley and the highlands during the 1970s and 1980s resulted in a strong increase in agricultural production. The agricultural sector accounts for approximately three-quarters of water consumption. However, high subsidies on water in the Jordan Valley have contributed to increased and inefficient use.

Until recently, the cost of supplying irrigation water to the Jordan Valley Authority, including operation and maintenance costs, was 23 fils per m³ (1 000 fils = 1 dinar), but it was sold to the farmers at only 6 fils per m³. At the same time, the long-term marginal cost of water was estimated to be 230 fils per m³. The subsidies on water, along with an overall restricted trade environment, resulted in a high rate of effective protection that distorted resource use. For example, the production of bananas (which consume a lot of water) increased by 400 percent between 1982 and 1992. Under the recent structural adjustment programme, the government is introducing graduated tariffs on water.

There is a need for water to be transferred from the Jordan Valley to the highlands using the existing pipeline to its full capacity and utilizing the present water supply more efficiently between and among the different user-sectors. Water can be saved by improving on-farm irrigation management. One option is to convert the surface irrigation systems into pressurized water delivery. This would require investments in extension and training on the new system's maintenance and use.

Groundwater in Jordan is also being depleted at an unsustainable rate. Unless the present rate of depletion is reduced, groundwater is estimated to last for only another 39 years. To address the problem, the government has created "basin protection units" that are expected to establish greater controls and larger levies on the use of groundwater by industry, and to stop the groundwater supply from being put to inappropriate uses. A classic example of resource mismanagement is the subsidizing of wheat production that uses water from the non-renewable Disi aquifers. The same water could be allocated to much higher-value uses.

Past policies have contributed greatly to overstocking and overgrazing, which have been major causes of widespread rangeland degradation and serious threats to the natural pastures of the steppe lands. The absence of a regulatory framework for user rights coupled with the subsidizing of inputs in the livestock sector, although benefiting producers, have also contributed to natural resource degradation. Sustainable environmental considerations require policies to arrest – and indeed reverse – the desertification process.

Food policy. Since the late 1960s, a primary objective of the agricultural policy in Jordan has been to achieve self-sufficiency in strategic crops. At the same time, prices of basic food items have been controlled in a bid to keep the cost of living down. The two, often conflicting, objectives led to a mix of interventionist polices that, in some cases, resulted in an inefficient use of resources and an increase in food imports. The regulatory regime included policies for: subsidizing producer prices, especially for wheat and barley; low water prices in the Jordan Valley; subsidizing agricultural credit; a regulated cropping pattern in the

irrigated areas; and specific subsidies to encourage the planting of fruit-trees.

The granting of subsidies contributed to a rapid growth in the production of fruit and vegetables, allowing Jordan to meet domestic requirements and export a surplus. However, input and output subsidies and trade restrictions resulted in a high rate of effective protection for certain commodities and, consequently, to resource misuse. The subsidies on barley encouraged its use as livestock feed and increased the viability of goat and sheep production, which increased fourfold since 1962, putting pressure on rangelands. As a result, between 1981 and 1992, the area under wheat declined by one-third whereas that for barley increased by over two-fifths. Greater producer profitability for fruits, especially with increasing opportunities for supplementary irrigation from groundwater development and water harvesting, has caused land previously under wheat to be used for the cultivation of fruit. This has had an adverse impact on food self-sufficiency in wheat.

The Ministry of Supply (MOS) is the sole importer for many basic goods such as wheat, wheat-flour, rice, sugar and milk powder. Until 1993, the government was the sole importer of apples, onions, potatoes and garlic. Monopolies on procurement and distribution enabled the government to control the subsidies provided to producers and consumers and to encourage domestic production by protecting the local producers from foreign competition.

Whereas output subsidies are being gradually reduced or eliminated as part of the recent economic reform programme, consumer subsidies have been maintained. Retail prices are subsidized for wheat-flour, lentils, chickpeas and barley. The nominal protection coefficient (NPC) at the retail level for wheat-flour sold to bakeries in 1994 was 2.9 indicating that the domestic price level was one-third that of the international price.

The future challenge in Jordan's agriculture is to regain sustainable growth through the adoption of outward-looking policies and productivity increases brought about by the efficient use of land and water resources. Many of the problems in the agricultural sector stem from the lack of a systemic land and water policy. At present, the lack of attention to demand management practices is compounded by a

proliferation of competing public institutions in agriculture. These institutions need to be brought together within the umbrella of an holistic agricultural sector strategy that focuses especially on land and water issues.

Policy reforms

Since the mid-1980s Jordan has faced economic difficulties. The decline in the price of oil led to a steep decline in workers' remittances and in foreign assistance from the Persian Gulf countries. A concomitant rise in foreign debt and interest payments compounded the difficulties faced by Jordan during the global recessionary period of the 1980s. By the end of the decade, the problems of declining growth rates, inflation and mounting external indebtedness needed to be addressed.

In 1989, the government requested a rescheduling of its debt and adopted a structural adjustment programme (SAP) supported by IMF and the World Bank. The SAP included a comprehensive economic reform programme to remove macroeconomic imbalances, minimize sector distortions and re-establish economic growth. The Jordanian dinar was devalued in 1989 and, as a result of the economic reform, policies were undertaken to decontrol agriculture, food and industrial prices; restructure tariff and trade policies; deregulate interest rates; remove consumer subsidies; and provide further incentives to the private sector in a move towards restoring the efficiency of the economy.

The conflict in the Persian Gulf adversely affected the newly undertaken reform programme and imposed a serious burden on the Jordanian economy caused by the loss of agricultural export markets in the Persian Gulf states and the return of more than 300 000 Jordanian migrant workers. Nevertheless, the economic reform programme was successful in meeting the macroeconomic targets. After registering negative and declining rates of growth in the late 1980s, the economy rebounded with a rate of output growth of 5.8 percent in 1993. The strict control over government expenditures accompanied by a strong revenue performance in 1993 resulted in a decline in the budget deficit to 6 percent of GDP in 1993 while the rate of inflation fell to 5 percent compared with a high of 21.5 percent in 1989.

As part of the ongoing reform, the government adopted an agricultural sector adjustment programme to improve efficiency, equity and sustainability. A major focus of agricultural reform is on removing subsidies in order to establish a market-oriented and competitive sector based on principles of sustainable natural resource use. Correction in relative agricultural commodity prices and greater private-sector involvement are expected to contribute to improving the rural incomes and sustainable development of agriculture in the long term.

In the area of water policy the government is focusing on rational allocation and use of water. Initiatives include the development of management plans for surface irrigation systems in the Jordan Valley and for groundwater basins (e.g. full utilization of the existing Deir Allah pumping scheme and conservation of the Disi fossil aquifers); modernizing and upgrading surface and groundwater monitoring systems; protecting water resources from pollution; managing groundwater to ensure sustainable yields for renewable aquifers; adopting a progressive pricing system to secure the financial viability of water delivery agencies; and establishing a strong institutional framework for the implementation of water management policies. In 1994, a bill was presented to parliament reflecting progressive water tariffs.

Producer subsidies are being removed on all crops. The 1994/95 prices for wheat and barley, both of which were until recently subsidized, indicate a zero subsidy. The government plans to liberalize trade in barley and to phase out public-sector involvement.

In a bid to remove consumer subsidies, prices were decontrolled for certain food items. In 1994 the government removed price controls on chickpeas to be followed by removal of controls on the prices and margins of the major fresh and processed agricultural commodities. All controls on retail price margins of fresh fruit and vegetables were to go, as were price controls on frozen poultry, chilled meat, tomato paste and lentils and controls on the retail prices of fresh poultry, red meat, table eggs and fresh milk.

A trade liberalization programme was launched to remove the public monopoly on trade, including marketing and distribution of agricultural commodities. The government has removed the Agricultural

Marketing and Processing Company's (AMPCO) import monopoly of potatoes, apples, onions and garlic. It has also removed import and export licence requirements on many fresh and processed agricultural products. The weighted average tariff rate was reduced from 34.4 percent in 1987 to 25 percent in 1992. Another significant step towards a more liberalized regime is Jordan's planned entry to the World Trade Organization (WTO). Joining WTO will imply further adjustments in the trade regime including the removal of non-tariff barriers and the government monopoly on import of other food products and the promotion of agricultural production and trade according to the principles of comparative advantage.

The impact of peace on water resources and agricultural production

One result of the peace treaty with Israel is expected to be the additional flow of water into Jordan from the Yarmouk and Jordan Rivers. This would have a positive impact on the country's current and future water balance and would contribute towards agricultural development.

As a result of the treaty, available water resources in Jordan are expected to increase by 230 million m^3 annually, a 25 percent addition to the country's present supply of water, which would increase the per caput availability by 63 m^3 per annum. A rapid rise in the standards of living and population growth has exerted a tremendous pressure on the limited water resources of Jordan in the past. In 1993, the domestic water supplied, amounting to 205 million m^3, was consumed by 3.7 million inhabitants. Currently, Jordan's average per caput domestic water consumption, at about 85 litres per day (l/c/d), is considered a bare minimum, given the country's per caput income and overall development level. Of the additional 230 million m^3 of water, 70 million m^3 are expected to be diverted to meet the shortfall in the domestic sector, to which the government attaches a high priority.

The increase in the per caput share of water from the current 85 l/c/d to 120 l/c/d is expected to reduce the concentration of waste products and, consequently, the treatment and conveyance cost of waste water by 30 percent. Increasing the quantity of irrigation water diverted to the King Abdullah Canal from the Yarmouk

River and fully utilizing the irrigation infrastructure are expected to lead to improvements in the quality of treated waste water, thus reducing the cost per m³ of irrigation water in the Jordan Valley by 40 percent.

Furthermore, improving the quality of the Jordan River water is expected to have a significant environmental impact on the region. At one time the river was rich with several types of fish, which supplied the local population with food and was a natural home to migrant birds and other wild life.

The peace agreement is expected to widen opportunities for economic resource and information integration between the signatories and to contribute towards greater development of the agricultural sector in line with principles of comparative advantage. Freedom of agriculture information exchange, the transfer of expertise on the possibilities of desert cultivation and utilization and the use of saline water with new kinds of seeds for desert cultivation are expected to be the dominant factors in regional agricultural cooperation.

Trilateral cooperation in desert agricultural activities among Israel, Egypt and Morocco has been taking place for some time. A pioneer project was initiated in the Egyptian and Moroccan deserts implementing Israeli expertise in the utilization of new brands of seeds and irrigation techniques. In the recently held Casablanca Summit in Morocco, a joint Jordanian-Israeli project under discussion was the integrated development of the Jordan Rift Valley. This project proposes to exploit the difference in natural elevation between the Red Sea and the Dead Sea by building a canal between them and generating hydroelectric power while also using Red Sea water for desalinization projects and for the ecological protection of the declining level of the Dead Sea.

Although the treaty has helped to alleviate Jordan's water supply problems by outlining proposals and initiating cooperation, it is imperative that these proposals be carried forward in the interest of development in the region. Regional cooperation will mean eliminating disparities in national income and in the acquisition of advanced technology. Investment in research and development in demand management and water conservation techniques and tools will come about if efforts are made towards greater regional

cooperation and integration. At the same time, Jordan will be able to benefit most from this benign economic climate if domestic economic policies are conducive to providing macroeconomic stability and growth and contribute to a more efficient utilization of scarce resources in the agricultural sector.

REGIONAL REVIEW
II. Developed country regions

CENTRAL AND EASTERN EUROPE AND THE NEW INDEPENDENT STATES OF THE FORMER USSR

REGIONAL OVERVIEW
Recent trends in economic and agricultural sector performance

In 1994, the countries of Central and Eastern Europe progressed further towards market-oriented economies.[50] A general trend of economic stabilization and improvement has been observed. Average GDP grew by almost 4 percent[51] and inflation rates decelerated considerably in 1994, although the level of unemployment remained high in most countries.

The performance of the agrofood sector also showed signs of recovery in most Central and Eastern European countries. Had it not been for the drought in Poland, aggregate agricultural output for the whole region would have grown for the first time in the transition period. Provisional figures for 1994 suggest an aggregate increase in total grain production in the region for the second consecutive year, with an increase of an estimated 8-9 percent following that of 6-7 percent in 1993. Cereal production was higher than in 1993 in most countries of the region, the exceptions among the major producers being Poland and the Baltic republics, all of which suffered from drought. Output in the livestock sector continued to decline in most Central and Eastern European countries, largely as a result of continuing adjustment to decreased demand. Supplies became tight in some countries leading to further increases of consumer prices, e.g. for milk in Poland and pork in the Czech Republic. In general terms it appears that the decline in livestock production may now have bottomed out, as indicated by some degree of herd buildup in, for example, Poland and Albania.

[50] This overview was contributed by the OECD Directorate for Food, Agriculture and Fisheries. It draws on ongoing work coordinated by the OECD Centre for Cooperation with Economies in Transition (CCET) and relevant OECD publications including: OECD. 1995. *Agricultural policies, markets and trade in the Central and Eastern European countries (CCECs), selected New Independent States (NIS) of the former Soviet Union, Mongolia and China – monitoring and outlook 1995.* Paris; OECD. 1994. *Review of agricultural policies: Hungary.* Paris; and OECD. 1995. *Review of agricultural policies: Poland.* Paris.

[51] OECD estimate.

CENTRAL AND EASTERN EUROPE

The economic situation in the 12 New Independent States of the former USSR differs markedly from that of Central and Eastern Europe. In 1994 Russian Federation GDP fell by 15 percent,[52] and there were even larger declines in some other New Independent States. A further drop in economic activity is expected in 1995. Although most New Independent States have made progress in controlling inflation, it still remains high.

In most of the New Independent States, the performance of the agricultural sector continued to deteriorate in 1994. Gross agricultural output in the four principal food-producing New Independent States (Belarus, Kazakhstan, the Russian Federation and Ukraine) has fallen by between one-third and one-half over the last five years and there are doubts whether it will recover in 1995. Much of the difficulty in 1994 can be attributed to unfavourable weather conditions. Drought affected yields in the southern Ukraine, some major Russian grain areas and northern Kazakhstan, while Belarus reported a harvest failure. Yet some of the problems can be attributed to the cumulative effects of disruptions in input supply, marketing and agricultural credit. The livestock sector has been particularly hard-hit since 1991. Herd size and overall production have decreased significantly and continue to decline.

Domestic demand for food continued to contract in the Central and Eastern European countries as well as in the New Independent States. Particularly affected have been high income-elasticity products such as meat and dairy products, where the total fall has been around 20-30 percent. However, before 1991 consumption of these products had been very high relative to per caput GDP because of huge consumer subsidies, so major shifts in consumption with the removal of these subsidies were to be expected.

Food supplies in Central and Eastern European countries and in most of the New Independent States were generally satisfactory. In rural areas of the New Independent States food supplies were quite stable because of small-scale private plot and garden production. Although an inefficient distribution and marketing system led to somewhat irregular supplies of certain products in larger cities, there were no major breakdowns in supplies of basic foods, which also seem unlikely to occur in the foreseeable future.

[52] OECD estimate.

Farm structural reform

During the prereform period, large state or collective farms worked almost all of the farmland in all of these countries, with the exception of Poland where private family farms predominated. Different strategies have been followed for putting land into private ownership and/or operation:

- Restitution recognizes the rights of former owners. In Bulgaria, for instance, as far as possible the actual land parcel was returned to its former owner. Alternatively, as in Hungary, legitimate claims were compensated by some other means, such as vouchers, rather than by physical restitution. Approaches that respect previous property rights are difficult to implement because of the poor state of precommunist land registration records and institutional inability to solve disputes and settle claims. In addition, many claimants lack the agricultural and managerial skills and the capital required to start farming individually.
- "Mass" or "spontaneous" agricultural privatization has divided land among many people without regard to former ownership. This occurred, for example, in Albania, Romania and the Baltic states. Workers on state and collective farms and other rural residents were all given small plots of land. In Romania and Albania, for example, the old collective farms have been totally replaced by small-scale private farming.
- Share privatization, widely used in the New Independent States, also divides up the land and assets of existing farms among current farm workers. Former collective and state farms establish equal shares of land for all their employees and pensioners as well as for workers in such "social assets" as schools, clubs and medical clinics on the farm's territory. At the same time, non-land production assets were to be divided into shares proportional to the number of years of service. However, ownership is not necessarily followed by demarcation of an individual plot of land and physical transfer to the new owner.
- The creation of new individual farms continues in the Central and Eastern European countries as well as in the New Independent States alongside the

reorganization of collective and state farms. Local authorities grant individuals a specified amount of land from either formerly unused land or land taken from large farms because it was underused. In many cases, the new individual farmer is then eligible for state-subsidized credits to buy or build what is needed for working the land.

The use of diverse reorganization strategies has led to a variety of new farm types; in all countries new individual enterprises have been established, ranging from family farms to new cooperatives and corporate (joint stock) farms. The latter are more frequent in the New Independent States. In these farms, land and asset shares have been recommitted to the new enterprise in return for stock certificates. Their internal operations have not changed very much, so it is doubtful whether these corporate farms will be able to survive in the medium and long term.

Concern is frequently expressed about the fragmentation of large farms into many very small, presumably higher-cost and less efficient farming enterprises. A distinction should be made, however, between fragmented ownership and fragmented operation. The former does not necessarily imply the latter. With the exception of Romania and Albania, excessive fragmentation of agriculture has not occurred. Hungary and the Czech Republic are good examples of fragmented ownership not turning into fragmented operation. In these countries very few new or restored owners have become new small farmers and the land has largely been leased to transformed cooperatives.

Many of the old large-scale farms wasted resources and had very high overhead and management costs. Evidence from the Organisation for Economic Cooperation and Development (OECD) countries suggests that, after a certain farm size is achieved, there are few additional economies of size to be gained by further expansion and that optimal farm size also depends very much on the product mix. Other factors, such as quality of management, technical skills and access to credit, become more important determinants of efficiency than size. Therefore, the concept of an "optimal" farm size has little meaning and can mislead policy-makers into attempting to achieve or retain some physical size of farm.

Land markets and financial reforms

The establishment of functioning land markets is a very
sensitive and important issue. In the Central and Eastern
European countries, land has not been bought and sold
for more than 50 years. In many New Independent
States, a land market has never really existed.

Advocates of market-oriented reform have stressed
the importance of creating land markets by permitting
mortgages to facilitate structural adaptation. Creating a
land market that permits land to be used as collateral,
however, will not by itself lead to a functioning system
of agricultural finance. Education and institutional
development, such as the establishment of an efficient
banking sector, will also be needed to stimulate a
private agricultural credit market. Financial institutions
play a crucial role in the development of the agrofood
sector. In order to enhance the establishment of
functioning institutions, many countries provide
incentives for bank recapitalization and implement
prudential regulation measures and privatization. Some
modest success has been achieved in the Central and
Eastern European countries, whereas in the New
Independent States financial sector reform has barely
begun.

Privatization in the upstream and downstream sector

Progress with the restructuring of upstream and
downstream agrofood industries has been very mixed,
but is in many cases lagging behind the privatization of
the agricultural sector. While privatization of the mostly
smaller downstream enterprises, such as the retail
sector, has been quite successful in many countries,
large state-owned supply and processing industries,
such as meat-packing, grain storage and similar
facilities, are more difficult to privatize, particularly as
they are often burdened with heavy debts and
characterized by poor technical standards and
overcapacity. In spite of this, a large number of food
processing industries have now been quite successfully
privatized in the more advanced Central and Eastern
European countries.

The availability of foreign capital is another important
determinant of the progress in privatizing up- and
downstream industries. Hungary, for instance, which
was very open to foreign investors, has seen significant
progress in the privatization of these industries. Poland,

in contrast, has been slower in privatizing larger-scale businesses as a result of a more restrictive approach to foreign investors.

The persistence of inefficient monopolistic up- and downstream enterprises continues to affect the farming sector because monopolistic powers can be exercised by these companies in the absence of any competitors. In addition, the modernization of the food industries is important for trade prospects for agricultural goods, since export opportunities are better and achievable profit margins higher for processed and high-quality products than for raw materials and low-quality products.

Trade relations and policy issues
Most Central and Eastern European countries have tried to reorient their agricultural trade towards western European countries after the dissolution of the Council for Mutual Economic Assistance (CMEA) trading system. Preferential agreements have been concluded to facilitate the access to West European markets. However, exports of agricultural products from Central and Eastern European countries have still been very limited as a result of difficulties in meeting western quality standards and in competing with subsidized products. Instead, imports, especially of value-added agricultural products from West European countries, have increased. As a consequence, the aggregate agricultural trade balance of the Central and Eastern European countries has deteriorated significantly compared with prereform levels. The slight improvement of the trade balance in 1994 resulted mainly from increased exports to the New Independent States.

Association agreements, so-called Europe Agreements, have been concluded between the EC and six "associated countries" – the four Visegrad States (the Czech Republic, Hungary, Poland and Slovakia), Bulgaria and Romania. For the Baltic states and Slovenia, Europe Agreements were initialled and are expected to be formally signed in the course of 1995. The agreements will gradually lead to free trade in most goods and services. Completely free trade is, however, not envisaged for agriculture and food products, which will remain subject to certain quotas and tariffs.

Although varying by country and product, there has been an apparent underutilization of many of the

agricultural tariff quotas under the Europe Agreements. Some quotas were very underused in 1992 and 1993, partly because of differing veterinary standards and product shortages resulting from unfavourable weather conditions, but also because the cumbersome administrative arrangements for some products deterred exporters from Central and Eastern Europe from taking full advantage of the concessions. Utilization was somewhat greater in 1994, and the Action Plan for Coordinated Aid to Poland and Hungary (PHARE) programme is now assisting the countries to overcome problems caused by a lack of market information and limited experience in such trading.

Some transition economies have adopted agricultural market regulation systems inspired by OECD country models such as, for example, the Common Agricultural Policy of the EC. However, as these countries face severe budget constraints as well as consumer resistance to higher prices, they have not been fully applying these new mechanisms and so far have kept the level of support to agriculture below the OECD average. The experience of OECD countries, however, has shown that once such mechanisms are in place they can easily become vehicles for delivering support that is highly economically distorting without being efficient in achieving the main policy objectives for rural areas.

There are a number of reasons why high price supports and their associated protective trade policies would be particularly inappropriate in the development of a competitive market-oriented agriculture in transition economies, whether or not those economies are prospective EU members. High price supports would impose high costs on taxpayers and on low-income consumers who, in all transition economies, spend a large part of their incomes on food. In addition, such policies would be economically distorting and would weaken competitiveness at a crucial point in the development of transition into market economies.

Belarus, Kazakhstan, the Russian Federation and Ukraine are still adjusting their trade relations to reflect their recent independence. Under the Soviet system, the flow of goods was determined administratively, not by market signals, so the collapse of the USSR severely disturbed the flow of goods among the New Independent States. Some previous production specializations, such as Belarus' focus on meat and

dairy production using feedgrain produced in other parts of the former USSR, have already become difficult to sustain. Attempts to re-establish and expand trade ties based on intergovernmental agreements rather than market exchanges have repeatedly been made among the successor states of the former USSR, loosely organized as the Commonwealth of Independent States (CIS). In the absence of functioning currency markets, most trade between the New Independent States continues to take the form of large-scale barter arrangements.

At the end of November 1994, the CIS Council of Foreign Trade Ministers approved in principle the creation of a CIS-wide free-trade zone. In March 1995 the CIS agricultural ministers agreed to recreate a common agricultural market. Although these plans included the removal of barriers to intra-CIS trade, a formal customs union has been postponed. These decisions clearly reflect the tension between the desire of the other former USSR states to regain and enlarge their share of the Russian market and their desire to avoid compromising their independence and once again becoming subordinate to a Russian centre.

In the New Independent States, governments continued to provide large subsidies to the farm sector. Very few, if any, of even the least productive farms have ceased operations or stopped receiving their share of available state-distributed production resources. Since very few of the large farms in the New Independent States can compete with, often subsidized, western exports, agricultural interests, especially in the Russian Federation, have been successfully lobbying for higher protective tariffs and market regulations along western lines (export subsidies, threshold or intervention prices, etc.). Yet these countries are unlikely to be able to afford to sustain such protectionist measures, which will weaken their competitiveness.

Implications of the Uruguay Round
Hungary, Poland, the Czech Republic, Slovakia and Romania are World Trade Organization members. Other Central and Eastern European countries and New Independent States are in various stages of application for membership.

The Uruguay Round further liberalized world trade, which should lead to increased economic welfare and

**CENTRAL
AND EASTERN EUROPE**

improve the entire region's agricultural trading position. World Trade Organization members from Central and Eastern Europe were allowed, as were developing countries, to offer tariff ceiling bindings essentially unrelated to base period conditions, rather than tariff bindings based on estimates of the tariff equivalents of trade restrictions in the base period. Many Central and Eastern European countries therefore bound tariffs at very high levels compared with previously practised tariff levels, thus keeping open the possibility for future tariff increases. Although governments may decide not to use this margin, it is likely that producer interests will press for taking fuller advantage of the opportunity to increase protection. Governments will need to resist such pressures in order to avoid economic distortions and increased costs to consumers and taxpayers.

A PROFILE OF KAZAKHSTAN'S AGRICULTURAL REFORMS

Geography and history

Almost three-quarters the area of western Europe, Kazakhstan is the second-largest, after the Russian Federation, of the 15 former USSR republics. Kazakhstan lies south of a 6 000-km long border with the Russian Federation.

Kazakhstan's history and economy are closely tied to Russia. Russia settled Kazakhstan in the nineteenth century, establishing the present-day capital, Almaty (known as Alma-ata before independence in late 1991) in 1854.[53] Today, Kazakhstan is the only former USSR republic with a titular nationality that does not constitute a majority of the population – comprising, as it does, only about 42 percent in the country as a whole and less than 30 percent in most of the *oblasts* (provinces) that border the Russian Federation. The percentage of Kazakhs is, however, increasing, largely because of the outmigration of Kazakhs of European origin. In 1994, Kazakhstan lost over 1.5 percent of its population of nearly 17 million.[54]

Resources in agriculture

Land resources. Over 80 percent of the land area of Kazakhstan is classified as agricultural land. Of this, 80 percent is pastureland, about 35 million hectares (18 percent) are arable and 4.5 million hectares (2 percent) are meadowlands. There are also approximately 120 000 hectares of orchards and vineyards. Kazakhstan irrigates approximately 2 million hectares of land. The country had half the pastureland but only 15 percent of the arable land of the former USSR.[55]

Kazakhstan's overall average precipitation is only 250 mm per annum. The two major agricultural zones are in the wetter north and in the south, where crop farming depends almost entirely on irrigation. The north's fertile *chernozem* soils have been cultivated with spring grains since the nineteenth century. The Virgin Lands Campaign (1954-60, see Box 5) expanded cultivation to more marginal land.

The warmer southern agricultural zone grows both spring and winter grains, irrigated by waters from the Tyan'-Shan and Altai mountains. Much of agriculture was expanded by large-scale irrigation works during the Soviet period. A relatively small amount of cotton is

[53] M. B. Olcott. 1987. *The Kazakhs.* Stanford, CA, Hoover Institute Press.

[54] *Panorama,* 15 April 1995.

[55] Goskomstat Respubliki Kazakhstan. 1994. *Zemledelie v respublike kazakhstan,* and *Sel'skoe khoziaistvo respublike kazakhstan* (stat. sbornik), both Almaty, Kazinformtsentr.

BOX 5
TWO SCENARIOS OF REDUCED DRYLAND FARMING
IN NORTH KAZAKHSTAN

Figure 10

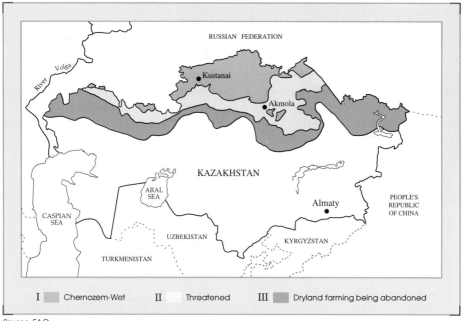

I ▨ Chernozem-Wet   II ▢ Threatened   III ▩ Dryland farming being abandoned

Source: FAO

During the Virgin Lands Campaign in Kazakhstan (1954-60) 25.5 million hectares of fragile virgin grasslands were ploughed up and seeded. In just a few years the *increase* in area sown to spring wheat in Kazakhstan roughly equalled the total combined wheat area of Canada and Australia.

From a peak of over 25 million hectares in the mid-1980s, sown grain area declined (rapidly since 1991) to only 20.7 million hectares in 1994. A concept paper of the Kazakhstan Agricultural Academy of Sciences foresees further reduction, based on emerging economic relationships, to 16.3 million hectares. This development would largely eliminate production in Region III of the map. The poorly developed light-chestnut soils of this region characteristically receive less than 300 mm of annual precipitation and yield under 500 kg per hectare. An alternative scenario developed by the Institute of Soil Management suggests that long-term dryland grain farming is sustainable on only 13 million hectares, mostly on the *chernozem* soils of Region I, a region characterized by 350 to 400 mm of annual precipitation.

Sources: Glavnoe Upravlenie Geodezii i Kartografii and Institut Zemeldelia Akademii Nauk Respubliki Kazakhstana.

BOX 6
THE CENTRAL ASIAN REPUBLICS:
AGRICULTURE, TRANSITION AND DEVELOPMENT

For centuries the five Central Asian Republics (CARs) Kazakhstan, Kyrgyzstan, Tajikistan, Turkmenistan and Uzbekistan have shared a common history and geography. The dominant physical feature of the area is its aridity, making the great river system flowing from the high mountains of the northwest frontier of the Indian subcontinent into the Aral Sea of fundamental importance. Today, much of the region's population lives in the oases along the rivers. In the past, the area has sustained important civilizations based on irrigation and forming part of the overland route across Asia.

During the 70 years of USSR membership, the CARs were closely integrated into the Soviet planning system, producing and processing raw materials for export. Although each had separate republic status, the planners in Moscow treated the region as a whole, determining the location of economic activities, transportation networks and water policy.

Since their independence from the former USSR in 1991, the CARs have shared two common challenges: the transition to a more market-oriented economy and the need for economic development. The CARs are facing problems similar to those of other countries in transition to a market-based economic system. These include how to establish macroeconomic stability with an appropriate incentive and property rights structure, how to stabilize the aggregate price level and how to allow economic agents to claim financial returns based on their efforts. However, agriculture is playing an especially important role in the CARs because of the sector's past contributions and its present fragile state.

The USSR centrally planned model collectivized and specialized agriculture, transforming the CARs into monoculture economies based primarily on cotton. (The exception was Kazakhstan, where cereal farming was greatly expanded under the Virgin Lands Programme.) From 1960 until the early 1980s, planners expanded the total irrigated area of the five republics by 60 percent or some 3 million hectares, dedicated mostly to cotton. The CARs produced 80 percent of the USSR's cotton output, with production concentrated in Uzbekistan, Turkmenistan and Tajikistan.

This irrigation-based cotton monoculture resulted in negative economic and environmental consequences. For example, the rapidly expanding irrigation projects reduced the river flow that reached the Aral Sea to less than one-tenth the 1950s volume. By 1990, the volume of the Aral Sea had fallen to less than a third of its 1960s volume and the surface area had declined by 45 percent, while the salinity content nearly tripled. Salinization is the major cause of declining crop yields. Average cotton yields in the CARs declined from over

2 800 kg per hectare in the late 1970s to 2 300 kg by the late 1980s, in spite of increased application of fertilizers. While fertilizer application could not reverse the declining yields, it did increase contamination of underground water.

How to balance a fragile resource base with their rapidly growing populations' need for jobs is the key agricultural development issue facing all the CARs; and one that requires an agreement among the five republics. For instance, even to stabilize the Aral Sea at its current reduced size involves decreasing irrigation withdrawals throughout the region. All the CARs have experienced large production losses in the early 1990s and the prospect of further unemployment is politically difficult to address.

Other sustainable agricultural issues also require immediate policy attention, but are less daunting. For example, livestock productivity throughout the region is about half that of of western Europe, suggesting productivity gains are possible. However, since much of the pastureland has been degraded, herd sizes will have to be reduced to ecologically sustainable levels.

Source: R. Pomfret. 1995. The economies of Central Asia. Princeton, NJ, Princeton University Press. Pomfret analyses the CARs as a regional economy and also each country's economic performance, structure and policies both before and after independence.

grown here, as are both winter and spring grains, fruit, vegetables, tobacco, sugar beet, potatoes, soybeans, rice and maize for grain.

Livestock. Its extensive pastureland allows Kazakhstan to support high numbers of ruminants. The structure of meat consumption in Kazakhstan has remained fairly stable; approximately 46 percent of meat consumed is beef (compared with 44 percent for the former USSR), 18 percent is mutton (5 percent in the former USSR), 4 percent horse meat, 17 percent pork (33 percent in the former USSR) and 13 percent poultry (compared with 16 percent in the former USSR).

Labour, nationalities, capital and farm organization before the reforms. At the beginning of the 1990s, Kazakhstan had approximately 2 100 state farms, with an average area of 80 000 hectares, 14 000 hectares of which were arable. In 1991, the "average" state or collective farm owned 90 tractors, 35 grain combines, 50 trucks, several thousand cattle, 10 000 sheep and 700 to 800 pigs. Most of the approximately 400 collective farms were created from farms pioneered before the revolution.

In 1993, 1.3 million people were directly engaged as full-time workers in agricultural enterprises, somewhat more than the number of employees in industry. Kazakhstan ranked eighth among Soviet republics (after the Transcaucasia and Central Asia) in terms of the share of population employed in socialist and private agriculture and second among Soviet republics (after Moldova) in the share of agriculture in gross social product (25.8 percent).[56]

Kazakhstan's roles in agricultural production and trade in the former USSR

In the 1980s, Kazakhstan produced just over 7 percent of total Soviet agricultural gross product, third after Russia and the Ukraine. Kazakhstan produced 12-13 percent of the grain and a higher share of the valuable durum and hard spring wheats used for pasta. However, Kazakhstan's overall grain yields have exceeded 1 tonne per hectare in only one-third of the years since 1954. In addition to variable, often disappointing yields, Kazakhstan's grain crops have suffered from frequent transportation and quality problems, thus being

---

[56] A. Illarionov. 1990. Economic potential and the levels of economic development of the Union Republics, *Voprosy Ekonomiki,* 4.

partly responsible for the USSR's dependency on foodgrains imported from abroad.

Approximately 10 percent of Kazakhstan's former annual meat production of nearly 1.5 million tonnes was exported, much of it to the populous neighbouring Central Asian Republics. Besides meat, also wool, skins and hides are important livestock exports. The republic imported protein meal, vegetable oil, sugar, canned and processed foods and dairy products.

Kazakhstan participated in the highly integrated Soviet[57] agricultural inputs complex, producing some dryland implements, and about 10 percent of the former USSR's phosphate fertilizer. Kazakhstan imported other implements, such as wheeled tractors and grain combines, as well as feed additives, veterinary medicines and plant protectorants, including large amounts of herbicides for grain production in northern Kazakhstan.

Although western Kazakhstan produces oil, which it exports to the Urals region, most petroleum products for northern Kazakhstan's agriculture come from western Siberia. Movement towards world prices for Russian oil has been the single most important factor affecting Kazakhstan's agriculture and leading directly to a reduction of sown and harvested area.

The political and macroeconomic context of agricultural reforms and policy

Political context. The most important political institution in Kazakhstan has been the presidency. Unlike the Russian Federation, where the central bank was at first under the control of parliament, the National Bank of Kazakhstan (NBK) has been under the control of the presidency. This has allowed the president relative freedom to pursue consistent macroeconomic policy. In October 1994, after parliament's vote of no confidence in the old government, the president appointed a western-trained Kazakh economist as prime minister. The cabinet appears committed to stringent fiscal and monetary policies, more rapid privatization and competition.

Kazakhstan has been an important proponent of closer economic and political ties among the former USSR countries. Ready to sign the "Union Treaty" that would have preserved the USSR, the president of Kazakhstan asked to be included as a charter member

[57] C.J. Foster and D.J. Sedik. 1994. *Former USSR: situation and outlook series.* (May) p. 74. Washington, DC, United States Department of Agriculture, Economic Research Service.

CENTRAL
AND EASTERN EUROPE

of the Commonwealth of Independent States (CIS) when the USSR broke up in 1991. Kazakhstan adopted a separate national currency, the tenge, in November 1993, when its parliament could not agree to the Russian Federation's conditions for its remaining in the rouble zone.

Kazakhstan formed a customs union with Uzbekistan and Kyrgystan in 1993, and another with the Russian Federation and Belarus in early 1994.

Stabilization policy. Inflation in the second quarter of 1994 averaged 35 percent per month and hit 46 percent in June of the same year, while the tenge depreciated to one-tenth its January value. In mid-1994, the president of Kazakhstan declared his support for "shock therapy". As a result of restrictive macroeconomic policies, inflation declined to 10 percent in December 1994, 8 percent in February 1995 and 3 percent in April 1995. The tenge, freely traded since its introduction, depreciated an average of only 4 percent per month on the interbank auction during the second half of 1994.[58]

To restrain the overall budget deficit, which had widened to 7 percent of GDP, the government reduced expenditures to 17 percent of GDP in 1994, versus 25 percent in 1993. Almost all remaining agricultural subsidies (including those on bread and mixed feed after October) fell to these cuts. NBK discontinued its practice of refinancing interenterprise arrears through money expansion, after such an operation in spring 1994 had fuelled inflation. Having begun the auction of credit in 1992, by December 1994 NBK was auctioning 70 percent of all credit. At the end of April 1995, the bank auction rate, to which refinancing was aligned, was 140 percent. In February 1995, directed credits (of which agriculture had been a primary recipient) ceased altogether.[59]

GDP in constant prices fell by one-quarter during 1994 and the real unemployment rate was estimated at 7.4 percent of the labour force in early 1995. However, along with the positive experience regarding price inflation, official figures showed industrial production turning up as of September 1994, and increasing by 1-3 percent monthly in the last quarter of 1994. Forecasts indicate a continued decline in GDP in 1995, but by less than half that of 1994. The government maintains that in the third and fourth quarters of 1994 the

[58] World Bank. 1995. *Republic of Kazakhstan: report on the status of the structural reforms.* Paris.

[59] Ibid.

standard of living as measured by the real average wage stabilized (Table 12).

Privatization and the creation of markets

The division of property rights is a difficult process taking place in a political setting which is not yet fully open and democratic. In addition, citizens of the former USSR emphasize the psychological difficulties of the transition. The Soviet state developed a peculiar interdependent relationship with managers, workers and consumers, which helps to explain the current mix of attitudes towards the creation of real private property rights and responsibilities. Key mechanisms in planned agriculture were the mandatory state procurement quotas and the reciprocal system of "material technical supplies" supported by planned prices and soft credits. Now, budgetary austerity has become the major force shaping the privatization of agriculture and the related issues which are discussed below.

Farm and production: prices and profitability.

Compared with 1993, Kazakhstan's aggregate farm production in 1994 declined 23 percent in real terms to 98.8 billion tenge (about US$2 billion). The decline had been 10 percent in 1993 and 2 percent in 1992. Grain production fell by 24 percent. Although it is becoming more and more difficult to measure accurately the increasingly private livestock output, official estimates indicate that meat production fell by 20 percent and milk production by 6 percent in 1994. The drop in livestock inventories during 1994 (numbers of cattle decreased by 14 percent, cows by 8 percent, swine by 19 percent and sheep and goats by 27 percent) presages further production declines in 1995. This disinvestment results in part from the cash crisis of many farm workers who were paid primarily in kind and sold livestock at distress prices.

Rapid inflation has made questionable the quality of statistics on cost and profitability. However, 1993 statistics showed that the profitability of state and collective farms (actual profit as a percentage of cost, including normed profit) was -1.3 percent, with crops generally profitable and livestock products unprofitable. The primary reason for declining farm profits is that input prices have risen more rapidly than farm prices since price liberalization in 1991-92. For example, in

**CENTRAL
AND EASTERN EUROPE**

TABLE 12

Macroeconomic performance

Indicator	1992	1993	1994	1995 (estimate)
GDP at constant prices (% change)	-13.0	-15.6	-25.0	-11.0
Consumer prices				
(Period average, % change)	1 381	1 571	1 826	165
(End of period, % change)	2 567	2 166	1 048	40
Wages and social benefits (tenge, end of period)				
Minimum wage/pension/ unemployment	2	30	260	900
Real minimum (December 1991 = 100)	10	7	5	13
Average wage	27	384	3 392	4 291
Real average (December 1991 = 100)	110	70	60	59
Exchange rate (tenge/US$)				
(Period average)	...	2.8	36.1	69.4
(End of period)	...	6.3	54.3	78.0

Source: State Statistics Committee and Ministry of Finance of Kazakhstan and World Bank staff estimates, May 1995.

[60] Disparitet tsen meshaet agrarnomu sektoru, *Biznis klub,* 18 October 1994.

[61] A. Deberdeev. 1995. *The role of agriculture in the transition process in Kazakhstan.* Symposium on the role of agriculture in the transition process towards a market-oriented economy, Wildbad Kreuth, Germany, 4-6 May 1995, Figure 1 and oral comments.

[62] Data from the Ministry of the Economy in *Kazakhstan agricultural sector review,* World Bank Report No. 13334-KZ, 12 December 1994. Washington, DC.

1992 it took 1.2 tonnes of wheat to purchase 1 tonne of fuel, a ratio that rose to 3.6:1 in 1993 and stayed at roughly the same in 1994.[60] In 1994, however, industrial and farm prices increased at about equal rates (20.4 times, versus 19.0 times), and the terms of trade for livestock in particular appeared to be rising in 1995, because of reduced supplies combined with consumers' stabilizing incomes.[61]

State budget subsidies and credit. During 1993, the Ministry of Economy estimated agricultural producers' subsidies from the budget at over 600 million tenge (about 2 to 3 percent of GDP). Approximately half of this represented subsidies for interest, operating expenses and fuel; the remainder was compensation for losses in livestock production.[62] In 1994, significant budget subsidies for agriculture were limited to the

input subsidy for mixed feed for some livestock producers and subsidies implicit in procurement quotas, which were retained only for grain products. In October 1994, these budget subsidies were removed, precipitating an immediate tenfold increase in retail bread prices.

In 1993, about one-third of NBK's directed loans had been for agriculture, at highly favourable rates (i.e. from 25 to 90 percent per annum, while inflation stood at approximately 2 000 percent).[63] In February 1994, NBK froze the interest on and refinanced approximately 10 billion tenge (then worth approximately US$500 million) of farm debt. By September 1994, agricultural debt totalled over 26.8 billion tenge, mostly owed to suppliers. A sum of 1.5 billion tenge (then worth US$30 million), equal to approximately one-half the 1994, wage bill was owed to workers on state farms.[64]

In August 1994, the president issued a decree requiring the Ministry of Agriculture and Agrobank to identify "chronically non-profitable" state farms and agrobusinesses and arrange their auction to persons who would take over their debts. Approximately 1 200 such firms were identified by early 1995, 256 of these were to be put up for early auction. Liquidation and restructuring was to be carried out by an agricultural restructuring fund formed to handle bad debt in the process of reforming Agrobank to put it on a commercial basis.[65]

Privatization. When the the USSR was dissolved and Kazakhstan gained independence in 1991, there was a phase of rapid privatization, initiated at the provincial level. This Stage I devolved too much power to the *oblast* governments, which in the north were at the time threatening to seceed from Kazakhstan to join the Russian Federation. A formal Stage II of the National Privatization Programme, announced in 1993 to last until 1995, sought to subject privatization to more clearly defined procedures overseen by the Republic State Property Committee (SPC) with its own territorial (as distinct from *oblast*) committees. A constitutional amendment eliminated the previous concept of municipal property, which had been under the control of *oblast* governments, leaving only two categories of property, state-republic and private.[66]

Procedures were outlined for the privatization of

[63] K. Gray and A. Kultaev. 1993. *Agricultural policy and trade developments in Kazakhstan in 1992-93.* OECD ad hoc Group on East/West Economic Relations in Agriculture, Paris, October 1993.

[64] K. Gray and A. Kultaev. 1994. *Agricultural policy and trade developments in Kazakhstan in 1993-94.* OECD ad hoc Group on East/West Economic Relations in Agriculture, Paris, September 1994.

[65] World Bank, op. cit., footnote 58, p. 181.

[66] Gray and Kultaev, op. cit., footnote 64.

small firms (of less than 200 employees) and large firms (of between 200 and 5 000 employees), as well as for case-by-case privatization of those national industries (primarily mineral) where foreign investment might be expected. Following criticism of SPC, in March 1995 the president of Kazakhstan removed authority for privatization from this body and assigned it to other state organs.[67]

By the end of 1994, approximately 10 percent of an estimated 30 000 small businesses had been sold by auction or tender. Compared with the Russian Federation, the mass privatization programme in Kazakhstan started late. The distribution of privatization coupons to citizens began only in 1994, but was largely completed by the end of that year. One-quarter of the coupons had been invested in just under 200 investment privatization funds which by April 1995 had acquired about 500 large enterprises.

In early 1995 the prime minister declared his support for accelerated democratic privatization by the coupon system, with the state acquiring less revenue from sales of state property. The government hoped to liquidate government shares in just under a dozen agriculturally related joint-stock or holding companies during 1995.

Farming and related agrobusiness have been treated somewhat separately, but within the general purview of the State Property Committee. The National Privatization Programme for 1993-95 has several distinctive features for farming and agrobusiness:

- On 1 January 1995 there were approximately 22 500 "peasant" farms, owned by individuals or families, some started under Soviet law. The number of these farms had doubled in 1993, with an additional 5 000 being added in 1994. Their size averages about 350 hectares and in total they have use rights to over 7 million hectares of agricultural land. Together with an associated group of almost a thousand agricultural cooperatives and small enterprises they control 5-6 percent of agricultural land. When small subsidiary and cooperative garden plots are added to the peasant farms, the land in individual or family control may now be 10 percent of Kazakhstan's total (Table 13).
- Farms, as well as inputs, food processing and storage enterprises, are treated separately from the

[67] Criticisms are detailed in A. Bilskaya. *Panorama*, 10 December 1994, p. 5; President's decree in *Kazakstanskaya pravda*, 21 March 1995, p. 2.

TABLE 13

Progress of the land reform in Kazakhstan in 1991-94: landholders by types and landholdings ('000 hectares)

	January 1991	January 1992	January 1993	January 1994	June 1994	January 1995
Peasant farms		2 480	8 877	16 020	20 110	22 512
Land area	104.0	1 615.1	5 355.2	6 424.9	7 123.5	7 828.4
Orchard						
('000s)	743.0	998.5	1 280.7	1 286.4	1 294.9	
Land area	59.0	81.9	107.6	112.3	113.3	
Gardens						
('000s)	499.3	790.2	962.4	989.6	1 099.0	
Land area	42.6	68.2	83.7	86.5	102.8	
Private plots						
('000s)	1 883.0	1 949.4	2 028.0	2 164.1	2 225.5	
Land area	193.6	199.0	231.3	246.5	250.0	
Agricultural cooperatives and small enterprises	16	132	919	872	916	
Land area	16.5	275.8	21 505	4 172.4	4 288.8	
Other non-state agricultural entities					646	727
Land area					42 671	47 782.3
Subsidiary agricultural enterprises					1 367	1 418
Land areas					1 880.9	1 918.7

Sources: Ministry of Agriculture and State Statistics Committee, Republic of Kazakhstan.

National Privatization Programme. All were temporarily held as part of holding companies organized along previous ministerial lines, with varying shares of state stock participation. By the end of 1994, two-thirds of the 2 120 state farms "belonging to" the Ministry of Agriculture had been privatized (Table 14). A total of 328 state farms were privatized during the first seven months of 1994, and 440 more during the next five months. This process, similar to the Russian re-registration conducted in 1992, is commonly recognized as a "changing of the signposts". For the most part, the physical division of assets according to workers' shares, particularly land-use rights, had not occurred.

**CENTRAL
AND EASTERN EUROPE**

TABLE 14

Privatization of state farms in the Republic of Kazakhstan, 1993-94

State farms at start = 2 120	1 July 1994	1 January 1995
Total privatized	923	1 363
Of which privatized during 1993-94 (Stage II)	473	891
From which were created:		
Total independent enterprises	1 355	4 344
Small enterprises	296	2 331
Agricultural cooperatives	32	487
Stock associations	122	295
Collective enterprises	698	1 082
Partnerships	56	148
Other	151	1
Non-privatized state farms	1 197	757

Source: Ministry of Agriculture, Republic of Kazakhstan.

- Farms in conjunction with SPC and the Ministry of Agriculture laboured throughout 1993 and 1994 to make a division on paper among farm workers and pensioners, of land and property shares, based on employment and accumulated pay. This process, which results in a certificate of ownership, was essentially completed by the end of 1994. Under the authority of a presidential decree of April 1994, some internal trading and pooling of shares had begun, in order to form independent associations and small enterprises from parts of farm assets. (Such enterprises include truck transportation companies, veterinarian clinics and repair shops.)
- At the same time, less egalitarian procedures were also being followed. In February 1994, the Cabinet of Ministers issued a decree, "On the sale of state agricultural enterprises into private property", which provided for the sale of state farms in closed auctions to small groups of people, usually the educated specialists of the farms. At the same time, the president signed another decree supported by the Ministry of Agriculture, "On the sale of part of the property of state farms into private property of their directors", which allowed directors with 20

years tenure to receive 20 percent of capital shares. This measure was extended and then subsequently dropped by the government, after criticism from parliament and the press.

Demise of state orders and emergence of a market for farm commodities. State procurement and subsidies for livestock products were eliminated in December 1993. Table 15 shows the effect of the elimination of subsidies and the freeing of state retail prices. In December 1993, average prices paid to farms by procurement agencies exceeded retail market prices by 30 to 100 percent, but these prices had converged by July. The State Statistical Committee (SSC) indicated that from January to October 1994 the volume of farm sales through channels other than the state system increased by 34 percent for meat and 57 percent for milk and remained almost constant for eggs, despite the decline in total marketings of each by approximately 20 percent, compared with the same nine months of 1993.[68]

State grain procurements, approximately 15 million tonnes in 1990-91, were reduced to 7 million tonnes in 1993 and 5 million tonnes in 1994. By late 1993, farms had experienced the harmful effects of inflation combined with slow payment from state purchasers. The finance ministry refused to provide credit for the entire 1993 grain procurement plan. Farms wanted to sell grain to Astyk (the state grain procurement and processing entity) at the posted state price, but reportedly sold grain for cash to private traders for half the posted state price. In October 1994, the government eliminated retail bread and wholesale flour subsidies. For 1995 the government has no mandatory grain procurement and plans to buy only 700 000 tonnes for state security stocks, etc. at commercial terms.

Food processing and storage. While a number of alternative processing and storage enterprises, including the growth of "mini" plants (such as flour mills and sausage and cheese plants) have developed on farms, special interest falls on the privatization of enterprises of the state processing and marketing system, which still have the bulk of processing and storage capacity.

By early 1995, the state had adopted a plan to auction off all but 19 of Astyk's 364 grain elevators and half its flour mills and macaroni plants by September

[68] Goskomstat respubliki kazakhstan. 1994. *Sotsial'no-eko-nomicheskoe polozhenie kazakhstana za yanvar'-oktyab' 1994 goda.* Almaty, November 1994.

CENTRAL
AND EASTERN EUROPE

TABLE 15

Average farm value of products by market channel before and after price liberalization, December 1993 to July 1994

	Tenge per tonne			Percentage change	
	Dec 1993	Jan 1994	July 1994	Jan/Dec	July/Dec
Livestock and poultry					
(carcass weight)					
Average all channels[1]	1 949	...	...	...	...
Procurement organs	2 103	3 292	11 558	157	550
Green Market	986	2 536	10 636	257	1 079
Dairy products					
Average all channels	336	704	2 366	210	704
Procurement organs	381	681	2 388	179	627
Green market	293	1 324	2 439	452	832
Eggs					
Average all channels	99	292	1 078	295	1 089
Procurement organs	104	292	1 092	281	1 050
Green market	181	285	1 037	157	573
Potatoes					
Average all channels	292	...	1 910	...	654
Procurement organs	315	...	2 339	...	743
Green market	401	...	2 203	...	549
Grain products[2]					
Average all channels	109	178 [3]	441	163 [3]	405
Procurement organs	138	190 [3]	1 100	138 [3]	797
Green market	97	155 [3]	632	160 [3]	652
Exchange rate: 1 tenge/US$5.7		9.3	45		

Source: Ministry of Agriculture, Republic of Kazakhstan. "All channels" includes traditional procurement organs, green (city) markets, barter and sales through restaurants. Effective procurement prices are overstated because of arrears in payment by procurement organs and high overall inflation.
[1] Estimated from data for price per live weight, using 0.59 as the average ratio of carcass to live weight for meat of all types in Kazakhstan, 1990-92.
[2] Not decontrolled until October 1994.
[3] February 1994.

1995. Additional plans were being developed for auctioning off food and meat and dairy processors which, after price liberalization, became desirable objects of private ownership.

The national privatization programme provided that a portion of shares in food processing enterprises be available on privileged terms to the farms supplying them. This policy of vertical ownership was apparently abandoned by SPC by early 1995.

This provision had been promoted by agricultural interests which thought that the refusal to accept unwanted production (of milk, etc.), which had become common by 1992, stemmed from the processors' exercise of monopoly power and not from the limits of market demand. However, the burgeoning excess stocks and financial losses of processors have since demonstrated the more pervasive problem of non-profit behaviour; competitive privatization is likely to lead to extensive cost cutting and commercial pricing.[69]

Trade in agricultural products in the "near" and "far abroad". From 1986 to 1990, Kazakhstan exported approximately 9 million tonnes of grain annually. The United States Department of Agriculture estimates that Kazakhstan exported approximately 7.7 million tonnes of its bumper 1992 crop, and about 6 million and 5 million tonnes from the 1993 and 1994 crops, respectively. Official statistics show no grain exports to the so-called "far abroad" (countries outside the former USSR), but other sources, including published state agreements, document sales to such countries as Poland, Lithuania, the People's Republic of China, Afghanistan, Iraq, the Islamic Republic of Iran and Turkey.[70] Some of these sales are handled by western grain traders who arrange credit.

Ascertaining the average grain price received by Kazakhstan's farms in order to make comparisons with world prices is not easy given poor statistics, the high rate of inflation and uncertain transport costs. The World Bank attempted to estimate 1993 state procurement prices as a percentage of world prices of about $130 per tonne. During harvest (September to October) state prices were approximately $65 a tonne, but this was reduced to about one-quarter of the world price after payment delay and inflation were taken into account.[71] Problems with ascertaining the price for

[69] The same observations have been made about food processors in the Russian Federation. O. Meliukhina and E. Serova. 1995. K probleme monopolizma v sfere pererabotki sel'skokhozi-astvennoi produktsii. *Voprosy Ekonomiki,* No. 1.

[70] N. Dudkin. 1994. Kazakhstani wheat. *Caravan Business News,* 1-30 June 1994.

[71] World Bank, op. cit., footnote 62, p. 183.

grain sold outside the state system arise from the fact that so much of it is bartered or registered at fictitious prices to reduce tax liability. In 1994, the state required a review of contracted export prices to reduce tax evasion and the incidence of individual farm directors selling grain cheaply and taking side payments from traders. However, these problems are likely to exist until full privatization is achieved.

The external trade of grain and agricultural products seems to be improving agriculture's terms of trade. All state trading agreements for grain and associated export licensing through the Ministry of Industry and Trade were eliminated in November 1994, and in January the president decreed that any person or firm could engage in the trade of any goods, except certain strategic ones. An official of the Almaty International Agricultural Commodities Exchange (AIACE) reported that by early 1995 average elevator prices paid to farms for wheat had risen to a minimum of US$77 per tonne and an average of $90.

At the same time, governments of the northern *oblasts* continue to "tax" grain exports in various ways. In addition, while Astyk has been virtually eliminated, exports of agricultural commodities (now including wool, hides and cotton) remain subject to price controls and hard currency taxation.

Long-term policy objectives
The exposure of Kazakhstan's agriculture to world prices for inputs and products has revealed a high-cost structure of production. Measures taken to restructure will affect the chances of Kazakhstan developing participatory democracy, a healthy and viable agricultural and food economy and a proper division of labour between market and government. The following specific policy areas, which have been the subject of domestic discussions and the observations of international agencies working in Kazakhstan's agricultural sector, are worthy of special attention.

Livestock restructuring for lower cost. At 71 kg per caput, Kazakhstan's 1991 meat consumption was sixth-highest in the USSR and about the same as that of the United Kingdom; higher than would have been predicted from Kazakhstan's per caput GDP (which was about one-quarter that of the United Kingdom) had it

been a market economy.[72] This level of consumption reflected both subsidies and the absence of competing consumer goods. Meat consumption declined to 59 kg in 1993 and 1994 and will probably continue to decline in 1995 as livestock herds have decreased and consumption levels in 1994 were largely maintained because of distress slaughter.

It is important that new levels of livestock product consumption be sustainable by market demand and that, in the process of arriving at this new equilibrium, restructuring reduces the cost of production and processing and improves distribution. A discussion of the prospects for poultry meat offers several lessons. Before 1991, Soviet pricing implicitly taxed poultry meat and subsidized red meats. While most other livestock products have been unprofitable, in part because of the increase of the relative price of grain, poultry meat has been just profitable because of a better feed conversion rate. New market prices, including higher relative feed prices and high real interest rates, should promote more efficient feed conversion for all livestock production and should especially promote poultry. A private feed industry, working with free market prices and responsive to a long-pent-up demand for protein, already shows signs of developing.

Concerns of sustainable agriculture. Kazakhstan has 28 million hectares of land susceptible to wind erosion and 80 000 hectares, including lands in the Aral Sea basin, which have been abandoned because of salinity. It is calculated that under the present methods used in northern Kazakhstan, for every tonne of grain produced, 1.5 tonnes of soil humus are expended. After 40 years of virgin soil exploitation, the humus content may have been reduced by one-third. Various research institutes disagree on what the optimal sown area in northern Kazakhstan should be (see Box 5, p. 175). Adjustments from past price patterns indicate that the area resown to grass will continue to expand, as will that of fallow and legumes in rotation.

Food processing. Kazakhstan needs to improve livestock products (including exported raw wool and hides) and cotton processing and to increase the level of packaging and processing in order to employ rural labour, compete with foreign imports and reduce retail

[72] D.J. Sedik. A note on Soviet per capita meat consumption. *Comparative Economic Studies,* 15(3): 39-48. Fall 1993.

food costs. As the economic crisis ends, these industries may begin to attract long-interested foreign investment on a commercial basis, as long as there are a free market and effective legal structures.

Finance and private property for land. Agriculture, like other Soviet economic sectors, was characterized by high, inefficient capital intensity, because investment in both fixed and variable inputs was financed by soft state credits.

A poll indicates that 75 percent of Kazakhstan's citizens now favour private landownership, and the constitutional prohibition against private landownership may be resolved by referendum in 1995.[73] Private landownership is given such importance because, first, full private landownership is a great ideological symbol, without which no entrepreneur is fully sure that the system has fundamentally changed. Second, landownership gives a "place" to ethnic Russians and others who are uncertain about their position in a possibly more nationalistic Kazakhstan. Third, landownership will encourage the development of a finance system for agriculture. Discussions in Kazakhstan reveal that entrepreneurs are afraid to invest their own money in agriculture without controlling the land. Although experience elsewhere shows that the value of agricultural land in transitional economies is low and so offers little mortgage security, borrowers who put up as collateral the land on which they have built are probably good credit risks.

A correct role for government in agriculture and rural communities. Many of Kazakhstan's branch ministries are being liquidated. The agriculture ministry will probably remain, although much changed, with a proper division of business (or, as it is put in Kazakhstan, *khozyastvennye*) from regulatory and informational tasks. While doing the vast amount of administrative allocation of capital investment distributing inputs and output plans, the Kazakhstan Ministry of Agriculture has not in the past done well those things which should now be emphasized. Among these would appear to be:

i) Market information and grading standards need to be provided. The previous system of state procurement obviated the advantages of discriminatory standards and postharvest care. Exposure to foreign markets has

[73] Reported by A. Kazahegeldin in an interview, *Rossiskaya gazeta,* 28 January 1995, p. 10; A. Nazarbayev, *Kazakhstanskya gazeta,* 14 April 1994, p. 1-2.

caused an increased interest in correctly identifying and certifying standards for grain, wool, hides, etc. and is orienting potential producers to higher-value grain grades, finer wool and better-treated hides. Likewise, farm managers, if they are to market what they formerly only produced, require information and analysis such as are readily available to western farmers.

ii) True marketing cooperatives or grassroots farm associations may do much of the above. In the Russian Federation, these efforts, although slow, may be ahead of those in Kazakhstan, where the private farm association is now moribund. An appropriate activity of a ministry of agriculture in a democratic Kazakhstan might be to encourage independent democratic cooperatives.

iii) Agricultural science, as in all former communist countries, is concentrated in an academy of agricultural sciences, separate from the ministry. These institutes need to be better integrated with teaching institutes, developing together research and extension programmes which are responsive to the needs of commercial farmers.

iv) The pressure for new *income and price support mechanisms* will become unavoidable when Kazakhstan achieves its expected future increases in wealth and tax revenue. Current circumstances have forced Kazakhstan to eliminate the expenditures that bribed farms to accept dependence on the state and caused an inefficient structure of production and farm organization. The country has benefited from its opened trade with established market economies and seeks to establish trade with CIS on open terms. At the same time, autarkic tendencies have emerged to curtail imports of food products in which Kazakhstan is deficit (e.g. vegetable oil and sugar). It would be important, both for Kazakhstan's own efficient development and for its future entry into the World Trade Organization to ensure that agricultural support policies conform with the non-distorting provisions allowed by the Uruguay Round's Green Box (see Box 11, p. 256). In addition, some of the following general principles should have a role in guiding agricultural policy:

- In late 1994, ideas of increasing gross production and exports still dominate most agrarian interests. Kazakhstan is only just beginning to realize that

farm prices and income are often negatively related to production, particularly for many farm products characterized by inelastic demand.

- When the residue of old thinking in terms of gross output is cleared, more attention will be paid to maintaining farm incomes. The total wage bill (much of it delayed for months) for the state farm sector in 1994 was in the order of only 2 billion to 3 billion tenge. Credit and budget subsidies of many times that amount were expensive ways of maintaining income.

- Modern economic development does not usually maintain unchanged price parities for farming. Lower terms of trade moderate the growth of per caput farm income which in turn stimulates exit from agriculture or to part-time non-farm activities. Kazakhstan currently has much underemployment, particularly in the rural parts of its south and southeast. Continued adjustments in cultivation are likely to affect the population of the northern steppe. At least 23 percent of the active labour force of Kazakhstan is engaged in farm work. In the long term this proportion must surely fall. Budget expenditures can be used either to try to keep the population in farming or to make labour more mobile by training and developing infrastructure to support rural industries, such as food processing, and jobs in other industries, such as minerals and fuels.

- The resolution of the land property issue and the final assignment of useful land shares to farm and service workers and pensioners have an implication for the ease of eventual transition from farming. Two distinct historical models of outmigration may serve to illustrate the issues. In one model, landless sharecroppers are pushed out by economic circumstances to become industrial labourers. In another model, farms are consolidated and families leave agriculture more smoothly and securely, typically transferring start-up capital for other enterprises, from land that is sold or rented out or that remains in the hands of the family.

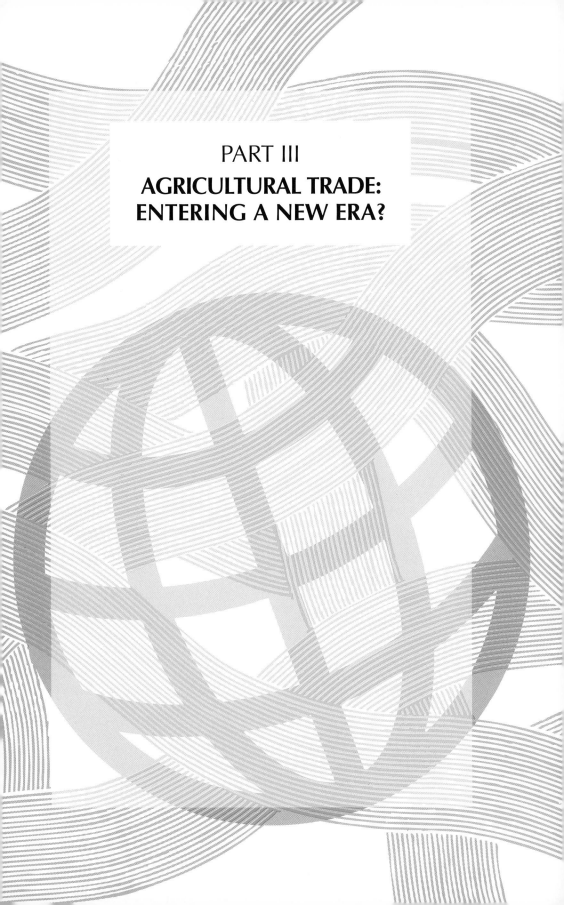

PART III
AGRICULTURAL TRADE: ENTERING A NEW ERA?

AGRICULTURAL TRADE: ENTERING A NEW ERA?
Introduction

The expansion of agricultural trade has helped provide greater quantity, wider variety and better quality food to increasing numbers of people at lower prices. Agricultural trade is also a generator of income and welfare for the millions of people who are directly or indirectly involved in it. At the national level, for many countries it is a major source of the foreign exchange that is necessary to finance imports and development; while for many others domestic food security is closely related to the country's capacity to finance food imports.

As with any activity that involves buyers and sellers, however, agricultural trade – perhaps more than any other trade – tends to be a source of conflicts of interest and international confrontation. One reason for this is that agricultural policies are frequently influenced by the interests of particular political constituencies within a country rather than by national, international or global interests. Related reasons are: the emergence and growth of widespread distortions in world agricultural markets; the food-security role of agricultural trade, which confers upon it a special political, socio-economic and strategic dimension; and, more recently, differing perceptions of the role of agricultural trade in environmental matters of transnational or global interest.

Agricultural trade policy has long reflected the widely held belief that, because of its importance and vulnerability, the agricultural sector could not be exposed to the full rigours of international competition without incurring unacceptable political, social and economic consequences. This view has led to high and widespread protection of the sector, which has been a cause of depressed and unstable agricultural commodity markets, in their turn, leading to further pressures for protection. In recent years, however, many developing countries have unilaterally taken steps towards the liberalization of overall and agricultural markets. Most of these steps have involved the development of structural adjustment programmes and regional cooperation schemes. In the former centrally planned economies, the systemic reforms underway have also led to greater external openness and this process, in particular the increasingly important role in international trade that China is likely to play, has far-reaching implications worldwide. On the other hand, for a number of developed countries, including such major traders as the United States and the EC, agricultural policy reform induced by domestic or international pressure has led to some reduction in trade distortions but not to significant trade liberalization as yet.

It was against this background of widespread protectionism and deep structural problems in the world agricultural trading system that the Uruguay Round of GATT negotiations took place. Its conclusion, and the creation of a new World Trade Organization (WTO), have been milestones in the recent history of international trade relations (even though the results of the Round fell short of expectations). Despite its shortcomings the Round was a momentous event for agricultural trade; first because, by its very conclusion, the worst was avoided; second, because agriculture was, for the first time, a major element in the negotiations; third, because it provides hope for at least some progress towards greater market liberalization and reduced domestic support in agriculture; and fourth, because the Round, and the newly created WTO, provide the framework for more discipline, stability and transparency in overall and agricultural trade. However, the impact of the Round on world agricultural markets may turn out to be small in the short term and protectionism in old and new forms is likely to remain high in the medium term and for longer unless further reductions are successfully negotiated.

At the same time as the international community was framing new multilateral rules for trade, many groups of countries were actively moving towards regional trading arrangements. In the recent past such arrangements have increased in number, country coverage and dynamism; and they include agriculture to a growing extent. The development of these arrangements has raised issues related to their position in the multilateral trading system, their degree of openness *vis-à-vis* third countries and the risks of regionalization of trade flows.

Another issue that has attracted increased attention, and may significantly affect future trade relations, is the role of international trade in environmental protection and the sustainability of production. This is a complex and controversial problem. Trade may be environment-friendly to the extent that it brings about efficiency in the use of resources. However, trading and the related acts of producing and marketing also put pressure on environmental resources. Appropriate environmental and trade policies can help ensure compatibility between trade and environmental objectives. However, resource limitations often impose difficult policy choices between immediate developmental and food security needs and long-term environmental concerns.

The problems and issues facing agricultural trade and the forces underlying agricultural trade policies can only be appreciated in the light of the major changes that have taken place in world markets during the past decades. The first Section of this chapter presents some basic data illustrating the main changes that have taken place since the early 1960s with regard to: the weight of agriculture in overall trade; the market shares of the different regions and countries; the real value and purchasing power of agricultural exports; and the direction and composition of agricultural trade flows. The second Section examines agricultural trade in the context of the major political and economic transformations that have taken place during the past decades, especially since the beginning of the 1980s. Section III discusses the new agricultural trading rules that emerged in 1994 after the conclusion of the Uruguay Round of GATT negotiations and their likely impact on world agricultural trade. Section IV discusses the movement towards closer regional economic integration through the development of regional trading blocs and the place of agriculture in this process. Finally, Section V examines the interfaces between agricultural trade, the environment and sustainable development and the conditions under which trade and the environment could be made mutually supportive.

AGRICULTURAL TRADE: ENTERING A NEW ERA?

I. Agricultural trade – changing trends and patterns

Amid the profound changes in the economic importance, structure, direction and composition of world agricultural trade during the past three decades, a number of paradoxical features have emerged. While losing importance in relation to total trade, agricultural trade has remained a key element in the economies of many countries. Nevertheless, it has tended to be those economies that depend less on agricultural trade which have made the largest gains in agricultural market share; while economies that are more firmly based on agriculture have not only lost market share, but in many cases have also seen their agricultural trade balances deteriorate in the face of persistently high or even increasing economic dependence on agricultural exports and food security dependence on imports.

Other general tendencies have been a protracted decline in the real international prices of agricultural products, which has negatively affected their purchasing power; greater geographic diversification of agricultural trade flows, along with intensified intraregional exchanges; and the increasing importance of value-added compared with primary products in total agricultural trade.

Declining importance of agriculture in world trade

The relationship between trade and output in general underlies the growing interdependence and integration of the world economies. This is the case also for agriculture. On a global basis, the long-term growth rate of agricultural trade has tended to be significantly greater than that of production.

This pattern was reversed during much of the 1980s, reflecting depressed exports and imports in the developing countries, particularly in Latin America and the Caribbean and in Africa. By contrast, the growth in agricultural trade continued to generally exceed that of production in the developed countries **(Figure 11)**.

Despite its relative dynamism, however, trade in agricultural products has tended to lag behind trade in other

Figure 11

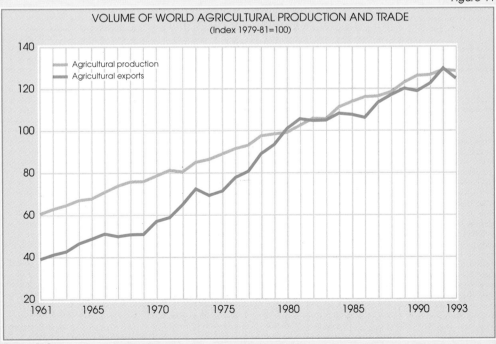

VOLUME OF WORLD AGRICULTURAL PRODUCTION AND TRADE
(Index 1979-81=100)

Agricultural production
Agricultural exports

Source: FAO

sectors, particularly manufactures, as industrialization proceeds. On a global basis, agricultural exports now account for less than 10 percent of merchandise exports, compared to about 25 percent in the early 1960s.

The tendency for agricultural trade to lose relative importance in external trade has been common to all regions, but in the developing country regions the process was particularly pronounced during the 1960s and early 1970s **(Figures 12 and 13).**

Thereafter, the share of agriculture in total exports has stabilized at around 2 to 7 percent in the Near East and North Africa region; and around 10 percent in Asia and the Pacific. More pronounced fluctuations in the share were recorded in sub-Saharan Africa and Latin America and the Caribbean, where the general decline in the

Figure 12

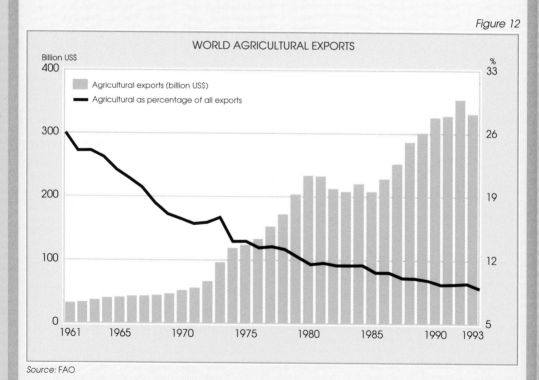

WORLD AGRICULTURAL EXPORTS

Billion US$

☐ Agricultural exports (billion US$)
── Agricultural as percentage of all exports

Source: FAO

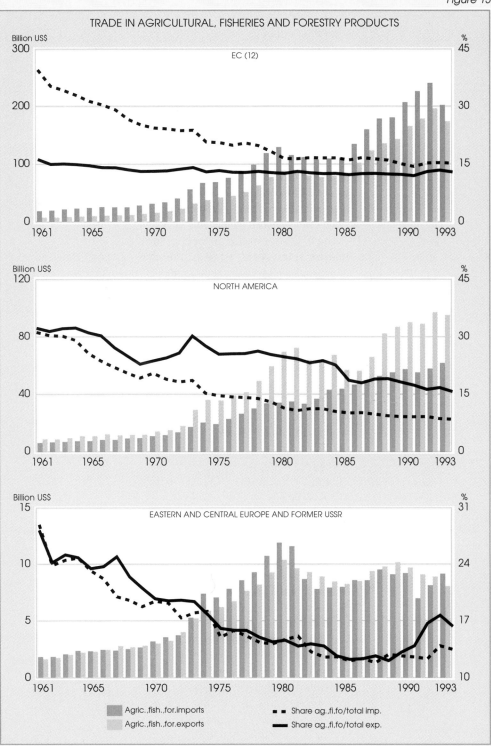

Figure 13

TRADE IN AGRICULTURAL, FISHERIES AND FORESTRY PRODUCTS

EC (12)

NORTH AMERICA

EASTERN AND CENTRAL EUROPE AND FORMER USSR

Agric.,fish.,for.imports
Agric.,fish.,for.exports

■ ■ Share ag.,fi,fo/total imp.
— Share ag.,fi,fo/total exp.

Source: FAO

agricultural trade share was punctuated by temporary upsurges (particularly during the late 1970s in the "commodity boom" years and in 1986, a year of high coffee prices caused by drought-reduced crops in Brazil and its suspension of export quotas) **(Figures 14A and 14B)**.

A similar pattern is observed on the side of imports. The declining weight of agriculture in total imports, which is a good indicator of a country's rate of development, was remarkably strong in the Asia and the Pacific region; less marked in the Near East and Latin America and the Caribbean regions (the latter having a comparatively low agricultural to total import ratio, however); and hardly noticeable in sub-Saharan Africa.

Agricultural exports have also tended to lose importance as a source of import financing. This long-term process has been interrupted only during exceptional periods, such as when particularly favourable conditions for agricultural exports prevail (as in the late 1970s); or, more notably, in the years following the debt crisis of the 1980s when many developing countries sharply contracted their total imports.

However, in Latin America and the Caribbean and in sub-Saharan Africa, agricultural exports still finance about one-fifth of the total import bill. Furthermore, economic dependence on agricultural exports has remained very high in many individual countries **(Figures 15)**. In 1993, 17 out of 46 countries in Africa depended on agriculture for half or more of their total export earnings. In Latin America and the Caribbean 16 out of 40 countries were in the same situation (nine of them in the Caribbean).

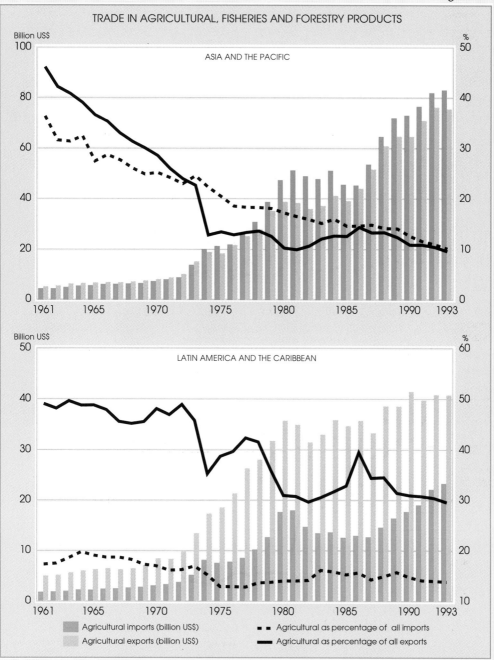

TRADE IN AGRICULTURAL, FISHERIES AND FORESTRY PRODUCTS

ASIA AND THE PACIFIC

LATIN AMERICA AND THE CARIBBEAN

Agricultural imports (billion US$)

Agricultural exports (billion US$)

Agricultural as percentage of all imports

Agricultural as percentage of all exports

Source: FAO

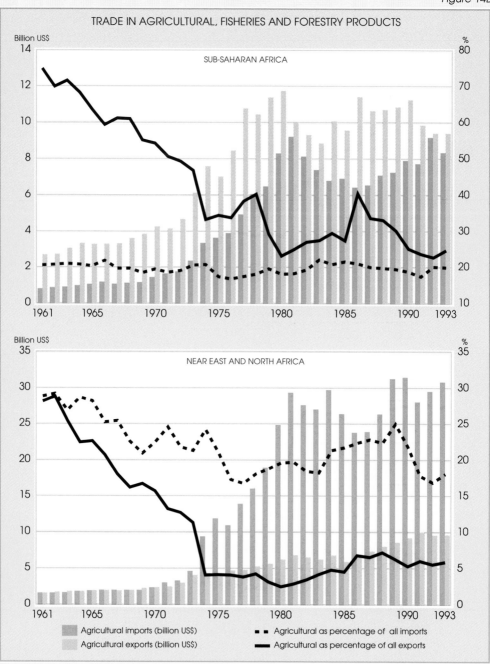

TRADE IN AGRICULTURAL, FISHERIES AND FORESTRY PRODUCTS

SUB-SAHARAN AFRICA

NEAR EAST AND NORTH AFRICA

Agricultural imports (billion US$)

Agricultural exports (billion US$)

Agricultural as percentage of all imports

Agricultural as percentage of all exports

Source: FAO

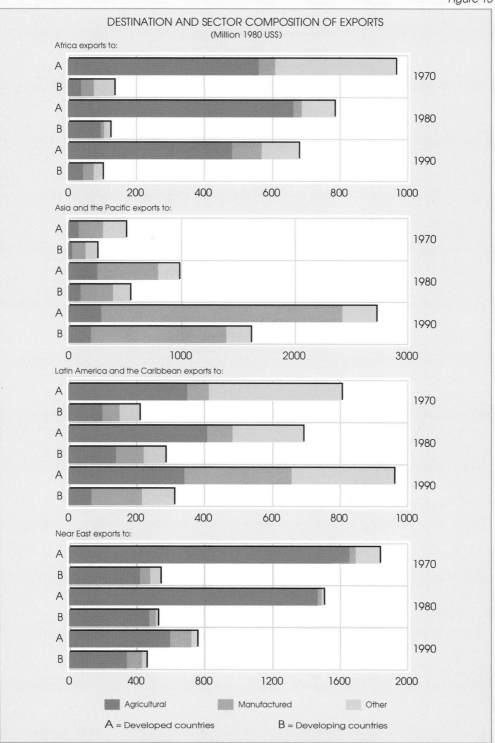

Figure 15

DESTINATION AND SECTOR COMPOSITION OF EXPORTS
(Million 1980 US$)

Agricultural Manufactured Other

A = Developed countries   B = Developing countries

Source: UNCTAD and FAO

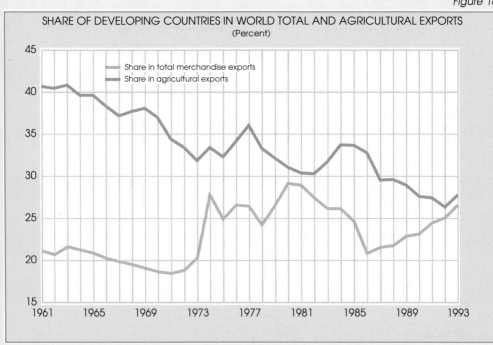

Extreme cases, where 80 percent or more of export earnings were agriculture-based, included Cuba and Paraguay in Latin America; and Burundi, the Comoros, Guinea-Bissau, Malawi, Uganda and the Sudan.

Expanding agricultural markets and contracting developing country share
The regional distribution of world total and agricultural trade has changed significantly since the early 1960s. While the developing countries gained market share for total merchandise exports (from about 20 to over 25 percent of the world total) their share for total agricultural exports has declined from over 40 to about 27 percent **(Figure 16)**.

The counterpart to the developing countries' market share losses was the increasing weight of the developed

Figure 16

SHARE OF DEVELOPING COUNTRIES IN WORLD TOTAL AND AGRICULTURAL EXPORTS
(Percent)

Share in total merchandise exports
Share in agricultural exports

Source: FAO

countries, mainly the EC, in world agricultural markets. Indeed, while in the early 1960s the EC-12 accounted for slightly more than 20 percent of world agricultural exports, this share is now around 45 percent. Most of this increase reflects intensified trade among EC member countries. Excluding intracommunity trade, however, EC exports still represent approximately 13 percent of the world total, up from 8 percent in the early 1960s. The EC has also remained by far the largest importing area in the world, although its share in world imports from outside the Community has tended to decline.

The United States, after having lost some market share during the late 1960s, managed to recapture it after 1973, when the export sector benefited from liberal fiscal and monetary policies and a weak dollar. However, from 1982 onwards the tightening of macroeconomic policies, the strengthening of the dollar after the second oil shock and the ensuing world recession resulted in a marked deceleration in the growth of United States exports.

All the developing country regions, with the exception of Asia and the Pacific, progressively lost world market share for their exports. That Asia and the Pacific has actually gained share in world agricultural exports since the mid-1970s is all the more remarkable as this is also the region that has been most successful in diversifying its export base away from agriculture. In contrast, despite the persistently strong agricultural component of its external trade, sub-Saharan Africa's presence in world agricultural markets has tended to lose significance since the early 1970s and

is now of a magnitude comparable to that of the Near East and North Africa. Latin America and the Caribbean experienced pronounced market losses since the second half of the 1980s, a period of slow growth in the volume of agricultural exports and of strong decline in export prices (**Figures 17 and 18**).

Will the developing countries remain net exporters?
Until the late 1970s, the agricultural exports of the developing countries as a whole exceeded agricultural imports by a significant and relatively stable margin. The economic crisis of the early 1980s caused a sharp decline in the demand for developing countries' exports and led to a temporary reversal of their agricultural net trade position. As the crisis progressed, however, financial constraints imposed a drastic cut in imports, including of food, and the developing countries as a whole emerged again as net agricultural exporters, a position they maintained until 1991. Generally disappointing export performances the following two years led, once again, to a reversal in the trade balance.

Regional situations, however, differed widely within this general pattern. Overall, Latin America and the Caribbean has maintained a strong agricultural surplus position although imports have tended to rise much faster than exports in recent years. Sub-Saharan Africa has recorded wide fluctuations in its agricultural export:import ratio, but recent trends suggest increasing difficulties for the region in maintaining its traditional net exporter status. Asia and the Pacific has moved into a net agricultural importer position since the mid-1970s,

Figure 17

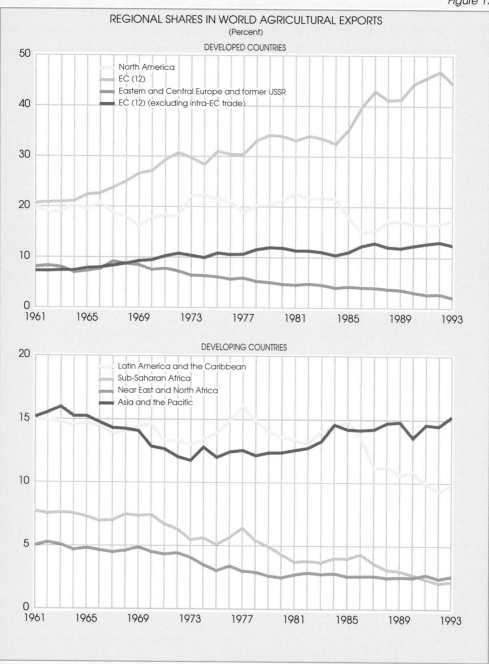

REGIONAL SHARES IN WORLD AGRICULTURAL EXPORTS
(Percent)

DEVELOPED COUNTRIES

North America
EC (12)
Eastern and Central Europe and former USSR
EC (12) (excluding intra-EC trade)

DEVELOPING COUNTRIES

Latin America and the Caribbean
Sub-Saharan Africa
Near East and North Africa
Asia and the Pacific

Source: FAO

Figure 18

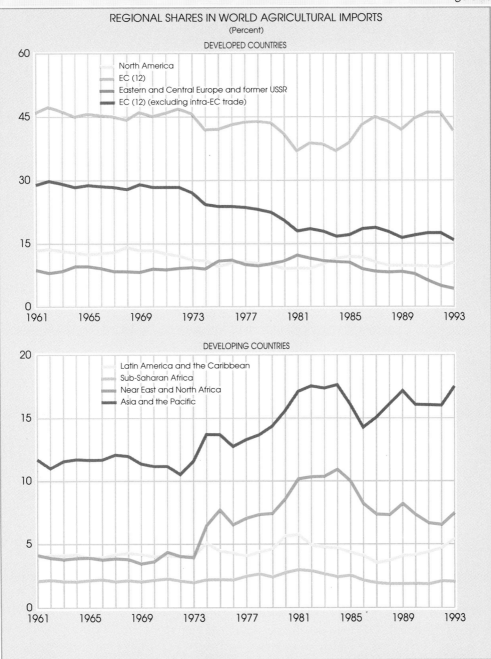

REGIONAL SHARES IN WORLD AGRICULTURAL IMPORTS
(Percent)

DEVELOPED COUNTRIES

North America
EC (12)
Eastern and Central Europe and former USSR
EC (12) (excluding intra-EC trade)

DEVELOPING COUNTRIES

Latin America and the Caribbean
Sub-Saharan Africa
Near East and North Africa
Asia and the Pacific

Source: FAO

with a steady expansion of both
imports and exports interrupted only
during the first half of the 1980s.
Finally, the Near East and North
Africa, a net agricultural exporter
during the 1960s, has seen food-
import dependence soar during the
1970s and early 1980s and remain
extremely high since then. The
agricultural trade gap widened
dramatically in the oil-exporting
countries in this region, but food
deficits of a structural nature also
emerged in several non-oil-exporter
countries (Figure 19).

Diversifying markets and intensifying intraregional exchanges

Two general tendencies have
characterized the direction of
agricultural trade flows during the past
decades. The first is a growing
geographic diversification of exports
and imports and the second is the
increasing intensity of exchanges
within the individual regions.

These general tendencies have been
far from uniform, however, and have
not resulted in large shifts in the
overall patterns of agricultural trade.
The developed countries' agricultural
trade has remained largely, and
increasingly, self-centred, with the
developing countries accounting for a
declining share of total imports. The
developing countries, on the other
hand, still depend to a very large
extent on developed country markets
both as suppliers of imports and as
outlets for exports.

Dependence on traditional
developed country markets,
particularly those of the EC, has
remained high in Africa. Indeed, the
developed countries currently account
for three-quarters of the region's total

Figure 19

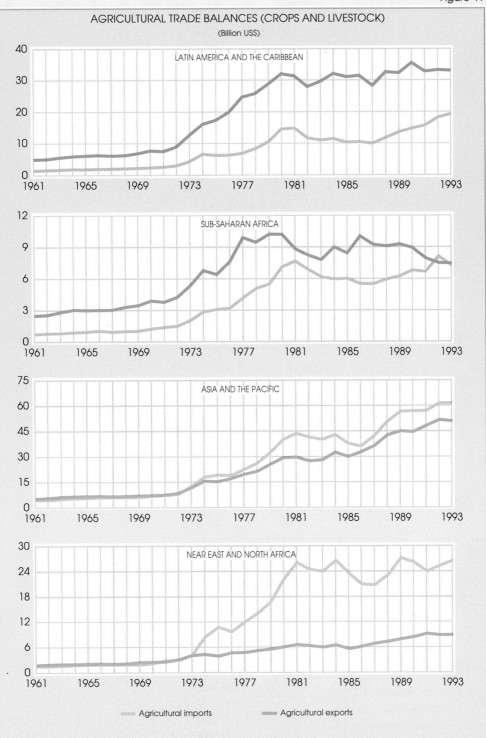

AGRICULTURAL TRADE BALANCES (CROPS AND LIVESTOCK)
(Billion US$)

Source: FAO

agricultural exports and nearly 70 percent of its agricultural imports. African agricultural exporters have increased the share of intraregional trade in total exports from 5 to 11 percent between 1970 and 1990. However, this has contributed little to reducing Africa's heavy reliance on food imports from the developed country markets.

All other developing country regions have shown varying degrees of market diversification and regional integration. The Far East already the most self-centred region for agricultural trade, intensified intraregional exchanges while also reducing the share of its total agricultural exports that go to the developed countries, particularly the EC. Latin America and the Caribbean maintained a fairly balanced export pattern between markets in the EC, North America, developing countries and the former centrally planned economies. Nevertheless, the region also significantly increased the developing country and intraregional share of agricultural trade, the latter by intensifying efforts towards regional economic integration. The Near East has tended to rely on the EC for an increasing share of its food imports, the respective shares of North America and the Far East remaining broadly equivalent.

The closely integrated agricultural markets of Eastern and Central Europe and the former USSR had tended to open significantly to imports, in particular from North America and the EC, even before the reforms of the 1990s and the breakdown of the traditional intraregional trading systems. By 1990 the EC had also emerged as the main outlet for these countries' agricultural exports (over 31 percent of the total, compared to 23 percent for intraregional exports). A growing share of the region's shipments had also been towards the developing countries. In the most recent years the breakup of the Council for Mutual Economic Assistance (CMEA) and the efforts by Eastern and Central European countries to tighten economic and political links with Western Europe, have led to an even further weakening of trade within the transition economies. The introduction in 1993 of a Central European Free Trade Area involving the Czech Republic, Hungary, Poland and Slovakia may reactivate intraregional trade of agricultural products to some extent (Tables 16 and 17).

Falling agricultural prices, increasing shipment volumes and dwindling purchasing capacity of agricultural exports
Throughout the 1960s and 1970s agricultural export unit values in the developed and developing countries followed virtually identical upward trends. Both groups of countries also shared in the decline in prices that followed the economic crisis of the early 1980s. However, while prices of products exported by the developing countries remained depressed until recently, those of the developed countries resumed their upward trend in the mid-1980s.

In contrast to these movements in prices, the volumes of exports showed a steady upward trend overall. However, the early 1980s marked a shift in the relative export growth patterns of the two country groups. Export volume growth decelerated

TABLE 16

Destination of agricultural exports by region (percent)

Exports from	Destination	Developed markets economies	EC	Canada/ United States	Developing countries	Latin America/ the Carribean	Africa	Near East	Far East	Eastern and Central Europe/ former USSR
World	1970	73	42	15	17	4	3	2	8	9
	1980	63	40	10	24	5	5	5	10	10
	1990	71	45	11	21	4	4	4	11	5
Developed market economies	1970	79	48	14	16	4	3	2	8	3
	1980	69	47	8	23	6	6	4	8	6
	1990	77	53	10	18	4	3	3	8	3
EC	1970	85	65	8	11	2	5	2	2	3
	1980	78	66	4	17	3	7	5	2	4
	1990	85	72	4	11	2	4	3	3	2
Canada/ United States	1970	72	28	21	23	8	3	2	13	2
	1980	58	25	12	29	12	4	2	15	7
	1990	65	19	21	28	9	3	3	16	5
Developing countries	1970	71	35	20	17	4	2	2	9	10
	1980	58	31	15	26	5	4	6	13	12
	1990	61	29	16	28	5	4	5	16	8
Latin America/the Caribbean	1970	77	33	29	12	9	1	0	3	10
	1980	60	30	24	19	10	3	3	4	18
	1990	65	32	25	21	12	2	3	5	12
Africa	1970	74	50	13	13	0	5	2	5	9
	1980	74	58	9	14	1	7	3	4	7
	1990	75	59	6	19	0	11	3	5	3
Near East	1970	55	36	7	24	0	2	19	3	18
	1980	40	30	4	38	0	4	31	5	17
	1990	50	37	6	40	1	5	29	4	9
Far East	1970	58	22	15	31	1	2	3	24	9
	1980	49	19	9	40	1	3	6	29	7
	1990	52	15	10	37	1	3	4	29	6
Eastern and Central Europe/ former USSR	1970	41	27	1	9	4	3	2	4	46
	1980	35	20	2	21	4	5	4	5	39
	1990	50	31	2	21	5	5	2	3	23

Source: FAO based on UNCTAD data.
Note: the figures in the shaded areas, representing subtotals for developed market economies, developing countries and Eastern and Central Europe/former USSR, should add to 100 horizontally. In most cases they do not, due to rounding and/or statistical discrepancies.

TABLE 17

Origin of agricultural imports by region (percent)

Imports by / Origin		Developed markets economies	EC	Canada/ United States	Developing countries	Latin America/ the Carribean	Africa	Near East	Far East	Eastern and Central Europe/ former USSR
World	1970	58	23	20	32	13	8	2	11	8
	1980	64	30	22	29	12	4	1	13	6
	1990	69	39	19	25	10	3	1	13	4
Developed market economies	1970	64	27	19	31	14	8	1	9	4
	1980	69	37	20	27	11	5	1	10	3
	1990	74	47	17	21	9	3	1	10	3
EC	1970	67	36	13	27	10	9	1	6	5
	1980	74	50	14	22	9	6	1	6	3
	1990	80	62	8	16	7	4	1	5	3
Canada/ United States	1970	55	13	29	44	25	7	1	11	1
	1980	53	13	28	45	29	4	1	11	1
	1990	62	16	37	36	22	1	1	13	1
Developing countries	1970	58	16	28	33	9	6	2	20	5
	1980	60	21	27	30	9	3	2	21	5
	1990	58	21	25	33	9	2	3	23	4
Latin America/the Caribbean	1970	62	14	40	30	27	0	0	3	7
	1980	70	14	52	25	22	1	0	3	5
	1990	62	17	41	32	28	0	0	4	5
Africa	1970	66	34	16	24	3	13	1	9	8
	1980	73	44	18	20	6	6	1	8	6
	1990	68	43	16	25	6	9	2	10	6
Near East	1970	51	22	17	39	3	6	16	15	8
	1980	58	31	11	35	9	3	8	17	5
	1990	61	33	17	36	8	2	11	15	2
Far East	1970	53	6	30	36	4	5	1	31	3
	1980	51	5	31	37	4	2	1	36	2
	1990	52	9	27	37	4	1	1	35	1
Eastern and Central Europe/ former USSR	1970	20	8	5	36	14	8	3	11	41
	1980	38	14	15	36	22	3	2	10	22
	1990	40	17	16	36	22	2	2	15	17

Source: FAO based on UNCTAD data.
Note: the figures in the shaded areas, representing subtotals for developed market economies, developing countries and Eastern and Central Europe/former USSR, should add to 100 horizontally. In most cases they do not, due to rounding and/or statistical discrepancies.

markedly in the developed countries (chiefly due to lower export volumes from the United States caused by economic policy shifts following the 1979 oil shock) and accelerated somewhat in the developing countries (reflecting, to a large extent, the booming export performances of Asia and the Pacific and the pressure to generate foreign exchange to alleviate debt in Latin America and the Caribbean). Nevertheless, because of the price increase differential the current value of agricultural exports rose on the whole much faster in the developed countries – roughly 50 percent between 1979-81 and 1991-93 – than in the developing ones where over the same period the comparable increase was only slightly above 20 percent **(Figure 20)**.

The increase in the agricultural export unit values of the developing countries also lagged behind that of other major traded products, resulting in a pronounced and almost uninterrupted deterioration of their real agricultural prices (or net barter terms of trade) in international markets after the world food crisis years of the early 1970s.[1] Taking 1979-81 as a base, the developing countries' net barter terms of trade had deteriorated by nearly 40 percent in 1993. All the developing country regions shared in the deterioration but to varying degrees **(Figure 21)**.

The general decline in agricultural commodity prices can be explained by many factors, including: governmental support and protection, particularly in the industrial countries, that provided incentives to production often well above those offered by international markets; the efforts of many countries to counter the decline in prices through expanding volumes of shipments; the plantings and investment made during the more favourable years that preceded the 1980s; and stabilization and structural adjustment policies affecting exchange rates, taxation and marketing systems, which in some cases raised prices paid to growers relative to international market prices.

Gains in productivity and/or the expansion of the area under export crops enabled developing countries to offset the decline in prices to a certain extent. Indeed, as noted earlier, the growth of their export volumes actually accelerated somewhat during the depressed 1980s relative to the previous decades.

Overall, however, prices fell to such depressed levels that they outweighed the expansion of production and export volume, thus reducing overall earnings. As a result, the purchasing capacity of agricultural exports (income terms of trade)[2] deteriorated for a large majority of developing countries. By 1991-93 the index of income terms of trade of the developing countries as a whole was 8 percent below the 1979-81 levels.

---

[1] Real agricultural prices are calculated by using the combined UN price index of manufactured goods and crude petroleum as a deflator.

---

[2] The income terms of trade, or purchasing power, of agricultural exports are the value of agricultural exports deflated by import prices of manufactures and crude petroleum.

Figure 20

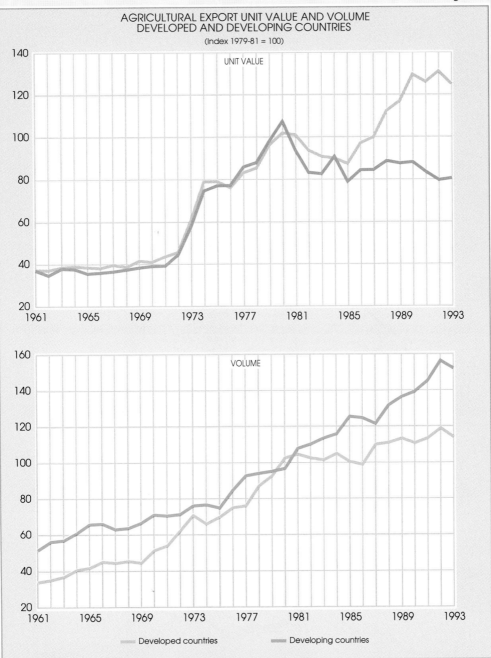

AGRICULTURAL EXPORT UNIT VALUE AND VOLUME
DEVELOPED AND DEVELOPING COUNTRIES
(Index 1979-81 = 100)

UNIT VALUE

VOLUME

Developed countries   Developing countries

Source: FAO

Figure 21

AGRICULTURAL EXPORT INDICES, DEVELOPING COUNTRY REGIONS
(Index 1979-81 = 100)

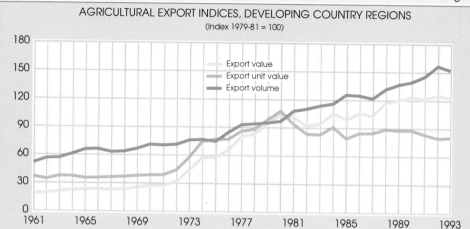

Export value
Export unit value
Export volume

NET BARTER TERMS OF TRADE OF AGRICULTURAL EXPORTS, DEVELOPING COUNTRY REGIONS
(Index 1979-81 = 100)

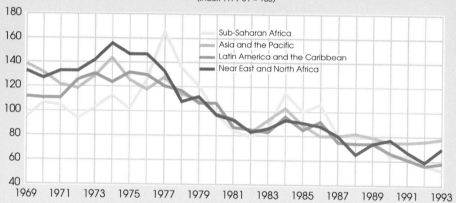

Sub-Saharan Africa
Asia and the Pacific
Latin America and the Caribbean
Near East and North Africa

INCOME TERMS OF TRADE OF AGRICULTURAL EXPORTS, DEVELOPING COUNTRY REGIONS
(Index 1979-81 = 100)

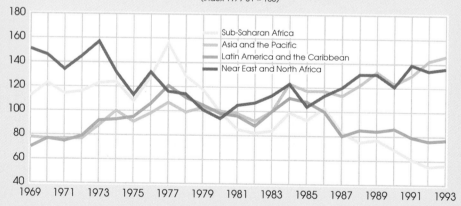

Sub-Saharan Africa
Asia and the Pacific
Latin America and the Caribbean
Near East and North Africa

Source: FAO

Within this general context regional
experiences diverged. Asia and the
Pacific benefited, on the one hand,
from a less traumatic fall in real export
prices than the other regions and, on
the other hand, from a strong
acceleration in shipment volumes
(which nearly doubled between 1979-
81 and 1992-93). At the other end,
sub-Saharan Africa suffered a collapse
in export prices coupled with widely
fluctuating, but overall stagnant,
volumes of exports. Latin America and
the Caribbean also experienced
declining export prices but maintained
a positive growth of export volumes.

To a large extent the different
regional export performances reflected
the market behaviour of the main
commodities exported by the
respective regions. Generally, the
international prices of products
exported by Asian countries were less
depressed and underwent less-
pronounced fluctuations than the
tropical products exported by Africa
and Latin America and the Caribbean.
For instance, the nominal dollar prices
of rice fell 13 percent between 1979-
81 and 1989-91, those of rubber fell
about 20 percent and those of palm oil
46 percent. On the other hand the
prices of tea and, more markedly, jute
and cotton, tended to strengthen. In
the cases of coffee and cocoa, the
main export crops for many African
and Latin American countries, prices
declined by respectively 56 and 58
percent during the same period.

Shifting from primary to processed exports

An issue of considerable importance is
the extent to which the developing
countries have been able to shift from
exports of non-processed primary

commodities towards value-added products. The different developing country regions recorded varying degrees of success on this account. In both Asia and the Pacific and Latin America and the Caribbean the share of processed products in total agricultural exports rose from around 10 percent in the early 1960s to about one-third of the total in recent years. This share has risen to considerably higher levels in the more industrialized countries in these regions. Thus, in Argentina and Brazil the comparable figure is about 50 percent while in Malaysia it is over 70 percent.

In sub-Saharan Africa, on the other hand, the share of processed products in agricultural exports has remained around 15 percent throughout the past three decades. Behind this stagnating pattern some countries showed pronounced temporal variations. In the case of Kenya the ratio of processed products to total agricultural exports was relatively high (at around 17 percent) during the 1960s and early 1970s, but declined to less than 10 percent over the following decades. In Côte d'Ivoire the ratio increased markedly between the early 1960s and the mid-1970s (from around 3 to 22 percent), but fell to around 15 percent during the 1980s. For most countries in the region, however, the general picture is one of a high and undiminished dependence on a limited range of primary product exports. In the Near East and North Africa, the high share of value-added products in the total generally reflects the strong weight of a few processed products in a relatively small agricultural export base. Processed shellfish and other sea products, as well as canned and preserved fruits and vegetables accounted for much of the total. Among individual countries the high share of processed products is largely explained by wine in Algeria (although this product has lost considerable importance in recent years); by processed fishery products and pistachios in Iran; and by tobacco, hazelnut and fruit confections in Turkey **(Figure 22)**.

Figure 22

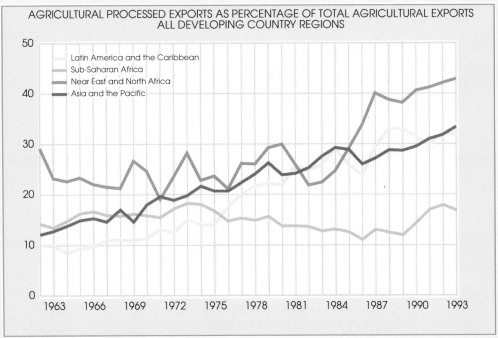

AGRICULTURAL PROCESSED EXPORTS AS PERCENTAGE OF TOTAL AGRICULTURAL EXPORTS
ALL DEVELOPING COUNTRY REGIONS

Latin America and the Caribbean
Sub-Saharan Africa
Near East and North Africa
Asia and the Pacific

Source: FAO

AGRICULTURAL TRADE: ENTERING A NEW ERA?

II. A changing world environment for agricultural trade

THE DEREGULATION OF THE WORLD ECONOMY

Trade being a relatively small part of the economic activity of most countries, the ways in which it is regulated and conducted are closely related to the policy orientations governing the overall economy. Thus, the major transformations that have taken place in many of the world's economies during the past decade, and especially since the late 1980s, are likely to have profound and permanent effects on trade policies and, indeed, on the way trade will be conducted.

The 1980s marked a move away from government intervention in developed, developing and centrally planned economies. Developed market economies began to reduce internal government intervention in a variety of ways and removed restrictions on capital flows and investment. More significant changes took place in the developing countries, which began to abandon their inward-looking trade and investment policies and embarked on major reforms. Developing economies reduced the government intervention that had caused exchange-rate overvaluation, reduced or removed capital controls and privatized state-owned enterprises. In the greatest shift of all, the political and economic system collapsed in the former USSR and in Central and Eastern Europe and these countries began adopting market-oriented principles of economic management. Starting in 1979 the People's Republic of China also began major internal reforms of its economic system. As a result, a large portion of the world economy, which had been under the control of state planning systems, moved towards a market system.

The developed countries had already removed many direct government controls over their economies in the years prior to the 1980s. They had been confident enough in their policy direction to sign the General Agreement on Tariffs and Trade (GATT) in 1947 and to adopt a set of common trade rules. Among other things, the GATT rules barred the use of quantitative import controls except in special circumstances, and this meant that tariffs became the only way of protecting non-agricultural products. GATT also prohibited the use of export subsidies in export competition for all but primary products. The original GATT, however, only covered trade in goods. Recognizing the difference in national policies related to agricultural markets, it set out exemptions for agriculture that were to persist for more than four decades. Export subsidies for agriculture were allowed, as was the use of quantitative import quotas, in recognition of the fact that many countries would keep internal markets for agricultural products isolated from world markets.

The developing countries began their major economic reforms in the 1980s. Although the form and pace of these reforms varied from country to country, they usually included the removal of controls and interventions on capital movements and exchange rates. In many cases, government-owned enterprises were sold to the private sector, thus ending the drain on public resources of supporting inefficient activities. Special measures were introduced to attract foreign investors, who had often been rebuffed in the past, and to encourage the repatriation of capital that had fled the country to avoid economic instability, uncertainty and government controls.

As internal reforms took hold, developing countries were in a position to reform and liberalize their foreign trade policies as well. Foreign exchange was made more freely convertible, import restrictions and tariffs were reduced and state trading entities dismantled. The various internal and trade reforms rendered national policies more compatible with GATT trade rules, and developing countries moved to join GATT and become active participants in the Uruguay Round of trade negotiations.

The shift in perceptions and policies also manifested itself with regard to intervention in international commodity markets (see Box 7).

A recent study concluded that, in contrast with earlier periods, the recent liberalization of trade was unidirectional and continual in most developing countries outside Africa. Liberalization was most rapid in Latin America and is beginning to accelerate in South Asia. East Asian countries varied in the speed of reform, but generally made continued progress towards neutrality and

BOX 7
INTERNATIONAL TRADE ORGANIZATIONS AND COMMODITY MARKETS

The first United Nations Conference on Trade and Development (UNCTAD) took place in 1964 to deal with the trade and development concerns of developing countries. The countries that led in the formation of UNCTAD had a different agenda from that of members of GATT. UNCTAD's activities centred on the development of a trading system for commodities that were of major concern to the developing countries through international commodity agreements. Commodity agreements were negotiated in the 1960s and 1970s for tin, rubber, coffee, cocoa, wheat and sugar. The interest in this type of agreement increased in the wake of the Organization of the Petroleum Exporting Countries' (OPEC) initial success in increasing and stabilizing oil prices through its producer cartel.

In the GATT Tokyo Round there was an attempt to extend the internal market interventions in agriculture, practised by many governments, into the international trade sphere. The EC proposed a series of international commodity agreements that would attempt to maintain minimum and maximum prices in world markets and allocate supplies to needy developing countries in the case of shortages. Agreements were proposed for grains, oilseeds, dairy products and meat.

It turned out that countries with markedly different internal systems and objectives were unwilling to adhere to an international system of commodity agreements. As a result of this, the Tokyo Round ended with modest agreement in agriculture and without effective international commodity agreements. The existing agreements in coffee and sugar were to collapse under the economic pressures of the 1980s.

In some ways the end of the Tokyo Round marked a turning point in the movement for government involvement in international markets. The world had already been forced off the fixed exchange rates of the Bretton Woods Agreement in 1973. Worldwide inflation, shortly followed by a widespread debt crisis and a collapse of international commodity prices in the 1980s, made many of the old interventions impossible and, in many cases, too expensive to maintain.

liberality. Only Africa has shown little progress in trade liberalization, with several countries actually reversing reform when confronted with renewed foreign exchange constraints and/or import competition.[3]

Changes in both developed and developing market economies were well under way before centrally planned economies began to make significant internal reforms. Centrally planned economic systems were generally linked to the political system and thus changes in political power were required before significant economic liberalization could occur. Incipient forms of internal reform had begun in these economies in the late 1970s and early 1980s. China had also begun some reforms in the late 1970s, including reform of the agricultural system and opening up to outside investors. By the late 1980s, the monopoly of the communist party over political power was broken in the former USSR and Central and Eastern Europe and the centrally planned economic system as it had been operated in these countries effectively ended. Economic reforms were initiated and have been pursued to varying degrees and with varying rates of progress. Generally these reforms have involved a reduction in government intervention in internal markets and more market-oriented trade policies.

In both developed and developing countries agricultural interventions were very firmly entrenched politically and this made them among the most difficult interventions to remove. The political influence of agricultural groups in the developed countries far exceeded their numbers in the electorate. These groups fought vigorously to protect government interventions that, in their view, increased their incomes and reduced competition from more efficient or more heavily subsidized producers. In many developing countries government interventions were heavily focused towards reducing the cost of basic foods to urban consumers, especially those consumers important to political stability. Moves towards agricultural reform came, as in the other parts of the economy, because the old system was not working well, was too expensive or because there were changes in political regimes.

[3] J.M. Dean, S. Desai and J. Riedel. 1994. *Trade policy reform in developing countries since 1985: a review of the evidence.* Study for the Development Policy Group. Washington, DC, World Bank.

THE TRANSFORMATION OF CENTRALLY PLANNED ECONOMIES

Although important, the economic reforms that took place in developed market economies and in developing countries were far less dramatic and profound than those that followed the collapse of the centrally planned economies and the political systems of Eastern and Central Europe and the former USSR.

Attempts at economic reform began in the 1970s and accelerated in the 1980s as economic conditions worsened. Then, in 1989, the political systems in Central and Eastern Europe and the former USSR began their sudden collapse, leading to the abandonment of the centrally planned system and a move towards a market-based economy. These interrelated political and economic events continue to have a significant effect on world agricultural markets and on world trading patterns.

A pricing system that kept consumer food prices well below world market levels and below the level that would balance supply with demand, combined with inefficient production and distribution systems, resulted in excess demand for food in many areas. Consequences of this excess demand were rationing, queuing and importing from outside the trading bloc. These imports were largely in the form of bulk commodities from Organisation for Economic Co-operation and Development (OECD) countries and had to be paid for in hard currency. (However, the former USSR also imported large quantities of sugar from Cuba on a barter arrangement for petroleum products.)

In all cases the collapse of the old economic and political system resulted in sharp initial declines in real per caput GDP (Table 18). This was accompanied by inflationary pressure as the central banks attempted to mitigate the economic decline or to prevent the collapse of state enterprises. Inflation ranged from serious to near hyperinflation, depending on the macroeconomic policies followed and the difficulties of adjusting to those policies. For the first time unemployment became a major issue in these countries, as inefficient industries disappeared or were restructured to function in a market economy while the unemployment and underemployment that had been disguised under the old system became impossible to hide. In most countries the retail prices of most products were freed, although in some cases the prices of certain basic food products, such as bread, are still subsidized or controlled.

The shift from a socialist to a capitalist economy and the consequent removal of most internal subsidies have resulted in shifts in relative prices and in food consumption patterns. The relative prices of meat, poultry and dairy products have risen and consumption of these products has declined sharply, as consumer incomes have fallen and unemployment has increased. These products are now readily available only for those who can afford them at the new unsubsidized prices.

Other factors are also likely to affect the demand for food. As public subsidies for items such as housing, transportation and other services are reduced or removed, some reallocation of personal spending is likely to occur, away from food and

TABLE 18

Indicators of economic and agricultural performance for selected countries in Central and Eastern Europe and the former USSR

18A

Real GDP

	1986	1987	1988	1989	1990	1991	1992	1993	1994
	(.. *percentage changes over preceding year* ....)								
Hungary	1.5	4.1	-0.1	0.7	-3.5	-9.9	-5.1	-2.0	...
Poland	4.2	2.0	4.1	0.2	-11.6	-7.6	2.6	3.8	...
Romania	2.3	0.8	-0.5	-4.3	-7.4	-15.1	-13.5	...	...
Former USSR	2.3	1.6.	4.4	2.5	-4.0	...	...	...	...
Russia	...	...	...	...	...	-13.0	-19.0	-12.0	...

18B

Open unemployment

	1986	1987	1988	1989	1990	1991	1992	1993	1994
	(................................ *percentage of economically active population* ....)								
Hungary	...	...	...	...	2	8	12	12	11
Poland	...	...	...	...	6	12	14	16	17
Romania	...	...	...	...	1	3	6	9	11
Russia	...	...	...	...	...	...	5	5	6

18C

Consumer prices

	1986	1987	1988	1989	1990	1991	1992	1993	1994
	(.. *percentage changes over preceding year* ....)								
Hungary	5.3	8.6	15.7	16.9	29.0	34.2	23.0	22.5	...
Poland	17.8	25.2	60.2	251.1	585.8	70.3	43.0	35.3	...
Romania	0.7	1.1	2.6	0.9	4.7	161.1	210.3	256.0	...
Former USSR	2.0	1.0	1.0	1.9	4.7	...	...	...	...
Russia	...	...	...	...	...	92.7	1 353.0	915.3	...

18D

Agricultural production

	1986	1987	1988	1989	1990	1991	1992	1993	1994
	(................................... *percentage changes over preceding year* ....)

Hungary	0.8	-0.7	6.1	-2.1	-5.7	6.6	-25.7	-7.3	6.4
Poland	5.7	-5.8	2.5	3.2	3.3	-5.9	-12.5	8.1	-16.4
Romania	-4.3	-9.4	5.9	-1.5	-10.3	0.8	-17.5	19.1	5.1
Area of former USSR	6.3	-0.1	-0.1	4.6	-0.3	-13.1	-7.7	-3.4	-20.6

Per caput food production

Hungary	1.2	-0.2	6.9	-1.5	-5.4	6.8	-25.6	-6.9	7.2
Poland	5.0	-6.2	2.4	3.5	2.9	-6.1	-12.6	8.1	-16.4
Romania	-4.4	-10.0	6.2	-1.3	-9.8	1.4	-17.5	19.7	5.0
Area of former USSR	6.1	-0.7	-1.1	4.5	-0.6	-14.2	-7.0	-3.8	-21.9

18E

Dietary energy supply

	1986	1987	1988	1989	1990	1991	1992	1993	1994
	(................................... *kilocalories per caput per day* ....)

Hungary	3 578	3 749	3 633	3 720	3 687	3 499	3 503	...	...
Poland	3 466	3 489	3 521	3 529	3 390	3 338	3 301	...	...
Romania	3 218	3 195	3 211	3 234	3 317	3 105	3 051	...	...
Former USSR	3 355	3 396	3 391	3 360	3 406	3 071	...	...	...

Sources: (for all Tables 18) FAO; IMF *World Economic Outlook*, October 1994; *Economic Survey of Europe*, several issues.

towards these other goods and services.

Thus, in the short to medium term, internal economic pressures will tend to reduce the demand for foodstuffs in the former Council for Mutual Economic Assistance (CMEA) countries and thus reduce the demand for imports. The time that will be required for income growth and food demand to reach levels comparable to those that prevailed prior to the reforms is difficult to predict. It will depend on a number of factors, generally related to the capacity of the countries concerned to maintain the political and social stability necessary to pursue and intensify consistent programmes of reform. The depth of the economic recession and related problems in several of these countries suggest that full recovery will be a much longer process than initially estimated. Whatever the extent and pace of such recovery, the levels and patterns of per caput food consumption are bound to be affected significantly and are not likely to return to those of the past.

This is so not only because of falling average incomes during the phases of transition, but also because different income distribution patterns are likely to emerge, with a wider gap between the higher and lower income groups.

While adjustments in demand have already been significant, and are likely to continue in the short to medium term, little progress has yet been achieved with regard to production and marketing systems, except for in some countries that are relatively advanced in the process of reform. Privatization has proved to be a difficult undertaking and will not solve *per se* many of the problems. In particular, in some cases public monopolies have simply become private monopolies. As the process takes hold, however, shifting to private ownership of the products in the marketing system should provide incentives for reducing waste and increasing quality. The appearance of imported consumer goods may also provide competition to internal processing and marketing activities.

The following section reviews various attempts at quantifying the foreseeable changes in supply and demand patterns in the transition economies, and the effects these changes are likely to have on trade.

THE YEARS TO COME

FAO projections to the year 2010 indicate that recovery from the sharp fall in agricultural output that took place in the initial years of the reform will be slow and that aggregate production growth between 1990 and 2010 may be only half that of the previous 20 years.[4] The sharp reduction in per caput consumption in the initial years of the reforms will probably be reversed, but future levels are unlikely to be above those of the prereform period. For example, the average annual per caput consumption (all uses) of cereals in these reforming countries is projected to be 660 kg compared with 780 kg in 1988/90 (in clean weight). This would be the result of slightly lower per caput food consumption of cereals and livestock products, little growth in livestock production, reductions in post-harvest losses, smaller quantities of cereals being used as seed and less cereal feed being used per unit of livestock output. In the case of meat, per caput consumption is expected to revert to near the prereform levels of about 70 kg, but with more poultry and less beef being consumed.

Overall, gross agricultural production growth is expected to decline, from an annual 1.2 percent during the period 1970 to 1990, to 0.4 percent yearly between 1988/90 and 2010. An even more pronounced decline is expected in domestic demand growth, from 1.4 percent to 0.2 percent during the same period.

---

[4] **FAO. 1995.** *World agriculture: towards 2010.* **Chichester, UK, FAO-John Wiley & Sons.**

Such differentials in domestic supply and demand expansion would result in significant shifts in the trade balances of the countries concerned.

In the case of cereals, from being large net importers in the past decades (their aggregate cereal net imports amounted to 40.3 million tonnes in 1979/81 and 36.4 million tonnes in 1988/90), these countries are expected to emerge as net exporters of 5 million tonnes in 2010.

Other estimates confirm the direction of changes in trade balances suggested in the FAO study, but some consider that the former centrally planned economies may emerge as far greater exporters by the year 2010. One noted analyst of the former USSR[5] estimated that consumption adjustments could reduce cereal use by as much as 35 million tonnes annually and that savings in post-harvest losses could amount to another 10 million tonnes annually or 5 percent of production. If feeding efficiency were to be increased by 15 percent (which represents about one-third of the gap between feeding efficiency in the former USSR and in Germany), 20 million tonnes would be saved annually. Meanwhile, improved seed and seed use could save another 10 million tonnes of cereals. Additional savings could be achieved by the use of improved pasture and hay to replace grain concentrates. While these estimated savings and improvements may not be additive they confirm that, even without the development of new varieties or animal breeds, the food deficit economies currently in transition are likely to become self-sufficient, if not net exporters, of a number of products.

Another recent study concluded that changes in the former USSR may have a significant impact on worldwide trade. Since livestock products were highly subsidized compared with grains, liberalization should raise the production of grain and reduce that of livestock (thereby reducing feedgrain demand). With demand for grain falling and producer prices and output rising, a surplus in grain seems inevitable. By the year 2000, the Russian Federation's net grain exports could amount to nearly one-fifth of those predicted for the United States.[6]

---

[5] D.G. Johnson. 1992. *World trade effects of the dismantling of socialized agriculture in the former Soviet Union.* Illinois, Chicago, University of Chicago, Office of Agricultural Economics Research.

[6] R. Tyers. 1994. *Economic reform in Europe and the former Soviet Union: implications for international food markets.* Research Report No. 99. Washington, DC, International Food Policy Research Institute.

THE COLLAPSE OF THE CMEA

At the very time when there is a perceptible trend towards the formation of new, or the expansion of existing, regional trading blocs, one of the oldest and tightest – the CMEA – has disintegrated. This bloc had been established by the former USSR to tie together the centrally planned economies of Central and Eastern Europe and of some other areas.

The foreign trade system organized by the former USSR was designed to complement the internal centrally planned and controlled economic systems of the other CMEA states. Trade was conducted by state entities and payments took place in nonconvertible roubles, with CMEA serving as a clearing-house system. CMEA was organized with some concepts of specialization in mind and with a view to maximizing self-sufficiency within the bloc. In general, the former USSR exported heavy manufactured goods, as well as oil, gas and other natural resources, to the countries of Central and Eastern Europe, which in turn exported consumer goods, including foodstuffs, to the former USSR. Exchanges took place at prices set by the state trading agencies rather than at world market prices.

The strength of this trading bloc can be seen by the fact that in 1988 all Eastern European countries except Hungary destined 70 percent or more of their total exports to other centrally planned economies, more than two-thirds going to CMEA countries. All except Hungary also received more than two-thirds of their imports from centrally planned economies, almost entirely from CMEA countries. Even Hungary sent half of its exports to CMEA countries and received 49 percent of its imports from them.

The pattern was similar for most agricultural exports and imports, which were also primarily effected among CMEA countries. Poland was an exception, because its agricultural trade, in contrast to its non-agricultural trade, was heavily oriented towards Western Europe and the United States.

Some countries, such as Hungary and Poland, had attempted to shift trade towards non-CMEA countries even before the demise of central planning. As the centrally planned economies broke down, the CMEA ceased to function and trade between the countries collapsed. What remains of it now is effected in convertible currencies and at world prices.

The effect of these changes on trade is already apparent. The members of the former bloc have changed from being major importers of cereals and oilseeds to being self-sufficient, or close to it, at lower consumption levels. Moreover, countries that were exporters of foodstuffs to the former USSR have now lost this market and are looking for other outlets.

Thus, one of the major events shaping agricultural trade over the period ahead will be the entry of over 350 million consumers and a massive amount of agricultural resources (which have, until now, largely been used inefficiently) into the market-oriented world trading system. This is occurring at a time when major institutional changes are being introduced throughout the system itself.

The problems of transition to market-oriented trading systems have been exacerbated by difficulties of market access. Despite major efforts to gain market share for their products, the transition economies have often been unable to surmount protectionist barriers, especially in the developed market economies and in particular for agricultural products. To make matters worse the transition economies have faced competition from subsidized agricultural products both in their own domestic and in third-country markets.

THE CASE OF CHINA

Some of the most momentous and far-reaching economic reforms have been, and are still, occurring in the People's Republic of China (Table 19). China is unique in several ways. It is the largest remaining centrally planned economy; its population, 1.22 billion people, represents one-quarter of the world's total; its booming economy is rapidly moving towards a market-driven system; and it is heavily involved in world trade, striving to join the world trade system, including the new World Trade Organization (WTO).

Underlying the economic reforms in China is a desire to maintain strong growth, allowing the country to turn itself from a poor developing economy dominated by subsistence-level peasant agriculture into a modern industrial economy. Prior to 1978 China was a traditional centrally planned economy. Agricultural activities were organized under the Rural People's Communes, which implemented government directives and managed small-scale enterprises and shops.

Stagnating levels of agricultural production and rising food-grain imports in the 1970s led to the initiation of agricultural reforms, which were essentially to move the food and agricultural sector of the Chinese economy towards a market system.[7] The reforms contributed to a significant increase in agricultural output which enabled China to turn

[7] An extensive review of the reforms is provided in *The State of Food and Agriculture 1994*. Rome, FAO.

TABLE 19

China: selected indicators of economic and agricultural performance

	1986	1987	1988	1989	1990	1991	1992	1993	1994
	(... percentage changes over previous year ....)								
GDP	8.3	11.0	10.8	4.3	3.9	8.0	13.2	13.4	11.8
Agricultural GDP	3.4	5.8	3.9	3.1	7.4	2.4	4.1	4.0	3.5
Inflation rate	7.0	8.8	20.7	16.3	1.3	3.0	5.3	13.0	21.7
Merchandise exports	2.6	34.9	18.2	5.3	19.2	14.4	18.1	8.8	30.5
Merchandise imports	-8.7	4.3	27.4	5.3	-13.3	18.5	28.3	34.1	10.5
Agricultural production	2.3	5.2	2.9	2.5	8.1	5.0	3.9	5.1	3.6
Per caput food production	2.7	2.3	1.0	1.5	6.8	2.7	3.5	5.1	3.5
	(... billion US$ ....)								
Agricultural exports	7 864	9 082	10 326	10 479	10 204	11 620	12 045	12 198	...
Agricultural imports	5 467	7 561	9 763	11 067	9 794	9 429	9 800	8 569	...
	(............................... kilocalories per caput per day ....)								
Dietary energy supply	2 587	2 597	2 567	2 597	2 654	2 679	2 705	...	...

Source: FAO and Asian Development Bank.

from being a net importer of food and agricultural products to being a net exporter.

At about the same time as the agricultural policy reforms were initiated, China began to open up its non-agricultural economy. It embarked on an export-led growth strategy, different from that of any other centrally planned economy, which led to a dramatic change in China's role in the international economy.

Thus, while China's total merchandise trade in 1977 represented only 1.4 percent of world trade, its share in 1993 had increased to 4.8 percent. From being only the world's 15th-largest exporting country in 1977 it became the sixth-largest in 1993. Over the same period, the country's share in world agricultural imports remained at 2.3 to 2.4 percent, while its share in world agricultural exports rose from 1.7 percent to 3.7 percent.

By the early 1990s China had become a substantial beneficiary of foreign aid, a large borrower on international capital markets and a major recipient of foreign direct investment. In 1993 net foreign direct investments reached almost US$26 billion. China has also taken substantial steps towards the convertibility of its currency.

Economic performances have been spectacular since the beginning of the reforms in 1978. The average annual real rate of GDP growth for the period 1979 to 1993 was more than 9 percent, leading to real GDP multiplying by more than 3.5 times between 1978 and 1993.

Although this outstanding rate of growth brought about significant improvements in the economic well-being of the population, a number of problems emerged. Inflation, for example, has been fueled by loose monetary policy combined with high levels of foreign investment. In addition, the dramatic growth has not been equally shared throughout the country and increasing disparities in income have emerged between the central/western and the eastern regions and between rural and urban areas. While the sweeping changes in agricultural policy contributed to a marked reduction in the absolute poverty level during the first half of the 1980s, the subsequent slowdown in agricultural growth caused the incidence of rural poverty to remain unchanged during the second half of the decade.[8]

The improvement in living standards and consumption patterns was brought about by booming growth in high-growth areas. The differences between urban and rural income levels are reflected in their different food consumption patterns. Over the past five years rural areas have remained dependent on high per caput consumption of cereals, whereas in urban areas cereal consumption was only half as high as in rural areas and has tended to decline. Conversely, urban consumers have had much higher per caput consumption of red meat, poultry, eggs and fishery products, and their consumption of these products has also grown faster than it has among rural consumers.

The Chinese experience raises a number of questions for the years to come. First, can China continue its extraordinary economic growth for a sustained period and can it do so without generating excessive inflation? Second, can the positive income and employment effects of high growth be extended to more of the population without further massive rural migration into the already overcrowded cities? Third, can the problems of Chinese agriculture be overcome so that it can continue to satisfy a major portion of the country's food demand as the population grows larger and richer?

Many observers, both within and outside China, are concerned about the impact that the huge population of China will have on both agricultural production and demand for imported cereals and other agricultural commodities. On the production side causes of concern are the rapid loss of cropland in areas of accelerated industrial growth; the serious competition for limited supplies of groundwater in the areas surrounding major cities; cropland erosion and contamination; and the exhaustion of

---

[8] *The State of Food and Agriculture 1994.* Rome, FAO.

the improved production technology that helped enable such remarkable progress in the 1980s. Per caput cereal production increased by 23 percent between 1978 and 1984, but the 1984 level has not been exceeded in the last decade except very marginally in 1990.

It has been suggested that Chinese demand for imported cereals might become so large in the early part of the coming century that it will constitute a threat to the stability of world prices and supplies available to other importers. A more realistic scenario is that China will become an increasingly active trader in world agricultural markets, producing some agricultural products for export and importing others. If China is able to maintain its export-driven growth at anywhere near its present relatively high rate it will have a major impact on international markets. In any event there is little doubt that China will have an important role in world agricultural trade in the next century.

AGRICULTURAL TRADE: ENTERING A NEW ERA?

III. The evolution of international trade rules

At the end of the Second World War economic policy-makers in the leading countries were searching for institutional instruments that would avoid the chaos and economic and trade warfare that had marked the 1930s. They believed that an institution was needed to help countries maintain international monetary stability and to avoid the competitive devaluations that had marked the Great Depression of the 1920s and 1930s. The International Monetary Fund (IMF) was developed for this purpose. The economic policy-makers also recognized the need for an institution to provide capital for the reconstruction and development of national economies. The International Bank for Reconstruction and Development (IBRD), commonly known as the World Bank, was created to this end.

The third part of this set of international economic institutions was to be the International Trade Organization (ITO). It was assumed that a repetition of the protectionist spiral of the 1930s could be avoided by developing a set of international trade rules to which all countries would subscribe.

The negotiations for the proposed international trade organization included an interim GATT that was to be enforced by ITO. This set of trade rules was based on two fundamental principles: reciprocity and non-discrimination. Reciprocity was enacted by agreements whereby one country granted tariff concessions to a trading partner in exchange for similar concessions from the partner. The non-discrimination principle, embodied in the "most favoured nation" (MFN) clause, states that any concession granted to one contracting party is to be automatically extended to all contracting parties.

GATT also included rules to limit protection of domestic industries from the competition of imported goods, rules to regulate competition in international markets, rules on the tariff levels that countries could apply to imported goods and rules for the settlement of disputes between countries over trade practices. These rules, along with the tariff concessions, have been revised several times in subsequent multilateral trade negotiations.

The proposed ITO never came into being, as the United States' senate did not ratify it. In spite of the international agreements on tariffs and trade rules, this left GATT without an institutional framework within which to operate. One of the major disadvantages of this was the lack of formal procedures for amending the basic rules to take new issues and problems into account. However, ambiguity had advantages as well as disadvantages, and the lack of a formal institutional framework allowed the flexibility to consider new approaches and address new issues – a flexibility that is often lacking in multilateral organizations.

Because of the difficulty of amending the basic GATT articles, a number of new agreements were developed that did not have the universal coverage of the basic articles. Indeed, in the Tokyo Round of negotiations in the 1970s new sets of rules were developed in several areas. These additional sets of rules were termed "codes", their acceptance was voluntary and not all contracting parties became signatories. In addition, some of these codes had their own special dispute settlement processes and countries could choose to their own advantage between these processes and the more universal ones of GATT. This complicated system of agreements and procedures was sometimes called "GATT *à la carte*".

By the early 1980s it had become clear that there were other major problems with the GATT system as it then existed. First, the rules covered a decreasing share of international exchanges as they only covered trade in goods, which had grown less rapidly than trade in services. Second, even within trade in goods there were major sectors that were effectively outside the normal rules, in particular agriculture and textiles. In the case of agriculture the exclusions went back to the beginning of GATT. For textiles, the worldwide Multi-Fibre Agreement was not envisaged in the original agreement, but had grown up as a substitute for the web of protectionist controls placed on textile imports by developed countries.

GATT was begun by some 23 countries only. With a few exceptions, centrally planned economies chose not to join the agreement, and China, which had been a founding member, withdrew. The former USSR did not join and built its own trading system with the centrally planned economies of Eastern and Central Europe, the Council for Mutual Economic Assistance (CMEA or sometimes COMECON).

A large number of developing countries also chose to stay out of GATT. In many cases this was because joining would have required the country to remove some of its internal and external controls over trade and investment.

By the mid-1980s the widespread domestic policy reforms and the accompanying trade liberalization undertaken by developing countries had enabled many of them to become members of GATT. The political and economic changes in the former centrally planned economies also induced them to apply for membership if they were not already members and those who were became more active participants. China's application for readmission to GATT, which would allow it to become a charter member of the new World Trade Organization, is likely to have a major and lasting effect on international trade.

THE URUGUAY ROUND

The Uruguay Round, completed in December 1993 after eight years of multilateral trade negotiations, is especially important for the future of trade. The agreement was approved by the 115 countries that were members of GATT in April 1994; most of these are developing countries. Never before had there been such large-scale participation of developing countries in a multilateral trade negotiation. Ratifying countries agree to abide by a common set of trade rules, although there are special exceptions for developing countries in terms of the timing and types of policy adjustment required.

The agreement sets up a new World Trade Organization (WTO) that supersedes GATT. The new organization will have responsibility for the rules relating to traditional trade in goods, services and trade-related intellectual property matters.

The establishment of WTO represents an ingenious way of overcoming the problems that had developed with GATT. Indeed, as a country ratifies the Uruguay Round agreement, thus joining the WTO, it will be accepting the entire package of agreements. One of these is the recognition of WTO and of its functions as the custodian of the agreements. New members of WTO will also be accepting the old GATT rules, as modified by the Uruguay Round negotiations, as well as the new rules concerning trade in services and trade-related intellectual property matters. At the same time, they accept a unified dispute settlement process that will apply to all agreements and, finally, they will agree to a trade policy review mechanism.

A major feature of WTO will be a new dispute settlement mechanism that, like the GATT dispute settlement process, will still attempt to obtain a negotiated resolution to trade disputes. However, the formal dispute settlement procedures have been changed to produce quicker and more certain outcomes in case of failure to reach a negotiated solution. The procedures have been speeded up by setting deadlines for each step. The outcome has been made more certain by removing the possibility for a country to block the consideration and approval of a panel decision that finds its trade policy inconsistent with its international obligations. It has been all too common in recent years for countries to block decisions adverse to their own policies by refusing to allow the consensus needed to approve a panel report. Now a panel report will be automatically approved unless there is a consensus to reject it. To block approval of a panel report under the new system will thus require the agreement of the complaining party. However, a new provision allows for appeal to a special panel of experts to review findings that one of the parties believes to be seriously flawed.

The new dispute settlement procedures should be of special significance to smaller countries and developing countries that have been disadvantaged under the old dispute settlement rules. Large countries or trading blocs have tended to use the consensus requirement to block adverse rulings and, because of their size and economic power, they have been insulated from unilateral retaliation from smaller countries outside GATT rules. At the same time, if smaller countries attempted the same blocking tactics they were often threatened with unilateral retaliation.

THE AGRICULTURAL AGREEMENT

The agricultural portion of the original GATT was drafted initially to be consistent with the agricultural policies of the major founders of GATT, especially the United States. At that time the United States' policy involved the maintaining of prices for domestic agricultural products at levels above the world market price. Production controls were operated on several of the supported commodities and import quotas were imposed to prevent the entry of lower-priced foreign products. This system led to the special exemption of agricultural products in Article XI of GATT, which allowed the use of import quotas for agricultural products that were subject to domestic production controls. This loophole was enlarged in 1955 when the United States threatened to withdraw from GATT unless it was granted a special waiver to Article XI that would allow it to apply import quotas whenever imports threatened to interfere with domestic price supports, regardless of whether production controls were being used. This was the famous Section 22 waiver, granted temporarily in 1955 and still in effect for several products in early 1995.

In addition, a host of other non-tariff barriers emerged in agricultural trade. These included the use of variable levies, minimum import prices and voluntary export restraints. Many countries applied quantitative import quotas, which were allowed under the balance-of-payment provisions of GATT only when there was a balance-of-payment problem, and left them in place long after the balance-of-payment problem had disappeared.

In the previous rounds of multilateral trade negotiations there had never been an attempt to revise the trade rules for agriculture, although there had been various attempts to develop international commodity agreements. In the Kennedy Round of the 1960s and the Tokyo Round of the 1970s, there were attempts to bring commodity agreements into the GATT framework and thus to extend government controls from domestic markets to the international sphere.

Strong export competition in the 1980s set the stage for the agricultural reforms of the Uruguay Round. The expanding markets and commodity boom of the 1970s was quickly replaced by a collapse of the growth in demand in developing countries and in centrally planned economies beset by debt and other economic crises. Production stimulated by high farm prices and high levels of subsidies continued to increase as markets contracted. As a result, in the mid-1980s the international prices of agricultural commodities fell to the lowest real levels in 50 years. Subsidy costs escalated in those countries that were attempting to support farm incomes. Incomes and export earnings of producers without subsidies and protection fell sharply.

Many countries became convinced that the major causes of falling incomes and escalating subsidy costs were the policies being followed by many of the OECD countries. Moreover, whereas it had been possible to reduce many of the existing government interventions in markets outside agriculture through domestic policy reforms, removal of the major interventions in the agricultural system could only be accomplished through international agreements to remove trade-distorting policies in agriculture. The risks of unilateral removal of intervention in agriculture by a single country were likened to those of unilateral disarmament. It was also pointed out that the agricultural protection programmes in one country were largely intended to offset the adverse effects of the subsidy programmes of other countries.

The rising tide of trade disputes in agriculture in the 1980s led to political pressure for major agricultural reforms in the Uruguay Round. Indeed, the Round started with agricultural reform high on the agendas of many participants, including a significant group that stated they would not complete the negotiations without a satisfactory agreement to reduce trade distortions in agriculture.

One element that created major political pressure for reform was a group of exporters, the Cairns Group, named after the city in Australia where they first met. The group, which included both developed and developing countries, threatened to block agreement on a number of issues of importance to other countries and thus exerted pressure to keep the agricultural reforms as part of the negotiations.

The negotiations turned out to be a contest between the advocates of fundamental reform and those of trade liberalization, with some countries, including the Cairns Group, hoping to get both (see Box 8). Advocates of reform were striving to get the GATT rules revised to remove the special exceptions for agriculture that accommodated the domestic farm policies of the major trading powers. Indeed, the reformers wanted GATT rules for agriculture to go further than rules for non-agricultural industries by barring trade-distorting domestic subsidies as well as special border protection and export subsidies.

The advocates of trade liberalization took a different approach. They argued that countries should have a right to pursue national agricultural policies that suited their own particular agricultural conditions, but that these policies should be gradually modified to limit or reduce their adverse impacts on trade. Advocates of trade liberalization were willing to negotiate increased import quotas for products under quotas, to limit or moderate the levels of internal support, to use production controls to limit surplus output and to apply market-sharing agreements in lieu of competition in export markets. They did not want international rules to limit either the domestic or the international trade policies they could follow in agriculture. The advocates of liberalization generally argued that gradual and moderate liberalization would be enough to restore balance to international markets, whereas the advocates of reform almost always pushed for substantial liberalization in addition to reform.

BOX 8

TRADE REFORM AND TRADE LIBERALIZATION

Trade reform starts with the goal of changing the rules, in this case the GATT rules that set out the acceptable policies countries can use to protect borders, support domestic industries or compete in export markets. Advocates of trade reform believe that comparability and transparency can best be achieved if everyone follows the same rules for policies that have a major impact on trade. The framers of GATT took this approach for industries outside agriculture. Some GATT rules also dealt with situations where a country could deviate from the general rules, such as when a country had balance-of-payment problems.

Trade liberalization is concerned largely with reducing levels of protection. It is measured by the extent to which the barriers maintain internal prices above world prices, changes in world prices are transmitted to internal markets and future levels of protection are predictable. Thus, liberalization can be achieved by enlarging quotas, lowering tariffs or reducing other non-tariff barriers. In the original GATT rules for agriculture, countries were allowed to use quantitative import quotas to protect high internal price levels as long as domestic production controls were in effect to

prevent domestic production from displacing imports. Countries using quotas were supposed to maintain the balance between domestic production and imports existing before the quantitative import quotas were imposed. In a similar vein, export subsidies were not to be used to gain more than an equitable share of the world market. Thus these rules were intended to maintain liberal trade regimes. In practice they were so poorly defined that they proved unenforceable.

IMPORT PROTECTION

In the end there were more reforms than liberalization in the Uruguay Round. The major reform was of the rules limiting the policies that can be used to provide border protection. There were five elements of the negotiations on import protection. One was the conversion of all import barriers to tariffs: a process known as tariffication. This became effective immediately. The second element was the reduction of existing tariffs and of those resulting from tariffication over an implementation period. The third was the immediate binding of all tariffs on agricultural products (see Box 9). The fourth element was the introduction of a special safeguard provision for agricultural products that was different from the general safeguard rules in GATT. The fifth was the provision of special access arrangements to allow minimum market access.

The new rules required that all quotas, variable levies and other import barriers be converted to common tariffs, as soon as the agreement took effect. These and existing tariffs had then to be reduced by a minimum of 15 percent each over the implementation period with the tariff reductions as a whole having to average 36 percent. Developing countries were required to reduce tariffs by 24 percent and were allowed ten years, instead of six, to implement the cuts. All tariffs were to be bound. Developing countries were also given the option, which many chose, of declaring bound tariffs to replace tariffs that had been unbound. These newly bound tariffs declared by developing countries were not required to be cut.

The tariffication of non-tariff barriers and the prohibition against future use of such non-tariff instruments represents a major reform of the trade rules affecting agriculture. It should bring transparency to barriers that have been hidden from public view and should also expose the high levels of protection enjoyed by agricultural producers in some countries. The question is, did the reform lead to any trade liberalization or do nothing to reduce the levels of protection? Alternatively, in the longer term will the reforms achieved lead to more liberalization than is now apparent.

The years 1986 to 1988 were chosen as the base years for tariffication. However, during that period world prices for many agricultural commodities were the lowest they had been in decades, implying an unusually wide gap between world prices and supported internal prices.[9] Because of the unusual situation in the base period, it became clear that the new tariffs would provide high levels of protection in normal times. In addition, many countries used what was called "dirty tariffication" in that the numbers they used to calculate their tariff equivalents resulted in higher tariffs than more objective

---

[9] **This gap is measured by the tariff equivalent, i.e. the level of tariff that would be required to provide the domestic industry with the same level of protection as is provided by the non-tariff border measure. The measurement is usually made in terms of price wedges, i.e. the difference between the world price at the point of import and the internal price of the same product.**

BOX 9
TARIFF BINDING

Under GATT rules tariffs may be "bound" or "unbound". Tariff binding means that, if tariffs are increased above the bound level, trading partners may have to be compensated. Unbound tariffs can be increased to any level. The applied rate is the tariff rate that a country actually applies to products entering the country at any given time. The applied rate may be below the bound rate since it reflects the current policy regarding protection. Applied rates often change with world market conditions. In theory the binding of any given tariff rate which was previously unbound represents trade liberalization because it prevents increases to higher levels of tariff. However, when the rates are bound at very high levels tariff binding does not represent significant liberalization.

calculations might have produced.

A recent study[10] showed that, for many products in many countries, the tariff equivalents tabled were significantly higher than the tariff equivalents calculated by OECD and the United States Department of Agriculture (USDA) for the same period. In other words, the reform process often resulted in levels of protection (at least potentially) above even the high levels that had been in effect in the mid-1980s. Even after the agreed-upon tariff cuts have been applied over the implementation period, the final bound tariffs will in many cases provide higher levels of protection than did the old system.

An examination of the tariff reductions across countries indicates a common pattern. Countries reduced tariffs on the least sensitive products

---

[10] D. Hathaway and M. Ingco. 1995. *Agricultural liberalization and the Uruguay Round.* Presented at The Uruguay Round and the Developing Economies, A World Bank Conference, 26-27 January 1995.

by a larger amount than they did on more protected products. Thus, very large percentage cuts were made in very low tariffs and minimum percentage cuts were made in high tariffs in order to achieve the agreed-upon average. As a result, the trade-weighted average levels of protection were not lowered as much as the simple averages indicated and the disparity in protection between commodities probably increased.

In addition, for products subject to tariffication, a special safeguard was agreed to operate for the duration of the reform process. The safeguard allows an additional duty to be levied if a country experiences an increase in the quantity of imports that is higher than a specified trigger level or if the import price in the domestic currency falls below a specified trigger price. The formulas for invoking the special safeguard are extremely complicated and it is difficult to judge in advance how much it may be used. The price trigger is very hard to predict since it is dependent on exchange rates.

Many of the developing countries did not apply tariffication, even on products previously subject to non-tariff barriers. Instead, they took advantage of a provision that allowed them merely to declare a new bound tariff where an unbound tariff had existed. Many of these newly declared bound tariffs provided levels of protection well above the levels that had existed during the base period.[11]

It was recognized that many of the tariffs resulting from the tariffication

process would be high enough effectively to block imports. In order to ensure minimum market access and to protect current access levels, countries that converted from non-tariff barriers to tariffs were required to provide a tariff quota amounting to actual imports during the base period or to 3 percent of consumption during that period, whichever was higher. The tariff for this quota quantity was to be low enough not to impede trade. The minimum quantity allowed under this lower tariff had then to be increased to 5 percent of domestic consumption over the implementation period.

There are, however, several problematic aspects of the minimum access agreements as presented in the country schedules. First, countries were allowed to aggregate individual tariff lines into product groups. Thus, as imports of products that exceeded the minimum access levels were grouped with similar products that fell short, in most countries and for most products the actual minimum access turned out to be no more than the current access. Despite an agreement that the minimum access quotas were to be provided on a non-discriminatory basis, countries were allowed to count existing special arrangements as part of their minimum access commitments and to allocate their minimum access to exporters that already had special arrangements with the importing country. For instance the EC counted its sugar imports under the Lomé Convention as meeting its minimum access requirements and the United States did the same for both its meat and its sugar import commitments.

The minimum access commitments will provide relatively little additional

---

[11] See Hathaway and Ingco, op. cit., footnote 10.

BOX 10
TARIFF QUOTAS

A tariff quota is an instrument that sets up a two-tier tariff designed to allow the import of a specified quantity of a product at a lower tariff. It is often used where the regular tariff is so high as virtually to prohibit trade except under extraordinary circumstances. The introduction of tariff quotas into markets where internal prices are well above world prices creates quota rents for exporters who get the right to share in the protected market or for importers who get special rights to import into the protected market. In many cases the quotas under the tariff quota system are allocated on the basis of special agreements or past participation in import quota regimes. This is the case for most United States and EC tariff quotas established as a result of the Uruguay Round. In some cases bilateral negotiations resulted in special tariff quotas on specific products of interest to the parties concerned which were above and beyond the minimum access agreement.

access and even less additional trade. Access is allowed but not guaranteed, for example, minimum access for maize into net exporting countries such as Thailand and Hungary or for wheat into Canada seem unlikely to produce more trade. There are a few notable exceptions to this generalization, however, such as the minimum access commitments for rice in the Republic of Korea and Japan, which will create a new market for exports of nearly a million tonnes annually by the turn of the century.

When the minimum access commitments for importing countries are examined critically, the prospects of expanding beyond current import levels appear very limited. The probable trade expansion is greatest for rice, but even there it is less than 10 percent of current trade levels.

There is no question that the agreement to move to a system of tariff-only border protection for agricultural trade represents a major reform of world trade policy for agriculture. For the first time the rules regarding border protection for agricultural trade have been brought partially into line with the rules for trade in other goods, and in the long term this is likely to have a substantial impact on national agricultural policies. However, agricultural trade seems likely to remain encumbered by a complex set of tariff quota systems until future negotiations result in substantial cuts in over-quota tariffs.

To achieve this reform of import protection policies, however, advocates of trade reform had to agree to limited import liberalization. In the absence of specific guidelines for the conversion of non-tariff barriers to tariff equivalents, the initial declared tariffs and the final bound tariffs are often very high. As a result, the rate of effective protection has not been reduced for many products in many countries.

EXPORT COMPETITION

The original framers of GATT expected that many countries would maintain internal prices for farm products above world levels, so they assumed that export subsidies would be required for these countries to compete in world markets. Thus, while export subsidies were forbidden for non-agricultural products, they had been allowed for primary products since the beginning of GATT. The only restraint on such exports was the requirement that a country should not use them to achieve more than an "equitable share" of the world market for the product in question. In other words, the allowable limit was to be defined by results, not by actions.

Over the years a number of complaints filed with GATT had established that the equitable share concept had limited or no operational content and thus provided no real restraint on the use of export subsidies. In the Tokyo Round an effort was made to refine the concept and to make it operational by imposing additional requirements, namely that export subsidies should not appreciably undercut prices. This effort achieved only negligible results.

Export subsidies for agricultural products, permitted in the original GATT rules, were used by a number of countries in the 1950s and 1960s. The United States, Canada and some other countries applied them for a limited number of products during that period. Major problems arose, however, with the increased scale of their use in the 1980s when the overall growth in world trade of cereals and other agricultural products slowed down substantially. The slowdown was the result of several factors (also discussed in Section I, p. 1). First, output improved in many developing countries, allowing them to meet growing demand from internal sources. Second, many developing countries faced a severe economic crisis in the 1980s that resulted in a slowdown in the growth of demand for imported cereals and other products. Third, the mounting economic difficulties of the former USSR and Central and Eastern European countries brought their import increases to a halt. Moreover, the EC moved from being an importer to being a real exporter of a number of agricultural commodities in the early 1980s.

By the mid-1980s, the United States found itself with a declining share of a stagnant world grain market (for which they blamed the EC export restitution programme) and, starting in 1985, once again resorted to export subsidies in an attempt to recapture that market share. This began an escalation in the use of export subsidies that was only ended by the Uruguay Round agreement.

In the mid-1980s, the combination of stagnant markets and widespread export subsidies drove world cereal prices to extremely depressed levels. This created great distress among producers in exporting countries where production and exports were not subsidized.

On the other hand, the cereal-importing countries, both developed and developing, were major beneficiaries of the low world prices that resulted from domestic support and export subsidies, primarily in the OECD countries. In particular, the former USSR gained from these subsidies, as did a number of countries in Africa and the Near East. However, farmers in these countries lost out as a result of the lower internal prices that were caused by subsidized imports.

A number of countries wanted an agreement in the Uruguay Round that would completely phase out the use of export subsidies for agricultural products. This, however, proved to be politically impossible as it would have required exporting countries either to let their internal prices for agricultural products fall to world market levels or to forego exports. The compromise position, reached after very difficult negotiations, contains some reform and some liberalization.

The final agreement does not require the elimination of export subsidies as it does for the use of non-tariff barriers. Instead it requires that over a six-year period developed countries reduce their spending on export subsidies by 36 percent and the volume of their subsidized exports by 21 percent from average 1986 to 1990 levels. Developing countries are required to make reductions of 24 and 14 percent respectively over ten years. The measurement and the reductions are on a commodity-by-commodity basis and are spelled out in schedules filed with the WTO by each country. Countries not using export subsidies during the base period (1986 to 1990) are prohibited from using them at all. Countries that used them during the base period are required to spell out the reduced limits on their use in future years and are prohibited from using them on products where they were not applied during the base period. The definitions of export subsidies in the agreement are fairly rigorous.

The liberalization resulting from

reductions in subsidized exports will, however, be delayed by an agreement that was reached in the closing days of the negotiations. According to the original draft agreement, the starting point for the reductions should have been the level of export subsidies in the base period 1986 to 1990 and the reductions should be made in equal amounts from that base level over a six-year period. However, the volume and spending on export subsidies for several products in 1992 were, for both the EC and the United States, well above their 1986-90 levels. This meant that an abrupt move to reduce the volume of subsidized exports to 3.5 percent (21 percent divided by six) below the 1986-90 levels would have created serious adjustment problems. Thus, the final agreement imposed the reduction of export subsidies from 1991-92 levels or from 1986-90 levels (whichever was higher) to the final target levels in equal instalments. The practical result has been to allow the United States and the EC to export additional wheat, dairy products, vegetable oil and rice using export subsidies over the next six years.

The impact of reductions in the volume of subsidized exports and of spending on export subsidies will vary depending on the quantity of product affected, the size of the subsidized amounts relative to total trade, the level of world commodity prices and the policy changes that have to be made by countries to accommodate the limits on subsidized exports. The size of the price gap between internal and external prices will determine the extent to which the expenditure controls constrain subsidized exports. For instance, in the EC spending constraints are unlikely to be binding for products that were affected by the recent reform of the Common Agricultural Policy, which lowered internal prices thus reducing the price gap. Instead, the binding constraint on EC exports of cereals will be the volume constraint requiring a 21 percent reduction in volumes of subsidized exports relative to the base period. If the EC were to allow its internal prices for agricultural products to fall to world levels, export subsidies would not be needed and the volume of products exported by the EC would depend entirely on domestic supply and demand conditions. However, while the EC's internal prices remain above world levels, constraints on the volume of subsidized exports may induce reductions in output or increases in stocks.

In the case of the United States the constraint on wheat export subsidies appears likely to be the spending constraints, since there is a significant difference between the world price level and the United States' internal price. However, if the United States allows the internal price to decline to the world level, export subsidies will not be needed so limits on export subsidies would not affect United States exports.

At this point it is impossible to predict how export subsidy limits will affect export volumes from individual countries or how great the impact of the changes will be on the prices of the commodities concerned. Considering the proportion of subsidized exports relative to total trade in the product, one could expect a marked improvement for wheat and wheat-flour (where the United States and EC subsidies have been used for half of the world trade), beef and veal (where subsidies have allowed the EC to become the world's largest exporter), pork, chicken-meat and processed dairy products. The international markets for coarse grains, oilseeds, vegetable oil and rice have been less affected by export subsidies and are thus expected to change little on account of the export subsidy limitations.

Relatively few countries account for most of the subsidized exports. The top five users of export subsidies for wheat accounted for 95 percent of subsidized wheat exports and subsidized over 50 million tonnes of wheat exports per year in the period 1986 to 1990. Even when all of the cutbacks are in place these five exporters will still be able to channel about 40 million tonnes of subsidized wheat into world markets, i.e. about 40 percent of current world trade in wheat. The equivalent figure for pigmeat is 53 percent, for coarse grains 22 percent, for poultry 25 percent and for beef and veal 34 percent.

While the export subsidy arrangement is not a tidy one and will be difficult to monitor, it is far more precise than the old GATT rules, under which the permissible limits to the use of export subsidies were very loosely defined. Moreover, the future trade expansion will occur without the distortions of direct export subsidies. This means that future market growth should increasingly benefit low-cost producers, including those in countries that cannot afford to subsidize their agricultural exports.

However, the export subsidy arrangement can enable only partial trade liberalization, as subsidies are rolled back by small amounts and large quantities of subsidized exports can still enter world markets. The separate treatment of agriculture in the GATT rules continues and the use of export subsidies now is explicitly approved as a trade policy.

DOMESTIC POLICIES

At the beginning of the Uruguay Round there was widespread recognition that to remove trade distortions in the world agricultural markets it was necessary to phase out the domestic policies at the basis of such distortions.

For a substantial period of the negotiations there was agreement on a balanced approach that would have reduced trade-distorting domestic policies by amounts commensurate with the reduction in import protection and export subsidies. As the negotiations progressed, however, a number of the developed countries with the highest level of trade-distorting domestic programmes began to back away from the idea of uniform commodity-by-commodity cuts in domestic policies, import protection and export subsidies.

At the end, the effective international controls over trade-distorting domestic policies were limited, as it was agreed that there would be no commodity-by-commodity roll-back of domestic support levels. Thus, the agreement requires that only the aggregate level of support provided via trade-distorting policies be reduced by 20 percent, while no individual commodity policy comes under control. The list of non-trade-distorting policies defined in the agreement would encompass the deficiency payments received by United States producers and the compensation payments received by producers in the EC under the reformed Common Agricultural Policy.

Several exempt policies are significant to developing countries. These include certain input and investment subsidies to agriculture, as well as stocks held for food security purposes. In addition the *de minimis* rule exempts programmes in developing countries that account for less than 10 percent of producers' total revenues – the limit for developed countries is only 5 percent.

This does not mean that there have been no significant changes in domestic policies during recent years or that further changes are unlikely. During the 1980s a number of developing countries drastically revised their agricultural policies to remove many of their trade-distorting aspects. In some cases these changes occurred in response to pressures from international financial institutions for structural adjustment programmes. In other cases countries responded to pressures from trading partners or acted unilaterally in anticipation of the results of the trade negotiations.

Many developed countries also made major policy changes. In the United States the rising costs of agricultural subsidies, combined with pressures to reduce federal budget deficits, resulted in policy changes leading to reductions in subsidies, and more, in 1990. To offset reduced support levels, however, a 1985 Act also introduced targeted export subsidies through the Export Enhancement Programme (EEP). In the EC a combination of external pressures and internal budget constraints brought about the most extensive reform[12] of the Common Agricultural

---

[12] **For a review of the reform of the Common Agricultural Policy, see *The State of Food and Agriculture 1992* and *1993*. Rome, FAO.**

BOX 11
THE "GREEN BOX"

The Uruguay Round added another term to the language of agricultural policy. Early in the negotiations there were discussions to set up two categories of policies, those that were to get the green light and those that would get the red light. The references then shifted to policies that fitted into the "green box", i.e. policies that were classified as not being trade-distorting. The concept of a red box was dropped, so now the only reference is to the "good" policies which fit into the green box.

Policy since its inception.

The Uruguay Round agreement does not require any country to give up its state trading organizations for agricultural products. Thus, states can retain their existing importing and exporting entities and those organizations that control internal markets. For example, under the agreement Japan is now required to import rice, but it can do so using its own existing food agency, which can determine the resale price of imported rice, thereby maintaining the desired level of internal prices. No requirements for transparency by state trading entities were added in the Uruguay Round.

Thus, what started as a bold attempt to bring major internal policy reform, especially within the OECD countries, ended up with somewhat more modest achievements in this regard. The agreement will bring about little or no reduction in the level of support for agriculture in developed countries. It has, however, resulted in some gains. For the first time in GATT history there is now official recognition and definition (by exclusion)[13] of policies that are trade-distorting (see Box 11). This, together with the requirement for an overall reduction in the aggregate spending on trade-distorting policies, will lead countries to provide any additional future assistance to the agricultural sector through policies that are less trade-distorting.

---

[13] The so-called green box defines non-trade-distorting policies, not subject to reduction commitments. By being excluded from the green box a policy is thus implicitly defined as trade-distorting.

THE PEACE CLAUSE

Another unique feature of the agricultural agreement is a section designed to reduce trade conflicts over agricultural issues by limiting the scope of GATT complaints that involve non-trade-distorting agricultural policies included in the green box; domestic support policies subject to and consistent with reduction commitments in the agreement; and export subsidies that conform to the reduction commitments. These provisions are to prevent a recurrence of the volume of complaints over agricultural trade issues taken to GATT during the 1980s.

The existence of a peace clause, however, is unlikely to guarantee an absence of complaints and trade conflicts. Trade conflicts are driven more by world market conditions than by trade rules and, as always, the future state of world markets is highly uncertain. It should be noted that there were virtually no trade conflicts on agriculture during the 1970s, when world markets were expanding and buoyant, whereas under the same trade rules in the 1980s there was a rash of trade disputes. Furthermore, when market conditions are highly competitive, countries may face domestic political pressures to take actions that are inconsistent with their Uruguay Round commitments. If this should occur, there are likely to be a number of disputes on the issue of whether obligations are being observed. In addition, some of the new rules added in the Uruguay Round may open up new areas of trade disputes, as countries test the limits and attempt to build interpretations of the rules.

THE COMMITTEE ON AGRICULTURE

The agreement calls for the establishment of a Committee on Agriculture to oversee its implementation. The exact duties and powers of the committee were not spelled out but were left to the new WTO. *Inter alia*, this new committee would keep track of the changes made by countries to bring their policies into compliance with their obligations. However, the committee is not a substitute for the formal dispute settlement mechanism, which is where major disputes over implementation will have to be settled.

This committee is also likely to lead the way in establishing the mandate for countries to enter negotiations for further reform at the end of the implementation period for the Uruguay Round. The committee would have the record of the implementation period and is therefore likely to have some judgements as to whether further reforms would be useful. Indeed, it was a special Committee on Agriculture of GATT that, by laying out the issues and investigating various ways to modify the rules, laid the groundwork for the agricultural negotiations of the Uruguay Round.

THE SANITARY AND PHYTOSANITARY AGREEMENT

Countries have developed a series of measures and import restrictions against products that come from certain areas or against products that might be carrying human, plant or animal diseases. These import controls have been justified under Article XX of GATT, which states, *inter alia*, that countries may adopt measures to protect the life of humans, plants or animals.

Of course, many of these import regulations have been legitimate protection against the spread of plant and animal diseases and against the imports of products that might threaten consumer health. Over time, however, a number of these import controls have been used as disguised trade barriers.

Restrictions were often directed against the exports of developing countries. The Uruguay Round has included an international agreement on sanitary and phytosanitary (SPS) measures, which allows countries to challenge these sanitary and phytosanitary regulations and will require member countries to make such regulations transparent.

Certain new trends in international trade will make the new SPS agreement even more important. Increasingly, environmental groups and food safety advocates have demanded that import controls be used to enforce the desired methods used to produce, process and market food. Such groups may call for import bans on goods produced in certain areas or produced using undesirable methods.

The SPS agreement includes the following key elements:

- Members have the right to take sanitary and phytosanitary measures necessary for the protection of human, animal or plant life or health.
- Members shall ensure that any sanitary or phytosanitary measure is applied only to the extent necessary to protect human, animal or plant life or health, is based on scientific principles and is not maintained without sufficient scientific evidence.
- Members are to base their sanitary and phytosanitary measures on international standards. Measures that comply with international standards deemed necessary to protect human, animal or plant life or health are presumed to be consistent with obligations under the agreement. The agreement establishes the standards, guidelines and recommendations of the Codex Alimentarius Commission, administered by FAO, as the international reference points in trade disputes over measures to protect food safety. The guidelines and recommendations developed within the framework of the International Plant Protection Convention, also administered by FAO, provide the reference points for the protection of plant health.
- It calls for international harmonization of sanitary and phytosanitary standards.
- It lays out principles of transparency, which have often been lacking.
- It allows for the new dispute settlement mechanism of WTO to be used to settle disputes over SPS issues.

The SPS agreement is likely to be interpreted and clarified over the years ahead. Some countries may lag in the revision of their SPS measures until it becomes clear that the new rules will be enforced. In addition, there are a host of new issues on the horizon and these may raise trade tensions.

The general nature of the SPS agreement means that interpretation of the rules will depend on the case law accumulated as a result of dispute proceedings. Initially this may mean a number of formal complaints as countries attempt to test and clarify the meaning of the agreement.

The new issues are in part the result of new technology in agricultural production or marketing. For instance, for nearly a decade the United States and the EC have been involved in a trade dispute over the use of growth hormones in beef production. Many groups are protesting the use of bovine somatotropin (BST) in the production of milk and want to ban imports of dairy products containing milk produced with BST. Groups in some countries want to ban trade in all products for which biotechnological methods are used. All of these proposals for trade restrictions fall under the purview of the new SPS agreement if they are claimed to be made in the interest of human, animal or plant life or health. Initially, as such proposals arise they are likely to go to dispute settlement until precedents are established. If the dispute is brought on another basis it would normally be considered, under the Agreement on Technical Barriers to Trade (1994), according to different decision-making criteria.

The agreement also calls for the establishment of a Committee on Sanitary and Phytosanitary Measures. This committee is to provide a regular forum for consultations, to oversee the implementation of the SPS agreement and, especially, to further the harmonization of countries' SPS systems. The committee is also charged with coordinating with the relevant international organizations in the field of sanitary and phytosanitary protection to ensure the best scientific and technical advice and to avoid unnecessary duplication.

The committee is to develop a procedure to monitor the process of international harmonization and the use of international standards and guidelines that it considers to have a major trade impact. Members are to be asked to indicate which of these international standards they use and, where they do not use them, to indicate reasons for non-use.

This means there will be a strong move towards establishing a set of common standards worldwide at the very time that some countries are under a great deal of domestic pressure to apply stricter standards. Indeed, environmental and food safety groups have been major forces of opposition to the ratification of the Uruguay Round results. These groups object to the idea of challenges to national SPS measures and to the harmonization of world standards.

THE IMPACT OF THE URUGUAY ROUND ON WORLD TRADE AND COMMODITY PRICES

FAO has attempted a quantitative assessment of the impact of the Uruguay Round agreement on agricultural markets and trade flows.[14] (The methodology behind the assessment is illustrated in Box 12.) The price effects of the Uruguay Round, according to this assessment, are summarized in Table 20. The figures shown represent forecast percentage price changes in the year 2000 relative to historical prices in the base period 1987 to 1989. The overall price changes shown are the result of two effects: that which would have taken place even without the Uruguay Round (baseline run) and that which is due to the Uruguay Round. The price change attributable to the Uruguay Round turns out to be positive for all commodities and, with the exception of oilmeal proteins, is in the range of 4 to 11 percent. The effect, although small, is sufficient to reverse a projected price decline for some commodities, under the baseline run.

Compared with the base period, both export and import prices in the developing countries increase in real terms. If carried back to domestic producers and consumers, these increases should give a boost to the traded goods sector *vis-à-vis* the subsistence crops and domestic services sectors, neither of which tend to be traded to any significant extent. Both import and export volumes are therefore likely to be affected

---

[14] FAO. 1995. *Impact of the Uruguay Round on agriculture.* CCP: 95/13. Rome.

TABLE 20

Change in world food prices by the year 2000 relative to 1987-89 levels

	Baseline	Uruguay Round	Total
	(.................. % ..:................)		
Wheat	- 3	+ 7	+ 4
Rice	+ 7	+ 8	+15
Maize	+ 3	+ 4	+ 7
Millet/sorghum	+ 5	+ 5	+10
Other grains	- 2	+ 7	+ 5
Fats and oils	- 4	+ 4	0
Oilmeal proteins	+ 3	0	+ 3
Bovine-meat	+ 6	+ 8	+14
Sheep-meat	+ 3	+10	+13
Pigmeat	+13	+ 11	+24
Poultry	+ 5	+ 9	+14
Milk	+33	+ 8	+41

Source: FAO.

positively or negatively according to the trade balance of the main agricultural commodities.

The effects of the Uruguay Round on the food import bills of developing countries are likely to cause a sizeable increase in these bills (Table 21, p. 263). For the low-income food-deficit countries (LIFDCs) as a whole the food import bill is projected to be US$9.8 billion (55 percent) higher in the year 2000. About $3.6 billion of this increase (14 percent) would be a result of the Uruguay Round.

The impact of the Uruguay Round on the poorest food importing countries causes particular concern. There will be cases where low-income developing countries have been recipients of targeted export subsidies that have allowed them to pay less

BOX 12

FAO'S METHODOLOGY FOR ASSESSING THE IMPACT
OF THE URUGUAY ROUND

FAO's assessment was based largely on the world food model (WFM) that covers all commodities in the cereals/livestock/oilseeds complex separated into 147 individual countries or country groups. For commodities outside WFM, single-commodity models were developed. In all cases the models simultaneously determine production, consumption, imports, exports and world prices.

The approach to the assessment was to compare the outcome in the year 2000 in the absence of the Uruguay Round provisions (baseline)[1] with the outcome incorporating Uruguay Round provisions. Projections to the year 2000 are driven by income growth, productivity changes and demographic trends. Income is exogenous to the model. GATT has made a number of estimates of the effect of the entire Uruguay Round agreement on income growth and

these predicted gains ranging from US$109 billion to $510 billion.[2] The World Bank/OECD has estimated gains of around US$213 billion.[3] For the purposes of the FAO study the World Bank/OECD figure was taken as the main scenario.

Prices in each country are linked to world market prices by tariffs and other policy effects. For the Uruguay Round scenario, the reduction in tariffs changes these price linkages. The modelling has been done in terms of the primary commodity (e.g. wheat) and the tariff changes for the derived products (e.g. wheat flour) have been aggregated into an average wheat-equivalent tariff. It has usually been assumed that applied tariff changes will reflect changes in the

bound tariffs. The reduction in export subsidies has been reflected in an increase to the consumer price in the recipient country that is in addition to any change in world prices caused by trade liberalization. Minimum access has been introduced in those cases where the model did not generate a sufficient volume of imports to meet the national commitments. The value of trade has been calculated by multiplying the volume of trade by an estimated world average export unit price for the year 2000, itself projected as the product of the index of world prices and the base year export unit value. Adjustments were made to take into account the decline in export subsidies and, to some extent, the loss of preferential margins.

[1] FAO. 1994. *Medium-term prospects for agricultural commodities: projections to the year 2000.* FAO Economic and Social Development Paper No. 120. Rome.

[2] GATT. 1994. *The results of the Uruguay Round of multilateral trade negotiations.* Geneva.

[3] I. Goldin, O. Knudsen and D. van der Mensbrugghe. 1993. *Trade liberalization: global economic implications.* Washington, DC, OECD and World Bank.

BOX 13
ALTERNATIVE ESTIMATES OF THE PRICE EFFECTS OF THE URUGUAY ROUND

Numerous studies have been made on the likely price effect of trade liberalization in the wake of the Uruguay Round. Results vary widely and are in some cases significantly different from those of FAO. In general, recent estimates based on the actual results of the Round show more cautious results in terms of prices than earlier estimates (see *The State of Food and Agriculture 1994*, Table 3, page 70). A recent World Bank study using the OECD model indicates in fact very modest price increases for most major traded commodities, as shown in the table below.

The study observed that, in the context of the instability and secular decline in world commodity prices, the predicted changes are barely significant. As a consequence, these changes would have a very minor impact on the welfare of the developing countries. For some commodities a modest price decline would be expected. Negative price changes would result from cross-elasticities between crops, with sugar, rice and cotton, which remain relatively more protected than other crops, occupying land previously devoted to less protected crops, such as the other cereals.

Effect of agricultural liberalization on agricultural prices to the year 2002 from benchmark levels

Commodity	Change
	(........ % ....)
Wheat	3.8
Rice	- 0.9
Coarse grains	2.3
Sugar	1.8
Beef, veal and mutton	0.6
Other meats	- 0.6
Coffee	- 1.5
Cocoa	- 0.7
Tea	- 1.4
Vegetable oils	- 0.3
Dairy	1.2
Other food products	- 1.4
Wool	- 0.9
Cotton	- 1.2
Other agriculture	0.8

Source: Goldin and van der Mensbrugghe, 1995.

TABLE 21

Food import bills of developing and low-income food-deficit countries (LIFDCs),[1] past and projected[2]

	Number of countries	Actual (1987-89)	Projected (2000)	Size of increase	Increase caused by Uruguay Round effect	
		(........................... US$ billion ....)			*(........... % ....)*	
WORLD						
All developing	137	40.0	64.7	24.7	3.6	15
LIFD	72	17.8	27.6	9.8	1.4	14
AFRICA						
All developing	52	6.0	10.5	4.5	0.5	11
LIFD	43	3.5	6.3	2.8	0.2	7
LATIN AMERICA AND THE CARIBBEAN						
All developing	46	8.0	12.7	4.7	0.3	6
LIFD	10	1.6	2.4	0.8	0.1	12
NEAR EAST						
All developing	19	11.5	16.8	5.3	0.8	15
LIFD	6	3.7	4.7	1.0	0.1	10
FAR EAST						
All developing	20	14.5	24.7	10.2	2.0	20
LIFD	13	9.0	14.2	5.2	1.0	19

[1] LIFD countries include those with a net deficit in cereals (averaged over the past five years) and a per caput income in 1993 below the cut-off point of US$1 345 used by the World Bank to determine eligibility for International Development Association assistance.
[2] Food comprises cereals, oilseeds and products, meat and dairy products.

than world market prices. With the reduction of these targeted subsidies these countries will increasingly have to pay world market prices at a time when world food prices are expected to increase. There is also some concern that, although the Uruguay Round agreement poses no limits on legitimate food aid, the volume of food aid, which historically has been linked closely to the level of surplus stocks, could be limited in the future as surplus stocks are run down. Clearly, some countries would be in need of assistance to improve consumption levels and, in particular, to compensate them for any increases in their food bills resulting from the Uruguay Round, especially when the country concerned has not gained in net terms in other sectors. With a view to these concerns, however, the Uruguay Round package contains special provisions for developing

TABLE 22

Effect of crop shortfalls and bumper crops on cereal prices, with and without the Uruguay Round [1]

	Wheat	Rice	Maize	Millet/ sorghum	Other grains
NORMAL CROP (1987-1989 = 100)					
Baseline (2000)	97	107	103	105	98
Uruguay Round (2000)	104	115	108	110	105
CROP FAILURE (percentage change above normal crop prices)					
Baseline (2000)	+25.8	+50.5	+24.3	+29.5	+24.5
Uruguay Round (2000)	+25.0	+50.4	+24.1	+29.5	+23.8
BUMPER CROP (percentage change below normal crop prices)					
Baseline (2000)	-19.6	-31.8	-18.4	-20.0	-18.4
Uruguay Round (2000)	-19.2	-31.3	-18.5	-20.0	-18.1

[1] An across-the-board shortfall (and bumper crop) of 5 percent below (and above) normal levels is assumed for 1999 and its effect on prices in the year 2000 is measured.

countries, contained in the Decision on Measures Concerning the Possible Negative Effects of the Reform Programme on Least-developed and Net Food Importing Countries. This decision recognizes the concerns of developing countries and provides for some redress via food aid, technical assistance to raise agricultural productivity and possibly short-term assistance to help in financing normal commercial imports.

An important consideration for food security is the impact of food production shortfalls, which occur quite often. In this connection, an important anticipated benefit of the Uruguay Round is the reduction of the impact of such shortfalls on price instability. The idea behind this view is that, by using tariffication and the reduction of tariffs to increase the number of countries that are open to world price signals, the shocks

(arising, for example, from unexpected production shortfalls) will be absorbed by a greater number of markets and this will cushion the effect of such shocks on world prices.

Table 22 summarizes the result of a simulation of the impact a 5 percent production shortfall for cereals (and a 5 percent bumper crop production increase) in 1999 would have on the year 2000, with and without the Uruguay Round. As expected, such a major shock in global production has a dramatic impact on world market prices. Contrary to expectations, however, the simulation shows that the Uruguay Round appears to have almost no effect in stabilizing cereal market prices. One of the reasons for the large effect on prices is that global stocks are not expected to be large in 2000, at just around 17 percent of consumption compared with what was often over 20 percent in the 1980s and early 1990s. These results indicate that countries need to be aware of the risks of occasional sudden price surges of basic foods and that when stocks are inadequate, a shortfall in production will push up prices rapidly with the poorer countries suffering the most.

The continuing problem of international food price instability will need to be carefully monitored in the future and the role of private versus public stockholding will need to be assessed.

AGRICULTURAL TRADE: ENTERING A NEW ERA?

IV. The development of regional trade arrangements

The past few years have seen a growing interest in regional trade arrangements (RTAs)[15] and a consequent concern with the prospect of a weakening of the multilateral trading system and the emergence of a small number of powerful regional trade blocs. Many have expressed the fear that these blocs would develop protectionist tendencies towards each other and (however inadvertently) towards third countries. Excluded countries would be forced to take shelter within other regional blocs. Many of the benefits of a broad multilateral trade system would inevitably be compromised, even if trade still stayed open within the blocs. Much agricultural trade flows among these blocs and could be affected by trade tensions arising from non-agricultural sectors and by general hostility in commercial policy attitudes.

However, such fears seem unfounded at present. The increased

---

[15] This section draws on a study prepared for FAO by T. Josling, *Implications of regional trade arrangements for agricultural trade,* forthcoming in the series of FAO Economic and Social Development Papers.

interest in regional trade pacts does not seem to have led to any marked regionalization of trade flows. It is true that intraregional trade has increased rapidly in recent decades and in Europe, for example, intraregional trade has outpaced trade with the rest of the world. However, the evidence shows that trade within many geographical areas is expanding no faster than that between such areas.[16] It is also clear that regional trade expansion is not always caused by a swing towards regionalism in trade policy.[17] The extent to which the proliferation of trade blocs has in fact led to regionalization of world trade is discussed fully by Lloyd,[18] who concludes that the larger amount of world trade flowing within these blocs is chiefly a function of the expansion of membership. Trade relations are readjusting in part as a reflection of the end of the Cold War and of the declining importance of superpower rivalry and security considerations in trade relations; in part as a reflection of the continued globalization of manufacturing operations in certain sectors; and in part as a means of competing for the limited funds available for investment. Trade blocs are a reaction to these forces.

It is also not obvious that greater intraregional trade is the result of shortcomings in the global trade system. The passage of the Uruguay Round makes it difficult to argue that the growth of regionalism has caused any obvious weakening of the rules of the multilateral system. Regional trade blocs have gone out of their way to emphasize their commitment to a strong multilateral system. New trade blocs have generally been formed with a careful eye to consistency with GATT. In the past, GATT itself has often turned a blind eye towards inconsistencies and few of the existing RTAs have been through a rigorous examination as to their compatibility with Article XXIV. Of some 70 notifications to GATT of the formation of a free-trade area, only four were declared fully compatible with Article XXIV, although none were rejected on the basis of incompatibility.[19] This rather casual application of the rules seems to be coming to an end and, as RTAs pursue more economic and less strategic motives, the examination of their compliance with trade rules will become more rigorous.

Countries in Asia and Latin America have recently emphasized that their integration plans conform to the concept of "open regionalism". This implies not only that regional trade arrangements contain no increase in trade barriers with outside countries (a condition that is relatively easy when the RTA is only a free-trade area) but also that they are undertaken along with a decrease in trade barriers to the outside world. Thus regional arrangements have often been included as part of a structural

[16] Josling, op. cit., footnote 15.

[17] D. Lorenz. 1991. Regionalization versus regionalism: problems of change in the world economy. *Intereconomics,* Jan./Feb., p. 3-16.

[18] P.J. Lloyd. 1992. *Regionalization and world trade.* OECD Economic Studies No. 18. Paris.

[19] Ibid.

adjustment programme that includes trade liberalization. Trade diversion may or may not be avoided altogether in this way, but it is likely to be minimized if third-country trade barriers come down at the same time. In addition, open regionalism usually implies a willingness to extend the RTA to include other interested countries.[20]

THE EXTENT OF REGIONAL TRADE ASSOCIATIONS

Regional trade associations have a long history and wide geographical coverage.[21] The prevalence of such arrangements can be seen from Tables 23A and 23B which list the most significant current free-trade areas together with their constituent countries. The 115 countries on the list include most of the Contracting Parties of GATT, as well as a few that are not GATT members.[22] The tables show that enthusiasm for RTAs varies by continent. The regions that are almost entirely covered by RTAs are Africa, Europe and the Americas. Asia and the centrally planned economies of Central and Eastern Europe and the

---

[20] In some Asian and Australian formulations, open regionalism includes the willingness to extend benefits on an MFN basis. Regionalism thus becomes part of a piecemeal multilateral negotiating process with the same ends as GATT or WTO.

---

[21] For a discussion of the current status of regional trade agreements see A. de la Torre and M.R. Kelly. 1992. *Regional trade arrangements.* IMF Occasional Paper No. 93. Washington, DC, IMF.

[22] Tables 23A and 23B do not include preference schemes, such as the Lomé Convention between the EC and the African, Caribbean and Pacific (ACP) countries and the Caribbean Basin Initiative (CBI) of the United States. The EC itself is included as a part of the European Economic Area (EEA), formed between the EC and EFTA. Switzerland has not ratified the EEA Treaty. Not all the free-trade areas in the list are equally effective, but all have been actively used in recent years as a vehicle for freer regional trade on a multicommodity basis. Many have plans for tariff harmonization, and some aim to liberalize capital and labour flows. Some are already in customs unions. In general the free-trade areas listed here do not plan full economic or political integration.

TABLE 23A

Country membership of major free trade areas, 1992[1]

Europe	Americas	
EFTA	**CUSTA**	**AP**
(European Free Trade	*(Canada-US Free Trade*	*(Andean Pact)*
Association)	*Agreement)*	Bolivia
Austria	Canada	Colombia
Finland	United States	Ecuador
Iceland		Peru
Norway	**NAFTA**	Venezuela
Sweden	*(North American Free Trade*	
Switzerland	*Agreement)*	**MERCOSUR**
	Canada	*(Southern Common Market)*
EEA	Mexico	Argentina
(European Economic Area)	United States	Brazil
EC-12		Paraguay
(Belgium	**CARICOM**	Uruguay
Denmark	*(Caribbean Community and*	
France	*Common Market)*	**CACM**
Germany	Antigua/Barbuda	*(Central America Common*
Greece	The Bahamas	*Market)*
Ireland	Barbados	Costa Rica
Italy	Belize	El Salvador
Luxembourg	Dominica	Guatemala
Netherlands	Grenada	Honduras
Portugal	Guyana	Nicaragua
Spain	Jamaica	
United Kingdom)	Montserrat	
Austria	St Kitts/Nevis	
Finland	St Lucia	
Iceland	St Vincent/the Grenadines	
Norway	Trinidad/Tobago	
Sweden		

[1] Bilateral preference arrangements are excluded.

former USSR have not yet developed regional trade associations to nearly the same extent.[23] Regionalism is itself therefore a region-specific phenomenon; different continents have approached the issue of regional trade from very different perspectives.

[23] Trade relations among the countries of the former USSR and between these countries and others in the region have yet to stabilize. CMEA, which acted as a framework for trade within Central and Eastern Europe and the former USSR, has been defunct since 1991.

TABLE 23B

Country membership of major free trade areas, 1992[1]

Africa		Asia and the Pacific	Near East
ECOWAS *(Economic Community of West African States)* Benin Burkina Faso Cape Verde Côte d'Ivoire The Gambia Ghana Guinea Guinea-Bissau Liberia Mali Mauritania The Niger Nigeria Senegal Sierra Leone Togo **ECCAS** *(Economic Community of Central African States)* Burundi Cameroon The Central African Republic Chad The Congo Equatorial Guinea Gabon Rwanda San Tome/Principe Zaire	**PTA** *(Preferential Trade Area for Eastern and Southern African States)* Angola Burundi Botswana The Comoros Djibouti Ethiopia Kenya Lesotho Madagascar Malawi Mauritius Mozambique Rwanda Seychelles Somalia Swaziland United Republic of Tanzania Uganda Zambia Zimbabwe **SACU** *(South Africa Customs Union)* Botswana Lesotho Namibia South Africa Swaziland	**ASEAN** *(Association of Southeast Asian Nations)* Brunei Darussalam Indonesia Malaysia The Philippines Singapore Thailand **CER** *(Closer Economic Relations Agreement)* Australia New Zealand	**ACM** *(Arab Common Market)* Egypt Iraq Jordan The Libyan Arab Jamahiriya Mauritania The Sudan The Syrian Arab Republic Yemen

[1] Bilateral preference arrangements are excluded.

As a consequence, the RTAs that have been set up vary widely. The extent to which regional trade institutions have been a significant factor in economic policy also varies greatly.

The trend towards regional trade liberalization has proceeded furthest in Europe. In the EC, a large and seamless "internal market" was largely in place by early 1993. Plans were laid for eventual economic and monetary union (EMU), together with cooperation on security issues and foreign policy, and the European Community became known as the European Union to emphasize this change. The negotiation of a European Economic Area, which includes the EC and the European Free Trade Association (EFTA) countries, and of association agreements, first with Poland, Hungary and the Czech and Slovak Republics and later with Romania, Bulgaria and Slovenia, effectively sets up an economic group of well over 20 countries. The accession on 1 January 1995 of three of the EFTA countries and the political decision to extend membership to include several of the Central European countries, over the next few years, makes this process of market integration more tangible. North America is following a similar process with the North American Free Trade Agreement (NAFTA) between Mexico, Canada and the United States, which builds upon the earlier Canada-US Free Trade Agreement (CUSTA) and promises a tariff-free zone for most commodities over a ten-year period.

Prompted by these activities, several regional schemes have been revived or formed in Latin America and Africa. In Latin America, the formation of the Southern Common Market (MERCOSUR) among the Southern Cone countries (excluding Chile) and the decision by the Andean Pact countries to form an Andean Common Market by 1995 have strengthened the level of economic cooperation in this region. The countries of the Central America Common Market (CACM) have signed a framework agreement for free trade with Mexico by 1996 and can be expected to negotiate terms with the other NAFTA countries. Also concerned about their future are the Caribbean Community and Common Market (CARICOM) countries, most of whom have preferential access to the United States through the Caribbean Basin Initiative (CBI) and to the EC through the Lomé Convention, but now face the prospect of the value of those preferences eroding. These countries may also be obliged to join a widened NAFTA to remain in contention for investment funds and to maintain access to the United States market. As a part of this strategy, the Caribbean states as a whole have recently formed an Association of Caribbean States (ACS), which includes most of the present CACM and CARICOM countries as well as Mexico.

In December 1994 the Summit of the Americas called for a Western Hemisphere Free Trade Agreement to be completed by 2005. This is to be achieved by building on several of the agreements that are already in place. Examination of the current agreements is already under way with a view to deciding what would be required to merge them into a single agreement.

In Africa, riddled with regional trade agreements since the colonial days, there is a new sense of urgency. South of the Sahara, the continent is now covered by four trade agreements: the Economic Community of West African States (ECOWAS) in West Africa, formed from the expansion of the French-speaking West African Economic Community (WAEC) to include English-speaking countries; the Economic Community of Central African States (ECCAS) in Central Africa, a revitalization of the Central African Customs and Economic Union (CACEU) arrangement of the 1960s; the Preferential Trade Area of Eastern and Southern Africa (PTA), which includes countries that were in the now defunct East African Customs Union (EACM) as well as those in southern Africa; and the Southern African Customs Union (SACU), which covers those countries closely aligned with South Africa. The Organization of African Unity (OAU) has agreed the ultimate objective of working towards an African Economic Community, based on these existing subregional groupings, by the turn of the century.

Discussions among the countries of Asia and the Pacific are also aimed at establishing a regional trade identity. The oldest Asian regional association, the Association of Southeast Asian Nations (ASEAN), has historically had a political and security, rather than an economic, focus. ASEAN countries have now agreed to establish an ASEAN Free-Trade Area (AFTA) that would liberalize internal trade in 15 years. Broader economic groupings have been suggested, most prominently by Malaysia, as a way of reacting to European and North American regional blocs.[24] The Asia-Pacific Economic Cooperation Council (APEC) was formalized in 1989 to act as a forum for the discussion of trade and trade-related issues in the Asia-Pacific area. More recently, however, APEC has set up a secretariat and called for a programme that would lead to regional trade liberalization. The APEC nations have agreed to a target for free trade among the countries in the region by the year 2020 or by 2010 in the case of trade between developed countries in the region. While this is not a binding commitment, it clearly marks an important policy direction that will be pursued. Other regional trade groupings are taking shape in Asia. A Central Asian bloc, including six former Soviet republics together with Afghanistan, Iran, Pakistan and Turkey, is in its infancy as the Economic Cooperation Organization (ECO). Another trade group links India, Pakistan, Nepal, Sri Lanka, the Maldives and Bangladesh in the South Asian Association for Regional Cooperation (SAARC).

---

[24] **The Malaysian suggestion would have led to an East Asian Economic Caucus, comprising ASEAN, Japan and several other countries in the region.**

RATIONALE FOR RTAs

The prevalence of free-trade areas implies that they fulfil some kind of political or economic need not satisfied by multilateral trade arrangements.[25] They seem to suit those countries that are balancing an open economic policy with a fear of economic competition from other countries. Part of the political attraction of trade blocs may be that they are perceived as both a step towards more open trade and as a line of defence against competitors. They are therefore likely to have widespread support in the business and political communities. As economic struggles replace the security concerns of the Cold War, economic alliances such as these may come to replace defence groupings as a focus for foreign policy. In international economic fora, this may lead to groups of states playing the role formerly filled by the superpowers.

The economic case for free-trade areas is less convincing than the political rationale. Economists warn that free-trade areas have negative as well as positive impacts on the performance of the trade system. Lowering trade barriers to a partner country improves resource allocation by allowing more competition for previously protected domestic industries. This trade creation is of benefit to the country concerned and contributes to the international division of labour through international trade. However, to the extent that the partner country gets preferential access to the partly liberalized market, there may be a less desirable consequence if that partner is not the most efficient supplier of the good in question. This trade diversion is a cost to both the importing country, as the foreign exchange cost of imports from the preferred partner is higher than from the efficient supplier, and to the world at large, as resources are not ideally allocated on the basis of comparative cost. Thus partial free trade has always been seen as a second-best economic policy, with its mix of liberalization and de facto discrimination against third countries that may be the more appropriate trade partners. Much of the argument about the role of RTAs in the trade system comes down to the anticipated balance between trade creation and trade diversion.

The positive economic case for RTAs rests on the notion that the process of removal of trade barriers may be easier in regional markets and hence is a step in the direction of freer trade with all countries. This case is strengthened in areas such as services, where little multilateral trade liberalization has been evident until now. Dispute settlement may also be easier in regional areas where legal systems and traditions are similar. In these areas, several of the free-trade areas are pushing ahead of the provisions of the Final Act of the Uruguay Round. Regional trade blocs could well have a growing role in trade liberalization.

---

[25] **For a recent discussion of the implications for the multilateral system of the increased interest in regionalism, see K. Anderson and R. Blackhurst, eds. 1993. History, geography and regional economic integration, in** *Regional integration and the global trading system,* **P.J. Lloyd, op. cit., footnote 18, p. 267 and A. de la Torre and M.R. Kelly, op. cit., footnote 21, p. 268.**

Although changes in trade barriers attract more attention, the most significant attribute of regional trade liberalization may be its role in stimulating investment. The attraction to investors at home is that domestic firms can invest in the partner economy, with less chance of discriminatory action by the host government, to take advantage of cost differences such as lower wage rates. Overseas investors can be encouraged with the assurance of access to an expanded "home" market for the finished product. As such, this motive for regionalism is a spin-off from the 1980s', "globalization" of business. In this respect, RTAs encourage profitable investment by reducing uncertainty. However, if they were possible, multilateral agreements on investment would be an even better stimulus to trade.

Combined with general multilateral liberalization, regional trade and investment liberalization can increase growth and employment and make better use of the world's resources. "Open regionalism" is the term that has been used to distinguish this form of export-oriented trade and investment liberalization from the closed integration models of the 1960s.[26] The concept implies that trade diversion is kept to a minimum by the reduction of trade barriers on third-country imports, while trade creation is maximized by the accompanying measures of internal liberalization.

The problems posed by such alliances stem from the defensive nature of much of trade politics. It is likely that this defensive posture might lead to regions using trade restrictions against other blocs. Moreover, even the most benign form of regional liberalization is likely to appear protectionist to outsiders. It is a fine line between encouraging partner investment and discouraging investment from third parties[27] and at times of economic hardship such subtle discrimination can easily turn to more blatant protection. This highlights the need for strong multilateral institutions and rules to oversee the trade blocs and their relationships to one another. The notion of making regional and multilateral trade rules and institutions complementary with each other is the most positive response to concerns over the threat to the trade system. A stronger multilateral framework would reduce the prospect of one bloc increasing discrimination against another. The beneficial aspects of regional trade liberalization could thus be reaped without the cost to the global division of labour.

---

[26] **For a discussion of open regionalism in a Latin American context, see C. Reynolds. 1992.** *Notes on the enterprise for the Americas Initiative and the Andean Pact: open regionalism in the Andes.* **Americas Programme Occasional Paper. California, Stanford University. A recent argument for its extension in the Pacific Basin is contained in F. Holmes and C. Falconer. 1992.** *Open regionalism? NAFTA, CER and a Pacific Basin Initiative.* **Washington, DC, Institute of Policy Studies.**

[27] **For example, a regional agreement against expropriation of property held by foreigners implies that the excluded parties have less protection. Investment costs for those countries will be higher to cover greater risks.**

THE TREATMENT OF AGRICULTURE IN RTAs

In many respects, agricultural trade should be a major stimulus to regional trade pacts. Regional flows of agricultural products improve the food security of the area by allowing production fluctuations to even out. Differences in resource endowments underpin much of agricultural trade and ensure that there will always be profitable trade between areas that have ample arable land in relation to population and those that have less. This trade will often be across regions rather than within a single region. Similarly, trade in crops that require particular climatic conditions will tend to be among rather than within regions. However, agricultural trade is taking on the patterns of industrial trade, including two-way trade within the same sector. Intra-industry specialization owes its justification to economies of size in particular processes and to the search for cheap and reliable components and materials. Under such a system, trade grows among countries that have similar resource endowments and are at similar stages of development. Trade in processed foodstuffs already moves among countries that produce similar products. This type of trade is much more likely to be generated either within a region or among countries that could form a region in the absence of political and infrastructural obstacles. This implies, for certain types of agricultural trade, a growing significance of the movement towards free trade areas.

Regional trading blocs and free-trade areas treat agriculture in various ways. Some ignore it, as if it were not really subject to the same set of circumstances as other sectors. In a few cases agriculture is treated as a regular sector of the economy and is subject to the same rules. In most cases, however, agricultural trade is only partially included in regional trading blocs and free-trade areas, as countries have taken care to frame free-trade areas so as to preserve as much as possible of the domestic autonomy of farm and food policies. Nevertheless the agricultural sector is bound to be profoundly affected by the existence of free trade with neighbouring countries. The issue is whether countries will allow national farm policies to change to take advantage of the possibilities that freer regional trade brings, or whether they will resist such changes and leave those policies to be modified by market pressures or to collapse under their own weight.

There are four major reasons for including agriculture in the provisions of a free-trade agreement. First, exporter members within the region will want improved access to importing markets for their agricultural goods. Only an alliance among food-importing countries is likely to be able to ignore intrabloc agricultural trade altogether. Second, food cost differences arising from different agricultural prices among countries within the free-trade agreement could both distort trade and investment patterns and cause problems of wage comparability. Third, if agriculture is excluded, the food sector will tend to remain national in scope, as a result of different raw material costs and regulations, and may not be internationally competitive. Fourth, to exclude agriculture from free-trade agreements leaves countries open to challenge under GATT. Article XXIV requires that such agreements cover *essentially all trade* among the partners.

On the other hand, there is in essence only one reason for excluding agriculture from the provisions of a free-trade area. Most domestic agricultural price policies require protection at the border in order to be effective. As a consequence, free trade poses a threat to the operation of such policies. Negotiations on freer trade are therefore likely to be complicated by domestic farm policy considerations. Politicians are often tempted to take the easy way out when faced with negotiating improved regional access to cherished domestic agricultural markets.

The situation is well illustrated by European experience. When the European Economic Community was established, agriculture was fully included in the aim of free internal trade. The exporting countries insisted on this as part of the bargain that allowed them to open up their industrial markets. In the treaty establishing the European Free Trade Association (EFTA) in 1960, agriculture was left out. With the exception of Denmark, which received some bilateral concessions in the United Kingdom market, no member of EFTA was an agricultural exporter. The EFTA-EC bilateral trade agreements (1973) again left agriculture out, as no EFTA preferences were being eroded by the accession of Denmark and the United Kingdom to the EC. In the more recent negotiations leading to the creation of the European Economic Area (EEA) in 1992, agriculture has been largely left out.

The various Latin American free-trade agreements have in the past focused mainly on industrial products, although the recent, more open agreements include provisions for agricultural trade liberalization. In Asia, regional groupings are less common and hence have less direct influence on agricultural policy. ASEAN has operated a collective agreement on food security, involving the sharing of rice stocks at times of shortage, but otherwise has had little agricultural content. Agriculture is to be largely excluded from the recently negotiated ASEAN free-trade area.

African free-trade agreements have generally included provisions for freer trade in agricultural goods, as these cover a large share of total trade for the countries involved. However, a variety of revenue duties coupled with parastatal control over many export commodities have made agricultural trade less than free, even when no tariff restrictions apply. Instead, the emphasis has often turned to the coordination of agricultural investment and to common approaches to prospective donors.

In North America, CUSTA (1990) included agriculture in the tariff-cutting activity, but not in the non-tariff barrier removal.[28] Neither the

---

[28] The exception to this was the liberalization of Canadian cereal import licensing, conditional on United States protection levels being less than those in Canada. This condition was met soon after the implementation of the agreement. The discrimination against sales of foreign wine in provincial retail outlets in Canada was also curbed by the Canada-United States agreement.

United States nor Canada thought of the other as a big potential market and the GATT Round seemed at that time to be taking care of agricultural trade issues. NAFTA (1992) was also overshadowed by the Uruguay Round. Market access has been improved by the provisions of two bilateral access agreements (United States-Mexico and Canada-Mexico) for agricultural products (to supplement the United States-Canada bilateral agreement that already existed. Some substantial liberalization will be achieved by this, as a schedule of tariff reductions over the next decade will give Mexico better access to United States and Canadian agricultural markets and vice versa. Non-tariff barriers are also to be phased out on United States-Mexico trade, leading to a relatively free internal market in at least a large part of the continent. Canadian-United States farm trade, however, remains governed largely by the pre-existing CUSTA and so is not truly on a path to liberalization.

Among the range of free-trade areas that exist, perhaps only the Closer Economic Relations (CER) Treaty between Australia and New Zealand fully incorporates agriculture. This was made easier by the sharp reduction in New Zealand's protection of the sector in the late 1980s and by the deregulation of marketing systems in the two countries over the last few years.

Agriculture is likely to be affected by the extent to which trade blocs can fit into the multilateral system without becoming inward-looking and protectionist. If the blocs pursue aggressive policies towards each other in non-agricultural trade, their agricultural trade relations are unlikely to be liberal. Moreover, if each country were to keep its own restrictive agricultural policy in the face of otherwise open intrabloc trade policies, it is not clear what scope would exist for global negotiations on types and levels of support. If, on the other hand, domestic policies are modified as a result of intrabloc trade developments, the international implications of such blocs could be benign. Indeed one could imagine a path to liberal international markets passing through regionally liberalized agricultural policies brought about by the forces of regional market integration.[29]

_____

[29] **For a further discussion of the question, see T. Josling, op. cit., footnote 15, p. 266.**

AGRICULTURAL TRADE: ENTERING A NEW ERA?

V. International trade, the environment and sustainable agricultural development

In recent years, the collision of environmental and trade interests has emerged as one of the most complex and divisive issues in world trade policy. While the debate is multifaceted, involving legal, economic and environmental perspectives, all sides are generally interested in promoting national and social welfare. Many supporters of liberal world trade believe that reducing trade barriers is environment-friendly as a way of allowing the world to use its resources more efficiently and, as long as impacts on the environment and on natural resources are appropriately priced, more sustainably. Moreover, by raising incomes, the reduction of trade barriers enables countries to spend more on preserving the environment. Trade supporters also point to numerous studies that show how protectionism often exacerbates environmental problems. For example, a variety of studies document how export bans, import restrictions and consumer boycotts of tropical hardwood products actually discourage conservation and encourage unsustainable rates of cutting.[30]

In contrast, some environmental interest groups argue that by contributing to economic growth and increasing the world's demand for natural resources, trade liberalization is a cause of the problem and not the solution. A few groups advocate trade restrictions to protect the environment. They argue that, unless accompanied by strict environmental regulations, trade-induced growth will further deplete and degrade the earth's oceans, air, fresh water, soils and climate. Not surprisingly, these groups tend to distrust regional and global trading agreements that are aimed at removing trade barriers. On the contrary, they support trade barriers and tighter restrictions in multilateral negotiations as a way of controlling excessive resource depletion and protecting consumers from potentially hazardous imported products, particularly food. Box 14 presents an overview of the trade and environment debate in forestry and highlights how environmental regulations may affect trade and how trade policies may affect the environment.

The growing debate over trade and the environment is raising new issues and concerns in global trade politics and is changing the way in which trade and environmental concerns are addressed in multilateral agreements. Three recent events illustrate the growing importance of trade and environment issues. First, in 1992, the United Nations Conference on Environment and Development (UNCED) outlined a work programme on trade and the environment in Chapter 2 of Agenda 21. As part of this

programme, OECD established a set of procedural guidelines for trade and the environment with the aim of encouraging member governments to work towards national trade and environmental policies that are more compatible with each other. Second, in 1993, Canada, Mexico and the United States signed an environmental side agreement to NAFTA. This side agreement represents an international precedent for subjecting trade agreements to environmental review. Third, in 1994, it was decided to set up a committee on trade and the environment within the WTO. This committee is to help ensure that trade rules are responsive to environmental objectives.

As with the overall goal of sustainable development, trade and environment issues pose long-term challenges for which adequate policy responses would often require better scientific knowledge than is currently available; but they also pose practical problems that require immediate attention. For many developing countries, the need to increase incomes at the same time as reducing environmental damage represents a real policy dilemma. The developmental and food security needs, together with the macroeconomic imbalances of these countries impose pressure on their natural resources in order to reduce food import dependence and generate foreign exchange from exports. These pressing needs for increasing incomes, economic growth and exports raise important questions about how to balance environmental protection, economic development and trade.

This section presents an overview of the linkages between trade and the

---

[30] *The State of Food and Agriculture 1994.* Rome, FAO.

BOX 14
FOREST TRADE AND THE ENVIRONMENT

Some environmental groups interested in protecting tropical forests argue that further trade liberalization is bad for the environment because it will increase the demand for tropical timber. These groups have encouraged some OECD countries to experiment with bans on the import of tropical timber products, or with a selective ban on those products that are not sustainably produced. Some 450 city councils in Germany and more than 90 percent of local councils in the Netherlands have banned the use of tropical timber. In the United States, the states of Arizona and New York prohibit the use of tropical timber in public construction projects.[1]

Despite their popular appeal, such bans are unlikely to encourage sustainable management in countries that export tropical timber for a number of reasons. First, recent empirical studies contradict the view that logging for the international timber trade is a major cause of deforestation and environmental degradation.[2] The evidence suggests that, in many countries, a large proportion of logging is for domestic consumption. Second, because the majority of tropical forests are cleared for agricultural use of the land; the majority of the wood then being consumed as fuelwood, only about 6 percent of the total amount of wood cut in the tropics enters the international timber trade.[3] Third, country case studies indicate that, however well-intentioned they may be, regulations such as bans on logging and exports aimed at protecting forests' environmental resources may be counterproductive and result in even higher economic and environmental costs.[4]

To date, most research demonstrates that a ban on tropical timber products is ineffective in reducing either tropical deforestation or the trade in unsustainable timber production. Log export bans have led neither to better

_____

[1] Global Environmental Change Report. 1991. 3(16).

_____

[2] E. Barbier, J. Burgess, J. Bishop, B. Aylward and C. Bann. 1993. *The economic linkages between the international trade in tropical timber and the sustainable management of tropical forests.* Final Report for the International Tropical Timber Organisation (ITTO). Yokohama, Japan.

[3] FAO. 1993. *The challenge of sustainable forestry.* Rome.

forest conservation nor to the development of efficient processing industries. The bans do not reduce the overall demand for logs; instead they shift the location of processing. While restricting log exports may stimulate short-term growth and employment in domestic processing, over time, they tend to result in undervaluing of logs (trees), losses in value-added and resource rents, processing over-capacity and inefficient production practices. For example,

[4] See, for example, J. R. Vincent. 1992. A simple, nonspatial modelling approach for analysing a country's forest products trade policies, in R. Haynes, P. Harou and J. Mikowski, eds. *Forestry sector analysis for developing countries.* Proceedings of Working Groups, Integrated Land Use and Forest Policy and Forest Sector Analysis Meetings, Tenth Forestry World Congress, Paris; J. R. Vincent. 1992. The tropical timber trade and sustainable development. *Science,* 256: 1651-1655; and L. F. Constantino and D. Ingram. 1990. *Supply-demand projections for the Indonesian forest sector.* Jakarta, Ministry of Forestry, Government of Indonesia and FAO.

when export bans cause log prices to fall, tropical forests are treated as an inferior land-use and timber as an abundant good.

For those tropical forest countries where timber exports are neither significant nor a major factor in deforestation (e.g. in Latin America), an import ban may have little impact on timber management or overall deforestation. In addition, a tropical timber import ban would have little impact on the economic incentives for sustainable management at the concession level and may actually encourage poor management practices. It is domestic policy that determines whether environmental costs are internalized and thus has most effect on user decisions.

Import restrictions affect the use of forest resources by depressing global demand for tropical timber products, reducing stumpage values in producer countries, discouraging investments in more efficient processing and in some cases eliminating incentives for better forest management. Moreover, import restrictions on processed wood products prompt producer countries to argue for subsidies and log export restrictions to compensate their domestic processors.

The forestry experience suggests that trade measures are not the most appropriate means of addressing concerns about deforestation and environmental degradation. First, domestic environmental policies can have substantial effects on timber production, trade and prices. Trade interventions, on the other hand, address these problems only indirectly at best. Second, the most direct impact of trade measures is on cross-border product flows and prices. As noted above, changes in these international flows may have very little influence on the main causes of deforestation and forest degradation in producer countries. However, trade policies can play a role in encouraging trade-related incentives for sustainable forest management. Such policies should be used in conjunction with and to complement forest sector policies and regulations that improve forest management. Certainly, other sectoral and macroeconomic policies that influence the pattern of deforestation and forest land-use must also be addressed.

environment in agriculture. It identifies conditions under which the goals of liberalized trade and environmental protection can be mutually supportive and it discusses the implications for domestic and international policy.[31]

HOW TRADE IS LINKED TO THE ENVIRONMENT

International trade may affect sustainable agricultural and rural development and the environment[32] in a number of ways. First, trade may encourage production activities to shift from places where the environment is less sustainable to places where it is more sustainable or vice versa. Second, increased trade liberalization changes the pattern and level of world consumption, production and income and these changes can affect the environment in ways that go beyond the shifting of consumption and production among countries. Third, trade influences the process of economic development, creating fresh opportunities for the profitable use of productive resources. For instance, international trade in agricultural products is large and an important source of foreign exchange earnings for many countries.

As incomes rise, demands on resources increase, but at the same time, income growth can also lead to more effective demands for better environmental quality. In addition, increased incomes make investment in resource-conserving strategies both more affordable and more attractive. Moreover, higher incomes are associated with lower population growth rates, reducing the pressure on environmental resources. Higher incomes and better employment opportunities widen the range of

---

[31] There is an important and growing body of literature on trade and environment, much of which focuses on agricultural, fisheries and forestry issues. See, for example, K. Anderson. 1992. *Agricultural trade liberalization and the environment: a global perspective. The World Economy*; and C.F. Runge. 1993. *Freer trade, protected environment.* New York, Council on Foreign Relations Press.

---

[32] Hereafter, reference to the environment includes implicitly the concept of sustainable agricultural and rural development.

choices thus leaving fewer rural people dependent on environmentally fragile areas, such as steep hillsides, for subsistence.

THE EFFECTS OF TRADE ON THE ENVIRONMENT AND THEIR MEASUREMENT

Trade shifts the incidence of environmental effects.

Trade geographically separates production from consumption. When environmental effects are national and not transboundary in their incidence and instead are mainly associated with production, trade may shift the environmental effects from one country to another. In addition, where consumption produces waste that has become an important part of the ecological cycle (for example, when nutrients are returned to the farmers' fields), trade's separation of production and consumption may put stable ecosystems out of balance. In some cases, production in one country may have environmental effects on neighbouring countries. For instance, water used for irrigation that then drains back into the river system raises the salt content for users in other countries downstream. In other cases, the act of production has beneficial global environmental effects. For example, planting trees that absorb and store carbon.

Although shifting the location of environmental damage may not affect total world environmental damage, it often poses problems of international concern. Where the negative effects are purely national, the unilateral action of one country to alleviate its own environmental problems may well raise costs to producers and hence cause a competitive handicap for its exports of affected products. If the country is big enough, the effect may be an increase in world trade prices, with consequences for all countries. In other cases, such as when an importer raises food safety standards, environmental protection measures may adversely affect exports from other countries.

Trade affects world production and consumption.
Trade causes global production and consumption to change. If there were no trade in coffee, for example, world consumption and production would be far less than it is, if only because coffee cannot be produced everywhere. The argument also applies to commodities that are produced in a far wider spectrum of countries than are tropical beverages. By exploiting comparative advantages, a country can enjoy higher levels of consumption and production which influence the ways in which natural and environmental resources are used and protected.

This basic interrelationship between trade and the environment implies that trade policy has an impact on the environment. Conversely, because environmental policy affects the supply and demand situation of commodities, it affects trade too. It is in recognition of this two-way relationship that UNCED called for mutually supportive environmental and trade policies.

Measuring the effects.
The impact of trade on the environment depends on the volume of trade, the share of trade in production and consumption and the environmental impact of production and consumption. Large volumes of forestry and fishery products are traded along with several agricultural commodities including cereals, sugar, fats and oils, oilmeals, cassava, meat, bananas, fresh citrus, cotton, pulses, dairy products, wine, coffee and rubber. At the global level,

the trade:production ratio is usually low, while for commodities such as tropical beverages and rubber world trade is the main stimulus to production. Trade in cereals accounts for little more than 12 percent of world production. Table 24 presents the shares of exports in world production for several commodities.

The trade:production ratio is often significant in some commodities for individual countries even when it is not significant globally. For example, while only 3 to 4 percent of world rice production is traded, exports account for more than 20 percent of production in Australia, the EC, Guyana, Pakistan, Thailand, Uruguay and the United States. At the same time, imports of rice account for more than 80 percent of consumption in as many as 43 countries (out of a total of 130 countries for which data were available).

The production and processing of commodities cause different amounts of environmental side-effects. These effects depend on numerous factors including technology, soils, topography, water quality and the ecosystem. There is no overall measure of pollution per tonne produced or consumed of a given product that can be applied to all countries and ecosystems.

Some work has already been done by several of FAO's intergovernmental groups[33] and FAO has also developed a methodology to be used as a standard tool in environmental impact assessment at the commodity level.[34]

---

[33] **FAO. 1994.** *International trade, environment and sustainable agricultural development: a progress report.* **CCP:95/14, Rome.**

TABLE 24

Shares of exports in world production for agricultural commodities, 1990

Commodity	Share	Commodity	Share
	(.... % ....)		(.... % ....)
CEREALS		**BEVERAGES**	
Wheat and products	19	Coffee and products	86
Rice and products	3	Tea	45
Coarse grains and products	12	Cocoa	82
LIVESTOCK PRODUCTS		**FIBRES**	
Meat and products	9	Cotton	27
Animal fats	19	Jute	17
Milk and products	10	Sisal	33
FRUIT		**OTHER**	
Oranges and products	35	Tobacco	31
Lemons and products	22	Rubber (dry equivalent)	85
Grapefruit and products	38	Sugar (raw equivalent)	20
Bananas	20	Vegetable oils and products	37
Apples and products	13		
Pineapples and products	26		
Dates	11		

Source: AGROSTAT.

However, at present there appears to be a basic shortage of hard data on the physical assessment of the environmental impact of production of individual commodities and on the financial cost of reducing the environmental damage caused by the production of commodities. This shortage greatly limits the ability to quantify the effects that changes in trade have on the environment and natural resource bases of participating countries.

_____

[34] FAO. 1994. *The economic assessment of production-related environmental impacts: an FAO manual.* ESC/M/94/7. Rome.

TRADE LIBERALIZATION AND THE ENVIRONMENT

In the absence of trade, each country has to meet its own requirements through domestic production. When trade becomes possible and when it is not distorted through subsidies or barriers, both the importing and the exporting countries gain; in the importing country gains to consumers exceed losses to producers; in the exporting country, consumers face a loss because prices become higher, but gains to producers exceed this loss as both the quantity sold and the revenue raised increase. This is a classic example of the gains from trade and implies that the world would benefit from liberalized trade because the gainers could compensate the losers and still be better off.

However, production processes require resources and these often include environmental resources. When the costs of pollution are taken into account the trade situation becomes more complicated. For the importing country any decrease in resource depletion or degradation associated with the reduced pressure on domestic resources of the (now) imported product represents an additional gain. Not only are there benefits in terms of resource reallocation in the market place, but the negative environmental consequences of producing the imported product are reduced as some production takes place in the exporting country.[35]

For the exporting country under the same assumptions the opposite is true. In effect, unless it is compensated, the exporting country is carrying part of the environmental cost of supplying the market of the importer and the welfare gain to its own citizens is thereby reduced.[36]

The next stage is to consider the implications of reducing

environmental damage through, for example, taxing the production process to reflect its environmental cost. The effect is straightforward for the importing country if it alone imposes such a tax. Its own production is reduced and more of its demand is met from imports. The gains from trade grow and, in effect, the environmental cost is transferred to the exporting country. If in that country too, similar environmental taxes are applied, the gains to the importing country may be reduced, but global welfare will increase. Production tends to occur where the sum of market and environmental costs is smallest.

This analysis suggests that in many cases trade liberalization and environmental concerns are compatible. Given an appropriate response to environmental protection, whether through market incentives or through regulation, and adequate services (information, training and extension), consumer needs can be met at lower environmental costs than in a protected market.

---

[35] Such an analysis is valid provided, of course, that the new uses of resources within the importing country are not more polluting than the former pattern of production was.

[36] Again, there is an assumption that, in shifting resources into export industries, the uses in which they were formerly engaged are not more environmentally damaging than the production of additional goods for export.

POLICY IMPLICATIONS

While there is a lack of hard data on interactions between trade and the environment, there are at least clear signs that in some situations these interactions are significant. The production of traded commodities affects the immediate environment, both positively and negatively. Similarly, environmental regulations often have effects on trade. The nature and magnitude of these interactions depend on the specific resource endowments, production technologies and socio-economic systems.

There are important differences between high- and low-income countries that are worth highlighting. First, the nature of environmental problems varies to such an extent among production systems that what is considered as an environmental "bad" in one system may be considered an environmental "good" in another. For example, in high population density areas of low-income countries manure has high value and is collected and traded as a commodity and as part of the general return on livestock investments. In contrast, in many industrial countries livestock waste is an undesirable side-effect and environmental regulations control its treatment, thereby raising production costs. Second, as incomes rise there is a corresponding shift in the allocation of both public and private resources towards the improvement of the quality of the environment. When market failure leads to environmental problems, richer countries are more likely to introduce measures to correct the situation. These measures, in the form of regulations, taxes and subsidies, may even be at the expense of economic growth and food

production. By contrast, low-income countries tend to emphasize economic growth and basic food production, even at the expense of environmental quality. Thus in many cases, the basic difference in reaction to environmental problems between high- and low-income societies is the ability, and not necessarily the willingness, to pay for the environmental goods. In other cases, global and local interests in natural resources may differ. For example local community interest in a tropical forest often focuses on its production values (as a source of land, food, wood and livestock feed), while global interests may focus on the biological diversity values of the same forest.

Domestic policy. Because of the considerable differences in resource endowments and levels of income among countries, universal prescriptions on domestic policy to control the environmental impacts associated with production and local processing of commodities are not feasible. However, some broad observations are possible and these can assist in the formulation of domestic environmental control policies.

The most obvious problem is related to cases where the excessive use of one factor of production, such as fertilizer, is caused by commodity-specific environmentally unsound subsidies. Clearly, reduction or elimination of such subsidies should be the first line of action. More broadly, environmental damage often results when producers lack incentives for taking proper account of the costs of resource use.

Environmental externalities can be

internalized through a regulatory approach, whereby quantitative standards are set and mechanisms are put into place to ensure compliance with these standards. Such approaches may be the only ones acceptable in certain circumstances where, for instance, public health or unacceptable levels of irreversible damage to resources are at stake. The alternative is to use market-based economic instruments (incentives and disincentives) and, in general, these are more cost-efficient than the regulatory approach and provide a continuing incentive to reduce environmental costs. The prerequisite, however, is the existence of markets and administrative structures that are adequately developed, and this can be a problem, especially in developing countries. In general, developed countries have greater experience than developing countries in undertaking policies to internalize environmental costs.[37]

Implications for international trade. The implications for trade policy depend on the various domestic policy responses of countries. As noted above, no universal prescriptions for domestic policy are possible. However, policy responses that are rational for an individual nation or area may become a source of friction within an international trading framework. Such policies may result in the denial of market access to certain imports (especially those from developing countries), based on the application of national health, safety and environmental standards. Evaluating whether domestic standards entail justified burdens on the international trading system involves weighing the benefits of environmental, health or food safety regulations against the trade distortions caused, including the loss of market access.

Further complications arise from the perceived effect of internalization as a potential cause of the loss of competitiveness. Indeed, the unilateral internalization of environmental costs at the producer level will tend to increase costs to the affected domestic producers relative to foreign competitors (as well as to domestic producers in other sectors). Thus, while unilateral internalization of environmental costs will improve resource allocation domestically, it can also affect trade flows because production of the affected goods will tend to shift to other countries that have not introduced similar measures. This, in turn, may create pressures from domestic producers in those countries that have introduced "green measures" for the imposition of trade barriers.

A country's internalization of non-transboundary environmental costs should not require reciprocity from other countries, to the extent that its principal objective is to improve welfare in the country itself. However, given the trade implications of such internalization, some harmonization of different regulatory approaches could "level the playing field" and make the internalization of environmental costs politically more feasible in the individual countries.

---

[37] **UNCTAD. 1994. *The effect of the internalization of external costs on sustainable development.* TD/B/40(2)/6.**

If environmental standards are harmonized at a high level, however, it is possible that developing countries will be unable to meet them. Conversely, harmonization at lower levels than currently prevail could pose a threat to the environment. It follows that a balance has to be struck between the advantages of harmonization and the advantages of allowing legitimate differences in national standards when these reflect differences in resource endowments, national preferences and the level of economic development.

The interrelationships between environmental measures and market access are numerous and complex. Some progress has been made on developing broad principles for measures and instruments that may be used to achieve environmental objectives while minimizing adverse trade effects. However, even if all policies respected such principles, there are still direct and indirect ways through which market access opportunities, especially those of developing countries, could be affected. By and large, these effects are linked to the costs to developing countries of adapting to new regulations related to specific product quality specifications and to the packaging and ecolabelling standards adopted by developed countries. In general, the effects on market access depend on whether the costs of compliance to environmental standards for the domestic producer are greater or less than those for the foreign supplier.[38]

Developing countries' access to world markets can also be affected by changes in demand in the developed countries, where consumers wish to have an assurance of the "environment-friendliness" of the production process, even when the final product is not distinguishable from those produced with more conventional technology. The effects on international trade of such shifts in demand depend on the extent to which the domestic market system can generate environment-friendly products compared to the foreign market.

Unilateral and multilateral trade policies. The adoption of environmental policies by an individual country on its own would raise that country's costs of production for the affected products. Unless other countries also adopt such policies, domestic producers of the products risk losing their market share. However, unilateral environmental measures, if taken by a sufficiently large number of individual countries or major producers, will affect world prices and, thus, other countries, benefiting exporters and increasing costs to importers of the product. Thus, even when an environmental problem is purely national in its incidence, there are likely to be effects on trade. The question arises as to which type of response to these problems is appropriate: unilateral or multilateral?

For countries that have adopted environmental policies leading to

---

[38] **An analytic framework on how these differentiated impacts could be measured is given in FAO. 1994. *The measurement of the impact of environmental regulations on trade.* CCP:95/15.**

higher costs, a unilateral response would be to levy import duties or to control the volume of imports in other ways. This may be done under Articles III and XX of GATT. Basically, Article III stipulates that internal taxation and regulations should apply equally to both the domestic and the imported product. Countries therefore have the option of imposing the same requirement on both the domestic and the foreign product, even though compliance costs might be greater for the importer.

Other environmental measures, however, may require special border protection to make them effective. For instance, a domestic policy to slaughter diseased livestock may require an import ban on diseased livestock to make the policy effective.[39] In these and similar cases Article XX of GATT may be invoked. This is perhaps the key article for dealing with the relation of trade to environment and sustainable development. It reads (in part):

> Subject to the requirement that such measures are not applied in a manner which would constitute a means of arbitrary or unjustifiable discrimination between countries where the same conditions prevail, or a disguised restriction on international trade, nothing in this Agreement shall be construed to prevent the adoption or enforcement by a contracting party of measures:
>
> (b) necessary to protect human, animal or plant life or health;

---

[39] Or even a regionally harmonized policy, e.g. to block the spread of large grain-borer in eastern and southern Africa.

(g) relating to the conservation of exhaustible natural resources if such measures are made effective in conjunction with restrictions on domestic production or consumption.

Thus unilateral trade actions to protect the environment or promote sustainable development are allowed under Article XX(b) and (g) provided they do not discriminate between countries nor act as a disguised restriction on trade. The extent to which this article can be used to justify trade measures taken in support of domestic environmental measures has been the subject of considerable discussion at GATT in the past and at the newly created Committee on Trade and Environment of WTO. Of great importance is the question of how wide a coverage is given by this article to the variety of concerns that go into the environmental and sustainable development agenda. If the article is interpreted too widely there is the risk of spurious environmental issues being used to justify trade restrictions. A too rigid reading of the article could limit the scope for genuine attempts to protect a country's environmental policy from being undermined. There has been debate on the force of the word "necessary" in Article XX(b) and under which conditions something that is sanctioned by an international environmental agreement could be considered as necessary for the purpose of invoking Article XX.

Other provisions of GATT/WTO also have a bearing on the use of trade policy to secure environmental ends. These provisions include: Article I on most favoured nation treatment and non-discrimination; Article XI on elimination of quantitative restrictions on imports and exports; Article XXV on waivers from other GATT articles; the Agreement on Technical Barriers to Trade (TBT); and the Agreement on the Application of Sanitary and Phytosanitary Measures (SPS).

The multilateral response to national environmental concerns has yet to be developed. The existing multilateral approaches to environmental matters have evolved to deal with transboundary problems but not with national concerns that may require multilateral support. The point at stake is that, while existing GATT articles allow an importing country to impose a domestic tax on imported products when the same is done on the domestic product and to impose some trade restriction to protect a certain category of domestic measures [covered under Article XX(b) and (g)], not all measures to protect the environment are likely to be covered. For instance, a tax on nitrogen fertilizer would penalize domestic farmers without providing an obvious way of counteracting this extra cost to them by, for example, raising the tariff on imported wheat. Thus a class of potentially important measures to support the environment could not be undertaken unilaterally without bearing the full trade impact of higher costs. This raises the question of whether there could be scope for multilateral environmental agreements to support national policies in this area.

Such international commodity-related environmental agreements (ICREAs) have been discussed at OECD. Among existing commodity agreements, only the International Tropical Timber Agreement explicitly includes environmental aspects, and it relies on the voluntary agreement of countries to promote environmental protection and reforestation together with research and development projects to foster reforestation. It contains no provisions for directly linking the costs of forest reconstruction and timber prices. In general, ideas on multilateral responses to national environmental problems are currently only at an early stage of development and much more work would be needed on them before they could be said to provide a valid approach to internalizing the costs of making production sustainable and the environment better.

CONCLUDING REMARKS

Markets alone cannot ensure environmental quality and sustainable agricultural development. Private values often do not take account of social costs and benefits and, while individuals have regard to the longer-term impact of production and consumption decisions for their families, these do not necessarily represent the interest of society as a whole. As a result, if the environment is to be protected, governments should have appropriate policies to modify the behaviour of producers, consumers and markets. Without such policies resource allocation is likely to be suboptimal. The range of policy options is very wide. Most will have to be applied to the respective resource directly and thus affect trade only indirectly via their effects on production or consumption.

In addition to national environmental issues, there are a number of transboundary environmental issues, which may or may not directly involve trade. Particularly difficult matters are raised when it is not the commodity itself that causes negative environmental effects but the processing and production methods that are damaging and that are, therefore, limited by trade measures in other countries. If appropriate national policies are not introduced and if damage is caused in other countries, multilateral action to encourage "good practice" could be considered via, for instance, international environmental agreements (IEAs). Such action, however, must be based on objective, scientific criteria and must recognize the authenticity of differences in valuation of environmental goods among countries.

Some principles to guide multilateral action are under discussion at the WTO Committee on Trade and Environment. These include, *inter alia,* non-discrimination, transparency, proportionality of the trade effect to the damage caused and least-trade restrictiveness, i.e. the choice of measures that have the minimum trade impact, given that the environmental goal can be achieved.

Special chapters

In addition to the usual review of the recent world food and agricultural situation, each issue of this report since 1957 has included one or more special studies on problems of longer-term interest. Special chapters in earlier issues have covered the following subjects:

1957
Factors influencing the trend of food consumption
Postwar changes in some institutional factors affecting agriculture

1958
Food and agricultural developments in Africa south of the Sahara
The growth of forest industries and their impact on the world's forests

1959
Agricultural incomes and levels of living in countries at different stages of economic development
Some general problems of agricultural development in less-developed countries in the light of postwar experience

1960
Programming for agricultural development

1961
Land reform and institutional change
Agricultural extension, education and research in Africa, Asia and Latin America

1962
The role of forest industries in the attack on economic underdevelopment
The livestock industry in less-developed countries

1963
Basic factors affecting the growth of productivity in agriculture
Fertilizer use: spearhead of agricultural development

1964
Protein nutrition: needs and prospects
Synthetics and their effects on agricultural trade

1966
Agriculture and industrialization
Rice in the world food economy

1967
Incentives and disincentives for farmers in developing countries
The management of fishery resources

1968
Raising agricultural productivity in developing countries through technological improvement
Improved storage and its contribution to world food supplies

1969
Agricultural marketing improvement programmes: some lessons from recent experience
Modernizing institutions to promote forestry development

1970
Agriculture at the threshold of the Second Development Decade

1971
Water pollution and its effects on living aquatic resources and fisheries

1972
Education and training for development
Accelerating agricultural research in the developing countries

1973
Agricultural employment in developing countries

1974
Population, food supply and agricultural development

1975
The Second United Nations Development Decade: mid-term review and appraisal

1976
Energy and agriculture

1977
The state of natural resources and the human environment for food and agriculture

1978
Problems and strategies in developing regions

1979
Forestry and rural development

1980
Marine fisheries in the new era of national jurisdiction

1981
Rural poverty in developing countries and means of poverty alleviation

1982
Livestock production: a world perspective

1983
Women in developing agriculture

1984
Urbanization, agriculture and food systems

1985
Energy use in agricultural production
Environmental trends in food and agriculture
Agricultural marketing and development

1986
Financing agricultural development

1987-88
Changing priorities for agricultural science and technology in developing countries

1989
Sustainable development and natural resource management

1990
Structural adjustment and agriculture

1991
Agricultural policies and issues: lessons from the 1980s and prospects for the 1990s

1992
Marine fisheries and the law of the sea: a decade of change

1993
Water policies and agriculture

1994
Forest development and policy dilemmas

FAO Economic and Social Development Papers

POLICY STUDIES GROUP, POLICY ANALYSIS DIVISION
Policy reform and the agricultural sector

65   Agricultural stabilization and structural adjustment policies in developing countries (A.H. Sarris, 1987)

66   Agricultural issues in structural adjustment programs (R.D. Norton, 1987)

84   Measures of protection: methodology, economic interpretation and policy relevance (P.L. Scandizzo, 1989)

90   The impact of stabilization and structural adjustment policies on the rural sector – case-studies of Côte d'Ivoire, Senegal, Liberia, Zambia and Morocco (P. Salin and E.-M. Claassen, 1991)

95   Guidelines for monitoring the impact of structural adjustment programmes on the agricultural sector (A.H. Sarris, 1990)

96   The effects of trade and exchange rate policies on production in agriculture (C. Kirkpatrick and D. Diakosavvas, 1990)

98   Institutional changes in agricultural product and input markets and their impact on agricultural performance (A. Thomson, 1991)

99   Agricultural labour markets and structural adjustment in sub-Saharan Africa (L.D. Smith, 1991)

100   Structural adjustment and household welfare in rural areas – a micro-economic perspective (R. Gaiha, 1991)

103   The impact of structural adjustment on smallholders (J.-M. Boussard, 1992)

104   Structural adjustment policy sequencing in sub-Saharan Africa (L.D. Smith and N. Spooner, 1991)

105   The role of public and private agents in the agricultural sector of developing countries (L.D. Smith and A. Thomson, 1991)

115   Design of poverty alleviation strategy in rural areas (R. Gaiha, 1993)

124   Structural adjustment and agriculture: African and Asian experiences (A. de Janvry and E. Sadoulet, 1994)

125   Transition and price stabilization policies in East European agriculture (E.-M. Claassen, 1994)

128   Agricultural taxation under structural adjustment (A.H. Sarris, 1994)

ENVIRONMENT AND SUSTAINABLE DEVELOPMENT STUDIES

107   Land reform and structural adjustment in sub-Saharan Africa: controversies and guidelines (J.-Ph. Platteau, 1992). French version: Réforme agraire et ajustement structurel en Afrique subsaharienne: controverses et orientations.

110   Agricultural sustainability: definition and implications for agricultural and trade policy (T. Young, 1992)

121   Policies for sustainable development: four essays (A. Markandya, 1994)

SELECTED

In preparation

- Growth theories, old and new, and the role of agriculture in economic development (N.H. Stern)
- Trade patterns, cooperation and growth (P.L. Scandizzo)
- A multidisciplinary analysis of local-level management of environmental resources (J.-Ph. Platteau and J.M. Baland). To be published by Oxford University Press.
- The economics of international agreements for the protection of environmental and agricultural resources: an economics perspective (S. Barrett)
- The implications of regional trading arrangements for agricultural trade (T. Josling)
- Credit policy, structural adjustment, and agricultural growth in sub-Saharan Africa (A.H. Sarris)

To acquire ESD papers please write to:
Distribution and Sales Section
Publications Division
Food and Agriculture Organization of the United Nations
Viale delle Terme di Caracalla
00100 Rome
Italy

TIME SERIES FOR SOFA '95 DISKETTE
Instructions for use

As in the past two years, *The State of Food and Agriculture 1995,* includes a computer diskette with time series data for about 150 countries, along with FAOSTAT TS software for access to and display of the time series.

FAOSTAT TS

FAOSTAT TS software provides quick and easy access to structured annual time series databases. Even inexperienced computer users can use FAOSTAT TS. No spreadsheet, graphics or database program is required. FAOSTAT TS is fully menu-driven, so there are no commands to learn. Users can browse through and print graphs and tables, plot multiline graphs, fit trend lines and export data for use in other programs. FAOSTAT TS is trilingual (English, French, Spanish) and uses a standard menu format.

FAOSTAT TS software is in the public domain and may be freely distributed. The data files accompanying the software, however, are under FAO copyright and users must attribute FAO as the source. FAO can provide only very limited support to users of this software and the accompanying data and cannot assist users who modify the software or data files. FAO disclaims all warrants of fitness of the software or the data for a particular use.

Technical requirements

FAOSTAT TS software requires an IBM or compatible PC with a hard disk, DOS 3.0 or higher, 300 KB of available RAM and graphics capability. Graphics support is provided for all common graphics adapters (VGA, EGA, MCGA, CGA and Hercules monochrome).

FAOSTAT TS will print graphs on Epson dot matrix, Hewlett-Packard and compatible laser printers. To use FAOSTAT TS with other printers, users can enable their own graphics printing

utility before starting the program. One such utility is GRAPHICS.COM in DOS 2.0 or later releases.

Because of its use of DOS graphics modes, if FAOSTAT TS is run under MS-Windows or OS/2, it should be set to run in a full screen DOS session.

Installation

Before running FAOSTAT TS you must install the software and data files on your hard disk. Installation is automated through the INSTALL.BAT utility on the diskette.
- To install from drive A: to drive C:
  - insert the diskette in drive A:
  - type *A:* and press ENTER
  - type *INSTALL C:* and press ENTER
  - press any key

A C:\SOFA95 directory is created and, after installation, you will already be in this directory.

Entering FAOSTAT TS

- To start the FAOSTAT TS software, if you are not already in the C:\SOFA95 directory (as after installation), change to this directory:
  - type *CD\SOFA95* and press ENTER
  - then, from the command prompt in the SOFA95 directory, type *SOFA95* and press ENTER

A graphics title screen will be displayed, followed by the main menu screen.
- If FAOSTAT TS does not start, graphs do not display correctly or the menus are difficult to read, your computer may not be compatible with the default functions of FAOSTAT TS.

The use of a command-line option may help. You may try to start FAOSTAT TS with the -E parameter to disable its use of expanded memory (type *SOFA95 -E*). You may also force the use of a particular graphics or text mode by typing its name as a parameter (for example, -EGA would force the use of EGA mode graphics).

Language choices

• The initial default language for FAOSTAT TS is English. To change the default language to French or Spanish:
   - go to the FILE menu
   - select LANGUAGE using the Arrow key (↓) and pressing ENTER
   - select your choice of language from those displayed and press ENTER

The language selected will remain the default language until another is selected.

Navigating the menus

The main menu bar consists of FILE, DATA, GRAPH, TABLE and HELP menus. Most menu options are disabled until you open a data file.

• Navigate the menus by using the Arrow keys (↑↓↔) and make a selection by highlighting an item and pressing ENTER. To back out of a selection, press the ESC key.

• If you have a mouse, menu items can be selected with the mouse cursor. The left mouse button selects an item and the right mouse button acts as the ESC key.

After you have made a menu selection, the menu will redraw and highlight a possible next choice.

• Several short-cut keys are available throughout the program:

Key	Action
F1	- *Help:* Displays context-sensitive help text.
ESC	- *Escape:* Backs out of the current menu choice or exits the graph or table currently displayed.
ALT+N	- *Notes:* Displays text notes associated with the current data file, if the text file is available. This text may be edited. Notes will not appear while a graph is displayed.

ALT+X, ALT+Q   - *Exit:* Exits FAOSTAT TS immediately, without prompting.

Help

• You will see context-sensitive help displayed at the bottom of each screen. Press F1 for more extensive help on a highlighted option.

• Select HELP from the main menu to access the help information. Introductory information on the software, help topics and an "About" summary screen are available from the HELP menu.

• The HELP menu options call up the same Help windows obtained by pressing the F1 key at any of the menu screens:
   - the FAOSTAT TS option displays the top-level help page
   - the TOPICS option lists the help contents
   - the ABOUT option shows summary program information

Opening a data file

• To display a list of FAOSTAT TS data files:
   - go to the FILE menu
   - select OPEN

All of the FAOSTAT TS data files in the current directory are displayed. Initially, only SOFA95 will be present. Other FAOSTAT PC data files, version 3.0, can be used with FAOSTAT TS.

• Use the Arrow keys to highlight the file you wish to view and press ENTER to select it. Files are shown with the date of their last revision. You can also highlight your choice by typing the first letters of the file's name. The current search string will appear in the lower left corner of the list.

• You can change the default data drive and directory from the file list by selecting the directory or drive of your choice.

If a current data file is open, loading in a new file will return FAOSTAT TS to its defaults (time trend, no trend line, no user-specified units or scalar). Only one file can be loaded at a time.

Once you have made a file selection, all the menu selections are activated.

Selecting a data series

• Use the DATA menu to select or modify a data series or to fit a statistical trend.

• Select a data series by choosing the name of a country and a data element from the scrolling menus. The first entry displays a list of country names, the second entry displays a list of data item names and the third displays a list of data element names.

If you type the first letters of a name in a list, the menu selection bar will jump to the matching name. For example:

- type *NEW* to skip to New Zealand
- press ENTER to select the highlighted name

Displaying graphs and graph options

The GRAPH menu allows you to view the data in chart form. You can display time trends and table or column profiles. Options under the GRAPH menu change the data series shown as well as its display.

For example, to show a plot of the data selected:

- go to the GRAPH menu
- select DISPLAY

Many options to modify, save or print a graph are available only while a graph is on screen. Use the F1 help key for a reminder of the options.

Graph action keys. You have several options when a graph is displayed:

• Press ESC to exit the graph and return to the main menu.

• Press F1 for help on the graph action keys. The help box lists the choices available while a graph is on the screen. You must exit the help box before making a selection.

• Press the Arrow and PAGEUP or PAGEDOWN keys to change the series displayed.

• The plus key (+) allows you to add up to three other series to the one displayed. Press the minus key (-) to remove a series. This is the way multiline charts are created:

- display an initial series
- press the + key to add subsequent series to the chart

• Press A to display a table of the axis data with statistics. Press T to show a table of the fitted trend data, the residuals and fit statistics (if a trend line is selected, see below).

• The INS key permits you to insert text directly on the graph. While inserting text, press F1 for help on your text options. You can type small or large, horizontal or vertical text.

• To print a graph, press P and select your printer from the menu. The print output is only a screen dump of the display, so the quality is limited.

• To save a graph for later printing or viewing, press S. The graph image will be saved in the common PCX bitmap format. You can use the PRINTPCX program or other software to view or print multiple images later. PRINTPCX also permits you to convert colour PCX images into black and white images suitable for inclusion in a word processing document.

Fitting trend lines

• To fit a statistical function to a data series, select FIT from the DATA menu. The options under FIT allow you to select the type of function, data year limits to include in the fit and a final projection year for a statistical forecast.

• By fitting a trend line (selecting the LINE option under FIT) with a projection (selecting PROJECTION under FIT), a statistical forecast can be plotted. Use the + key to add a new data series to the graph, which can be made with only a few key strokes.

Charting profiles

• The options under the GRAPH menu allow you to change the year span or style of the graph display (options LIMITS and STYLE, respectively), or to switch from a time trend to a table or column data profile (VIEWPOINT). The VIEWPOINT option is an easy means to compare data for a particular year.

Viewpoint

• If you want to change from a time series display to a country or item profile display for a given year, select VIEWPOINT from the GRAPH menu.

Select DISPLAY from the GRAPH menu, and the profile will be drawn.

The initial profile display is for the last year of historical data. To change the year, use the Arrow keys. Press F1 for help.

• For a tables profile (profile of data across countries), you can either choose the tables to be displayed or let FAOSTAT TS select the top members and array them in order. A limit of 50 items can appear in one profile.

By selecting TOP MEMBERS instead of SELECTED MEMBERS, FAOSTAT TS will sort the values in the file and display a ranking of table or column values.

Viewing tables

• The TABLE menu allows you to look at data in a tabular format and to define subset tables that may be saved and imported into other software packages:
- go to the TABLE menu
- select BROWSE DATA to view individual data tables from the current file

• When viewing tables, a help bar appears at the bottom of the screen. Press PAGEUP or PAGEDOWN to change the table displayed or press ALT+1 or ALT+2 to choose from a list of tables. Use the Arrow keys to scroll the columns and rows.

Series data

• The SERIES DATA option under the TABLE menu displays the last data series selected, including summary statistics. This is the data series used to plot a graph. To change the series, you must make a new choice from the DATA menu.

• The SERIES DATA screen can also be displayed while you are in a graph by pressing the letter A. If more than one series has been plotted, only the last series is shown. The range of years used for the series and statistics can be adjusted through the LIMITS option under the GRAPH menu.

• To view country or item profile lists and statistics, select VIEWPOINT from the GRAPH menu. You can quickly see a list of the tables with the greatest values (for example, countries

with the highest commodity consumption) by choosing a table profile from VIEWPOINT and selecting the TOP MEMBERS option. Then select SERIES DATA from the TABLE menu to view the list, or select DISPLAY from the GRAPH menu to plot a chart.

Trend data

• If the FIT option has been selected (from the DATA menu) for a time trend, then the values composing the trend can be displayed with the TREND DATA option. Summary statistics for the original series and for the trend as well as residual values are included. The list scrolls with the Arrow keys and you can toggle between the axis and trend data with the A and T keys.

Exporting data

• The EXPORT option under the FILE menu allows you to export FAOSTAT TS data into other file formats or to create custom tables for viewing or printing. By selecting EXPORT, you will jump into another set of menus.

• To select the tables and columns you want to view or save, go to the DATA menu. Select options with the + key. To undo all your selections quickly, select RESET MARKS.

• To arrange, view, save or print data, go to the options under EXPORT (in the FILE menu):
- VIEW: displays a temporary text file of the data selected. It is a convenient way to view a subset of the tables and columns in a FAOSTAT TS file and can also be used to see the effects of the ORIENTATION or LAYOUT selections before using the SAVE or PRINT option.
- SAVE: displays a list of file formats to let you save your data choices in a file. You will be prompted for a file name. If you need to export FAOSTAT TS data for use with other software, use this menu item. The WK1 and DBF file format selections are not affected by the LAYOUT option (see below).
- PRINT: prints your current table and column selections. Many printers cannot print more than five columns of FAOSTAT TS data.

Select VIEW to check the table width before printing.

- LAYOUT: allows you to display years across rows or down columns. The default is down columns.

o get back to the main FAOSTAT TS menu or clear your selections and create more tables, the RETURN option.

aking notes

o read or edit textual information on the rrent data file, select NOTES from the FILE enu. You can also call up the Notes box by essing ALT+N at any of the menus. The option)TES allows you to read or edit text associated th the data file.

DOS shell and exit

The DOS SHELL option under the FILE menu returns you to the DOS prompt temporarily but keeps FAOSTAT TS in memory. This is not the normal way to exit the program. It is useful if you need to execute a DOS command and would like to return to the same data file. The data file itself is dropped from memory and reloaded on return, so default values will be in effect.

Exiting FAOSTAT TS

• To exit FAOSTAT TS:
  - go to the FILE menu
  - select EXIT

The ALT+X or ALT+Q key combinations are short cuts to exit the program from almost any screen.